INSTRUCTOR'S RESOURCE
WITH TEST QU

to accompa

APPLIED DATA COMMUNICATIONS
A BUSINESS-ORIENTED APPROACH
SECOND EDITION

JAMES E. GOLDMAN
Purdue University

Prepared by

MARK W. SMITH, Ed.D.
Trident Technical College

John Wiley & Sons, Inc.
New York • Chichester • Weinheim • Brisbane • Singapore • Toronto

Copyright © 1998 by John Wiley & Sons, Inc.

Excerpts from this work may be reproduced by instructors for distribution on a not-for-profit basis for testing or instructional purposes only to students enrolled in courses for which the textbook has been adopted. *Any other reproduction or translation of this work beyond that permitted by Sections 107 or 108 of the 1976 United States Copyright Act without the permission of the copyright owner is unlawful. Requests for permission or further information should be addressed to the Permissions Department, John Wiley & Sons, Inc., 605 Third Avenue, New York, NY 10158-0012.*

ISBN 0-471-18086-6

Printed in the United States of America

10 9 8 7 6 5 4 3 2 1

Printed and bound by Malloy Lithographing, Inc.

CONTENTS

Preface v

General Information vii

Chapter 1: The Data Communications Industry 1

Chapter 2: Data Communications Concepts 17

Chapter 3: Basic Data Communications Technology 33

Chapter 4: Voice Communications Concepts & Technology 51

Chapter 5: Local Area Networks Concepts & Architectures 71

Chapter 6: Local Area Network Hardware 89

Chapter 7: Local Area Network Operating Systems 107

Chapter 8: Wide Area Networking Concepts, Architectures, & Services 129

Chapter 9: Internetworking 151

Chapter 10: Remote Access & Wireless Networking 173

Chapter 11: Enterprise Networks & The Internet 195

Chapter 12: The Network Development Life Cycle 217

Chapter 13: Network Security 235

Chapter 14: Network Management 257

Comments for Selected Figures 277

PREFACE

FEATURES

This instructor's resource guide consists of a short general information section followed with a chapter-by-chapter detailed set of information, and a final section of comments on selected figures from the text.

CHAPTER ORGANIZATION

Each chapter of this guide consists of the following sections:

Answers to Chapter Review Questions

Suggested answers to all of the text end-of-chapter material. In the interest of space, short answers are provided, but in many cases, students' answers should be more comprehensive.

Test Questions

Approximately 50-75 True/False, Multiple Choice, and Fill-In questions, with the text page reference provided next to the right answer.

Case Study and Answers

A brief introduction followed by detailed answers to the case study questions which appear in the text.

COMMENTS FOR SELECTED FIGURES

This final section of the instructor's resource guide contains brief explanatory notes on selected figures from the text which will be helpful for the instructor in preparing lecture material.

ACKNOWLEDGMENTS

I am indebted to a number of people for their assistance and support:

- Curt Snyder - for his help and friendship
- Bob Borns - unqualified support and a real friend
- My friends and colleagues at Trident Technical College - for their reminder of what teaching is all about
- Amy Hegarty - of John Wiley & Sons, for her assistance with the project

As always, I would especially like to thank my wife Linda for her love and support in all of life's endeavors, my grandson Shawn, who continues to be one of life's biggest joys, and finally to my daughter Hope and her husband Kevin of whom I am immensely proud.

GENERAL INFORMATION

OVERVIEW

This second edition of the textbook is again one of the most comprehensive and versatile available today in the field of Data Communications. It can be adapted for teaching a multitude of courses including: a one-semester Data Communications survey course; a one-semester PC Connectivity and Local Area Networking course; a one-semester Wide Area Networking and Business Telecommunications course; and possibly a one-semester MIS graduate course in Data Communications.

To aid the instructor, here is a listing of the courses the textbook can be used for, a brief course description, and the chapters which would contribute to a better understanding of the subject areas covered by the course.

COURSES FOR WHICH TEXT CAN BE USED

DATA COMMUNICATIONS course

Course Description:

Introduction to a wide variety of topics in the voice and data communications field. Vocabulary, hardware, concepts, issues, trends, and decision making as well as the link between business needs and the data communications field are stressed. Proper application of business data communications technology is a primary theme of the course.

Major Topics:

> State of the data/voice communications industry
> Current trends in data/voice communications
> Introduction to data communications hardware and its proper application
> Introduction to the OSI Model
> Introduction to the Top Down and Input Processing Output Models
> Familiarization with data/voice communications vocabulary
> Relationship between business demand, technology, and network design
> Data communications media/network options
> Local Area Network alternatives
> Circuit and Packet Switched Networks
> Introduction to Network Analysis, Design, and Management

Chapters Covered:

Chapter 1	The Data Communications Industry
Chapter 2	Data Communications Concepts
Chapter 3	Basic Data Communications Technology
Chapter 4	Voice Communications Concepts and Technology
Chapter 5	Local Area Networks Concepts and Architectures
Chapter 6	Local Area Network Hardware
Chapter 8	Wide Area Networking Concepts, Architectures, and Services
Chapter 12	The Network Development Life Cycle

Note: A two-semester course would continue with the remainder of the chapters.

PC CONNECTIVITY & LOCAL AREA NETWORKS course

Course Description:

Exploration of PC connectivity alternatives and the decision-making process for designing cost-effective local area networking solutions for a given application. Emphasis is on the use of these local area networking solutions in client/server architectures. Hands-on laboratory experiences emphasize problem solving and troubleshooting skills through network implementation.

Major Topics:

- Local Area Networks versus Multiuser Computer Systems
- OSI Model
- Media & Physical Topologies
- Local Area Network Standards
- Communication Protocols
- Network Communication Services
- Interconnecting LANs
- Novell Netware
- LAN Manager
- Windows NT & NT Advanced Server
- Banyan Vines
- Introduction to Network Management

Chapters Covered:

Chapter 1	The Data Communications Industry
Chapter 2	Data Communications Concepts
Chapter 3	Basic Data Communications Technology
Chapter 4	Voice Communications Concepts and Technology
Chapter 5	Local Area Networks Concepts and Architectures
Chapter 6	Local Area Network Hardware
Chapter 7	Local Area Network Operating Systems
Chapter 10	Remote Access and Wireless Networking

Note: This course would be supported by a laboratory for hands-on experience

WIDE AREA NETWORKING AND BUSINESS TELECOMMUNICATIONS

Course Description:

This course will explore the many alternatives available for connecting LANs as well as providing remote access to/from users not connected to LANs. Emphasis will be on the effect of telecommunications systems and networking decisions on business performance. Integration of internetworks (LAN to LAN) and micro to mainframe connectivity into client/server and client/host architectures will be emphasized. Enterprise networking and interoperability analysis and design will be stressed. Organization and management of large-scale telecommunications projects is investigated.

Major Topics:

- Internetworking Hardware and Software
- Wide Area Networking Technologies and Services
- Enterprise Networking Analysis and Design
- Telecommunications Environment, Trends Services
- Packet Switching, Frame Relay, Cell Relay Networks and Services
- Metropolitan Area Networks
- Interoperability Analysis and Design
- The Human Side of Telecommunications Project Management

Chapters Covered:

Chapter 8	Wide Area Networking Concepts, Architectures, and Services
Chapter 9	Internetworking
Chapter 10	Remote Access and Wireless Networking
Chapter 11	Enterprise Networks and The Internet
Chapter 12	The Network Development Life Cycle
Chapter 13	Network Security
Chapter 14	Network Management

Note: This course would be supported by a laboratory for hands-on experience

CHAPTER 1

The Data Communications Industry

ANSWERS TO CHAPTER REVIEW QUESTIONS

1. Technology, Regulatory, Carriers, Research, Residential Customers, Manufacturers, Standards Making Organizations, Vendors/Consultants, Business/Customers, and Judicial/Political/Legislative.

2. Manufacturers and Standards Making Organizations: Development process is often carried out at a significant expense to manufacturers often before standards are set. Hence, manufacturers have a big stake in the standards process. Business and Manufacturers: Business may demand faster transfer of data which manufacturers may or may not be able to supply (supply and demand then affect price). Carriers and Regulatory Agencies: A formal process of a series of proposals from the carriers to the state and federal regulatory agencies and the issuance of rulings and approvals in return. Carriers and Political/Judicial/Legislative: The judicial component initially brought about divestiture and deregulation which had a major impact on carriers. When special interest groups don't like the way some carriers are functioning they may bring pressure on the legislative and political components to control the telecommunications industry in a manner favorable to the special interest group.

3. They are an integral part of an overall Information Systems Architecture. The ultimate success of an implemented information system depends largely on the design of the network which forms the foundation of that system.

4. It provides the business requirements along with the business objectives which are passed down the top-down model where they are further refined and solutions proposed to meet these requirements.

5. The top-down model approach shown in Figure 1-11, requires an understanding of business constraints and objectives as well as information systems applications and the data on which those applications run. Figure 1-10 graphically illustrates the five layers: Business Model, Applications Model, Data Model, Network Model, Technology Model. Business requirements are passed down the model while solutions are passed up.

6. Intra-LATA (Local Access Transport Area) means all local phone traffic within a LATA as handled by Local exchange carriers, or the local phone company. Inter-LATA is traffic between local exchange carriers that must be passed off to long distance carriers. The

circuits between a residence or business and the local Central Office or **CO** are known as local loops. A central office is a facility belonging to the local phone company in which calls are switched to their proper destination. Competing long distance carriers wishing to do business in a given LATA maintain a switching office in that LATA known as a POP or Point of Presence. This POP handles billing information and routes the call over the long distance carrier's switched network to its POP in the destination's LATA. Divestiture broke up the network services of AT&T into separate long-distance and local service companies. AT&T would retain the right to offer long-distance services while the former Local Bell Operating Companies were grouped into new Regional Bell Operating Companies (to offer local telecommunications service).

7. The Telecommunications Act of 1996 seeks to encourage competition in all aspects and markets of telecommunications services including switched and dedicated local and inter-LATA traffic as well as cable TV companies and wireless services such as paging, cellular, and satellite services. The legislation directs the FCC to produce the rules which will allow LECs and IXCs to compete in each other's markets. Companies which seek to offer local access service in competition with RBOCs are known as Competitive Access Providers or CAPs. Perhaps most importantly, the law expressly preempts the authority of Judge Greene to dictate the operation of the telecommunications industry in the United States, while increasing the burden on the FCC to establish a fair and equitable market environment in which a variety of companies can compete in a deregulated manner. Figure 1-6 summarizes the major implications of the Telecommunications Act of 1996 from a variety of perspectives.

8. Understand and speak "business", understand and evaluate technology with a critical eye as to cost/benefit of that technology, work effectively with carriers and understand comparative value and proper application of available network services, and communicate effectively with technically oriented people as well as with business management personnel.

9. Divestiture broke up the network services of AT&T into separate long-distance and local service companies. Deregulation addressed the ability of "phone companies" in America to compete in an unrestricted manner in other industries such as the computer and information systems fields.

10. Regional Bell Operating Companies. Also a holding company of several smaller BOCs (Bell Operating Companies).

11. Data communications is in a state of change due to divestiture and deregulation along with the continuing trends of any of the particular components listed in question one and the net effect of the supply and demand forces of these combined components.

12. A ruling issued by Federal Judge Harold Greene in 1982 which, as a result, allows both AT&T and the RBOCs to enter into other industries by forming additional subsidiaries as well as offering local telecommunications service.

13. This enormously important event was primarily a judicial process, fought out in the courtrooms, largely fostered by one man, Bill McGowan, former president of MCI. Although the FCC, a federal regulatory agency, initially ruled in 1971 that MCI could compete with AT&T for long distance service, it was McGowan's 1974 lawsuit which got the Justice Department involved and led to the actual breakup of the telecommunications monopoly in America.

14. AT&T/RBOCs are now able to branch into unregulated industries, but are not familiar with customer driven markets; Users now find more competitive pricing, but coordinating multi-vendor services is a nightmare; Other Telecom Companies can now compete on a level (multi-billion dollar industry), but cost/overhead and infrastructure may not be present.

15. Important impacts include more competition and in some cases more competitive pricing of products and services; however, it is hard to coordinate competing vendors' services and products and may end in a lot of finger pointing among competing vendors.

16. Network services offered by phone companies are still regulated however, phone companies are now free to form joint ventures and compete in unregulated industries.

17. Local service rate changes are filed on the state level with a particular state's Public Utilities Commission and on a federal level with the Federal Communications Commission for inter-state service proposals and rate change requests.

18. The Open Systems Interconnection (OSI) model is a framework or an architecture in which standards can be developed, compared, and understood. It allows data communications technology developers as well as standards developers to talk about the interconnection of two networks or computers in common terms without dealing in proprietary vendor jargon.

19. Competing manufacturers have a strong desire to get their own technology declared as the standard due to the high cost of development of new technology.

20. By the time standards are actually adopted for a given technology (often a very political process), the next generation of that technology is sometimes ready to be introduced to the market.

21. Possible business impacts include the ability of one manufacturer of data communications equipment to design products which will work with another manufacturer's equipment. This impacts both price and competitiveness. On the negative side - if a manufacturer's technology is not declared as the "standard" it could spell financial disaster.

22. Figure 1-9 describes the interaction of the major components of the data communications industry with the law of supply and demand. Example: BUSINESS and USERS may

demand faster transfer of data. However, if RESEARCH has not supplied the TECHNOLOGY to accomplish these faster transfers, then MANUFACTURERS cannot produce and supply (sell) these products to BUSINESS and USERS while VENDORS and CONSULTANTS cannot distribute and recommend their use.

23. Benchmarking can be summarized into the following three major steps:
    1. Examine and document quantifiable improvements to business processes.
    2. Perform surveys to measure customer satisfaction with deployed network services.
    3. Compare actual implementation costs with the cost to purchase similar services from outside vendors in a process known as outsourcing. Alternatively, comparative costs could be determined by examining other companies in the same vertical market.

    Benchmarking the impact of networking technology is not an exact science. Although costs are relatively easy to quantify, the same cannot be said for benefits. Controlling all variables effecting business improvement is difficult at best.

24. Input-Processing-Output model is used to analyze a wide variety of data communications equipment and opportunities. Using this model, one need only understand the differences between the characteristics of the data that came IN and the data that went OUT. Those differences identified were PROCESSed by the data communications equipment being analyzed and determine the basic function of the piece of data communications equipment.

25. Receive the bits and pieces of data. Examine the bits and pieces of data. Decide how to process the data. Send the data to its proper destination.

26. Interfaces may be physical (hardware to hardware) in nature. For example:
    - Cables physically connecting to serial ports on a computer
    - A network interface card physically plugging into the expansion bus inside a computer.

    Interfaces may also be logical or software-oriented (software to software) as well. For example:
    - A network operating system client software (Windows for Workgroups) communicating with the client PC's operating system (DOS).
    - A client-based data query tool (Microsoft Excel) gathering data from a large database management system (Oracle).

    Finally, interfaces may cross the hardware to software boundary. For example:
    - A network operating system specific piece of software known as a driver which interfaces to an installed network interface card (NIC).
    - A piece of operating system software known as a kernel which interfaces to a computer's CPU chip.

27. The reason that these various interfaces are able to be bridged successfully, thereby supporting compatibility between components, is due to protocols. Protocols are nothing more than rules for how communicating hardware and software components bridge

interfaces or talk to one another. Protocols may be proprietary (used exclusively by one or more vendors) or open (used freely by all interested parties). Protocols may be officially sanctioned by international standards making bodies such as the ISO, or may be purely market driven (de facto protocols). Figure 1-12 illustrates the relationship between interfaces, protocols, and compatibility.

28. Law 4 states that if the network doesn't make good business sense, it probably makes no sense. A top-down approach to network analysis and design is undertaken which assures that the network design implemented will meet the business needs and objectives which motivated the design in the first place.

29. The Internet Suite of Protocols model, also known as the TCP/IP Protocol Suite, or TCP/IP Architecture, is a communications architecture that takes its name from TCP/IP (Transmission Control Protocol/Internet Protocol), the de facto standard protocols for open systems internetworking.

30. Like the OSI Model, the TCP/IP Model is a layered communications architecture in which upper layers use the functionality offered by the protocols of the lower layers. Each layer's protocols are able to operate independently from the protocols of other layers. Refer to Figure 1-14 for a graphical comparison of the OSI Model and the Internet Suite of Protocols model.

31. Certification as an indication of mastery of a particular vendor's technology may be important in some employment situations. Some concerns with certification programs are:
    - the amount of practical, hands-on experience required to earn a given certification
    - the amount of continuing education and experience required to retain a certification
    - vendor specific certifications do not provide the broad background required for today's multi-vendor internetworks

32. The Network Layer of the top-down model is the logical network design and is concerned with network functionality - What are we asking our network to do for us? The Technology Layer in the top-down model refers to the actual physical network design - How are we accomplishing the what of our logical network design?

33. The top-down model helps develop critical communication between sub-systems as well as between the individuals who developed these sub-systems based on requirements from one layer being passed down to the next layer and the solution passed back up the layer.

34. Insist that a top-down approach to network analysis and design be undertaken. One way to demonstrate the impact of implemented technology is by binding networking costs to business value through a process known as benchmarking.

35. Individuals with good business, interpersonal, and technological skills will be able to find jobs with business, technology, and carriers in data communications due to the multi-talented nature of jobs in these data communications areas.

36. The different columns of the model allow you to plug in new items as the business demands change. Profitability and productivity are the highest level of business demands. While they don't change, the business solutions, technology etc. will change.

37. In the past decade, over $1 trillion dollars has been invested by business in information technology. Despite this massive investment, carefully conducted research indicates that there has been little if any increase in productivity as a direct result of this investment. This dilemma is known as the productivity paradox. Clearly, something is wrong with an analysis and design process which recommends technology implementations that fail to meet strategic business objectives of increased productivity and should be of concern to the network analyst in order that he/she provide good business solutions.

TEST QUESTIONS

True/False Questions

1. Divestiture and deregulation are synonymous terms for the breakup of AT&T. F/7

2. Prior to divestiture, the regional bell operating companies (RBOCs) provided local and long-distance service. F/8

3. Co-location requires RBOCs to allow alternate carriers to install their equipment in the RBOC's central office in order to gain equal access. T/10

4. The ANSI standards making organization is an international group responsible for the OSI 7-layer model. F/12

5. The 1982 Modified Final Judgment represented the final rulings handed down concerning deregulation and divestiture. F/8

6. In today's data communication environment, the most important component is the technology and research component. F/5

7. Initial divestiture and deregulation of the telecommunications industry was the result of a purely regulatory process. F/8

8. Final standards are sometimes least common denominator implementations of competing proposals. T/14

9. The basic laws of supply and demand do not apply to the rapidly expanding and complex data communications industry. F/14

10. Sales and marketing people are governed by the same standards which apply to data communications equipment. F/14

11. The Telecommunications Act of 1996 seeks to encourage competition in all aspects and markets of telecommunications services. T/10

12. Ad hoc standards, created by task forces, interest groups, and consortiums, are produced quickly and pose few problems for manufacturers and consumers of telecommunications products. F/13

13. Network requirements which define what the implemented network must do, are also referred to as the physical network design. F/18

8   Chapter 1

14. If the network doesn't make good business sense, it probably makes no sense. T/16

15. The logical gap between components is commonly referred to as a protocol. F/19

Multiple Choice Questions

1. Which of the following are commonly referred to as phone companies?
   a. regulatory agencies
   b. public utilities
   c. EDI
   p.6 d. carriers

2. Vendors often add these to the standards their equipment must meet to give their equipment a competitive edge.
   p.14 a. extensions
   b. GOSIP
   c. MIB
   d. carriers

3. Which of the following allowed phone companies in America to compete in an unrestricted manner in other industries such as the computer and information systems fields?
   a. divestiture
   p.8 b. deregulation
   c. regulation
   d. tariff regulation

4. A facility belonging to the local phone company in which calls are switched to their proper destination is called a(n)
   a. long-distance carrier
   b. OSI
   p.7 c. central office
   d. none of the above

5. The OSI 7-layer Model
   a. is not a standard, nor a collection of standards
   b. works as a framework in which standards can be developed, compared, and understood
   c. allows for discussion about the interconnection of two networks in common terms
   p.23 d. all of the above

6. This model is a key model used to analyze a wide variety of data communications equipment and opportunities.
p.24
   a. I-P-O model
   b. Data Communications Industry System model
   c. Supply and Demand model
   d. ISO model

7. This model or approach is a key to assuring that implemented data communications solutions will actually solve business problems and not merely throw some technology at them.
   a. I-P-O model
   b. OSI 7-layer model
   c. supply and demand model
p.16 d. Top-down model

8. Which of the following standards making bodies contributed the OSI model to data communications?
   a. ITU
p.12 b. ISO
   c. ANSI
   d. IEEE

9. Which of the following standards making bodies is responsible for Local Area Network standards?
   a. ITU
   b. ISO
   c. ANSI
p.12 d. IEEE

10. This layer of the Top Down Model is where the physical network design would be placed.
   a. network layer
   b. business layer
p.18 c. technology layer
   d. applications layer

11. One way to demonstrate the impact of implemented technology by tying network costs to business value is through a process known as
   a. BPR
p.19 b. benchmarking
   c. prototyping
   d. layering

Chapter 1   9

12. This layer of the OSI model sets up the end-to-end connections.
    a. Presentation
    b. Transport
    p.22 c. Network
    d. Physical

Fill-In the Blank Questions

1. Competing long-distance carriers are allowed to sell long-distance services on a level playing field with AT&T as a result of divestiture known as _____.

2. A long-distance company's switching facility is known as _____.

3. _____ broke up the network services of AT&T into separate long distance and local service companies.

4. The _____ Model is a structured methodology followed in order to assure that the implemented network meets the communications needs of the intended business, organization or individual.

5. _____ are nothing more than rules for how communicating hardware and software components talk to one another.

6. The _____ Model allows data communications technology developers as well as standards developers to talk about the interconnection of two networks or components in common terms without dealing in proprietary vendor jargon.

7. In the top-down approach, the layer which deals with hardware-software-media analysis is the _____ model.

8. The sum of all of the protocols employed in a particular computer is sometimes referred to as that computer's _____.

9. Rulings are provided by regulatory agencies based upon carriers' <u>proposals</u>.

Answers

1. equal access p.9
2. POP or Point of Presence p.7
3. Divestiture p.8
4. Top Down p.16
5. Protocols p.20
6. OSI p.22
7. technology p.10
8. protocol stack p.20
9. proposals p.6

CASE STUDY AND ANSWERS

TELECOM COMPETITION - ROCHESTER, N.Y.: LAND OF THE FREE MARKET

Activities

1. Top-down model:

Business   Former Rochester Telephone Co. will sell long-haul, cable and cellular services in exchange for opening the local loop to competitiors.
Companies would like to find one carrier to handle all their telecommunications needs.
Large companies may now compete with small providers and vice versa.
Carriers are looking to consolidate services with other companies in order to provide decreased costs and better services to customer.
Bundling services to customers is now more common because of competition.

Applications   Carriers are trying to consolidate services to provide tailored, competitive packages to customer.
Internet access is required at ever increasing transmission rates.

Data   Data must pass over telecommunications systems securely and efficiently.

Network   A variety of services must be transmitted over the telecommunications network.
Customers must be able to have the bandwidth when they want it.
Redundancy must be built into the network.

Technology   Superior performance over fiber with redundancy using SONET rings.
Connections to the Internet using 10Mbps will be available.
Centrex service will be used.

2. Unanswered questions:

While competition is often mentioned, costs are not detailed.
How long must a company agree to contracted services?
What equipment must be purchased or rented in order to gain access to the carriers services?
How much of the technology in this case is "bleeding edge" technology?
How important for a business is it to be on the bleeding edge?

Business
1. Rochester Telephone gained the right to sell long-haul cable and cellular services.
2. They had to open the local loop to competitors, making Rochester the nation's first open market for phone service.
3. Frontier Corp. is the unregulated entity that has as a subsidiary Rochester Telephone.
4. Frontier put together an attractive bundle of local, long-distance, cellular and private-line services.
5. Time Warner Communications of Rochester, AT&T, and Citizen Telecom are competing.
6. These companies can lease services from each other also.
7. Time Warner Communications had a local cable TV network and stepped in as a local exchange carrier offering lower rates.
8. Time Warner had a better SONET network in place.
9. Alternative service providers must be able to provide missing services and bundle services uniquely for each customer. They must also be able to provide local and long distance services, cellular and private-line services.
10. The competitors' inroads into local dial-tone service is between 3% and 4%.
11. Rochester Telephone is installing more fiber in SONET rings; looking for a partner, perhaps a wireless provider, to compete against cable TV offerings; and researching a way to deliver high bandwidth to the home over its existing wires. They are also consolidating their central offices from 20 to five.
12. More services are offered at lower prices.
13. Local competition may not be good for standardization. It may also be short lived, meaning that some companies, which a business depends on for services, may go out of business, leaving the company at the mercy of the competition.

Application
1. Centrex is a business telephone service offered by a local telephone company from its local central office providing many services such as intercom, call forwarding, call transfer, toll restrict, least cost routing and call hold services, to the company's desks rather than the company having to buy or lease its own PBX.
2. Businesses which require fault tolerant service and do not want to implement and service their own PBX system would be very interested in Centrex. Also, businesses with several offices spread over a small geographic region can share one virtual PBX - Centrex.

Data
1. Cable modem access is to be offered at up to 10Mbps.
2. The maximum data rate of a V.34 modem over a dial-up local loop is a transmission rate of 28.8 Kbps and a overall throughput rate of 115.2 Kbps.

Network
1. SONET is Synchronous Optical Network with fiber-optic transmission rates from 51.84 Mbps to 13.22 Gbps.
2. Carriers are able to re-route data over different SONET rings in order to provide redundancy.
3. A T-1 is digital transmission link with the capability to transfer data at approximately 1.544 Mbps. It can be copper wire and is capable of handling up to 24 voicer conversations at one time (64 Kbps for each conversation).

Technology
1. In general, the lack of technology by one service provider creates a vacuum other providers will try to fill. This means that the providers will gain or lose market share accordingly. However, an alternative appears to be consolidation of services between providers, where they merge services that each does best and partner to provide the customer with the services desired.

CHAPTER 2

Data Communications Concepts

ANSWERS TO CHAPTER REVIEW QUESTIONS

1. Analog transmission involves a varying wave-like tone or frequency while digital transmission is represented by discrete, digitized electronic voltage levels representing 1's and 0's.

2. Asynchronous transmission: data is sent one character at a time, each character has a start and 1 or more stop bits, time between characters is unsynchronized and of random length. Synchronous transmission: data is sent as a block of uninterrupted characters, synchronization characters precede and follow the data block, synchronization is maintained via a clocking signal whether data is actually being sent and detected or not. Synchronous transmission is more efficient - see Figure 2-16.

3. A carrier wave is a normal or neutral wave used by a modem which manipulates or varies it to represent bits of data as 1's and 0's.

4. Amplitude, frequency, and phase.

5. A detectable event or signaling event represents the period of time in which a carrier wave can either be manipulated or left alone by a transmitting modem. The more signaling events per second (known as the baud rate) which a modem can perform, the more data which can be transmitted per second. When more than one bit/baud can be interpreted in a signaling event this will increase the bits per second (bps) transmission rate. If the baud rate of a modem was 2400 signaling events per second and the modem was able to interpret 4 bits per signaling event, then the transmission speed would be 9600 bps (2400 x 4).

6. More sophisticated modulation techniques are able to interpret more than one bit per baud allowing the modem to increase the overall bits per second (bps). Higher speed modems require higher numbers of bits/baud. This requires a higher number of constellation points. In order to obtain enough constellation points with sufficient intersymbol distance, more than one wave characteristic must be varied. For example, phase and amplitude are varied in QAM.

7. Half-Duplex - modems transmit in both directions, only one direction at a time. Full-Duplex - modems transmit in both directions, simultaneously.

8. Modulation of the carrier wave called a detectable event or signaling event can occur at different rates per second known as baud rate. When only one bit per baud is interpreted per signaling event the baud rate and bps are equal. However, the more sophisticated techniques allow for more than one bit per second to be interpreted, thus the bps can be higher than the baud rate. For instance, 2 bits per signaling event for a modem with a baud rate of 2400 signaling events per second allow 4800 bps to be transmitted.

9. Leased line is a line which bypasses the carrier's switching equipment to connect two or more locations. Dial-up line is the type of phone line which you would typically have installed in your home or place of business. Calls placed over dial-up lines through central office switches have connections built from available circuits which last only for the duration of the call. The quality of these available circuits may vary from one instance to another.

10. Encoding is transformation of humanly-readable characters into machine-readable characters. It is necessary to encode characters because computers can only work with discrete states (electronic bits) hence humanly-readable characters must be converted to discrete voltages of electricity representing coded characters which can then be easily transmitted, received, and examined by data communications equipment.

11. ASCII - American Standard Code for Information Interchange used primarily with microcomputers and non-IBM mini/mainframe computers, and EBCDIC - Extended Binary Coded Decimal Interchange Code used primarily with IBM mainframe computers.

12. Politics and competition between IBM and the rest of the computer industry lead to establishment of more than one encoding scheme.

13. BIT - Binary dIgiT - a 1 or 0 represented by discrete voltages of electricity in digital format.

14. Bits must be transformed by a modem from digital (discrete) electrical waves (sometimes called square waves) into analog (continuous) sine waves for transmission over voice-grade dial-up lines.

15. Parallel transmission is sending bits simultaneously down parallel transmission lines (along side each other) while serial transmission is sending bits one after the other down a single transmission line. Parallel transmission is used mostly to transmit data within a computer and between a computer's parallel port and a parallel printer while serial transmission is used mostly for data communications between computers.

16. Serial is used most often for data communications due to its ability to travel relatively farther distances than parallel.

17. A UART (Universal Asynchronous Receiver Transmitter) is a computer chip which performs parallel to serial conversion and vice versa so the data which is in parallel transmission in the CPU to serial transmission so it can go out the computer's serial port.

18. | DB-9 | DB-25 | Name | Abbr. | From | To |
     |------|-------|------|-------|------|----|
     | 5 | 1 | Protective Ground | PG | | |
     | 3 | 2 | Transmit Data | TXD | DTE | DCE |
     | 2 | 3 | Receive Data | RXD | DCE | DTE |
     | 7 | 4 | Request to Send | RTS | DTE | DCE |
     | 8 | 5 | Clear to Send | CTS | DCE | DTE |
     | 6 | 6 | Data Set Ready | DSR | DCE | DTE |
     | 5 | 7 | Signal Ground | SG | | |
     | 1 | 8 | Carrier Detect | CD | DCE | DTE |
     | 4 | 20 | Data Terminal Ready | DTR | DTE | DCE |
     | 9 | 22 | Ring Indicator | RI | DCE | DTE |

19. Breakout box.

20. The purpose of the I-P-O model is to provide a framework in which to focus on the difference between the data that comes into a modem (I) and the data that comes out of the modem (O). By defining this difference we know how the modem processed the data (P). By defining the input into a circuit and the required output from a circuit, it can be determined what process must occur to make the given circuit perform as required.

21. A phone number is dialed and the circuit between the originator and the Central Office (CO) within a Local Access and Transport Area (LATA) is then switched to the desired circuit number dialed. Once the call is complete and the phone is hung up, the circuit is terminated.

22. Bandwidth of a voice grade dial up circuit is from 300 Hz to 3300 Hz.

23. Originally the bandwidth was set to handle the range of the frequencies of human speech and hearing. This 3000 Hz is all the bandwidth with which the modem operating over a dial-up circuit has to work.

24. Shortcomings include: unpredictability of path and equipment which can lead to unpredictability of connection and circuit quality which can lead to unpredictability of data transmission speed and reliability.

25. Modem stands for Modulator/demodulator.

26. | INPUT | PROCESSING | OUTPUT |
     |-------|------------|--------|
     | 1's & 0's | convert digital data | Phone Network |
     | discrete voltages | to analog data | analog data |
     | digital data/discrete | discrete to wavelike | continuous wavelike |

27. A carrier wave is a "normal" or "neutral" analog wave which can be changed into two states representing 1's and 0's (modulated).

28. Each modem must conform to whatever standards are set. The modem at each end of a carrier wave must conform to the same standards.

29. The distance between the same spots on two subsequent waves is call the wavelength. The longer the wavelength, the lower the frequency and the shorter the wavelength, the greater the frequency.

30. Each change to a carrier wave called a modulation is a detectable event or signaling event.

31. .833 milliseconds (1 sec/1200)

32. .416 milliseconds (1 sec/2400)

33. Synchronous transmission uses a clock to maintain synchronization between modems so that data can be sent as a block of uninterrupted characters providing excellent efficiency.

34. Increasing the number of signaling events per second (baud rate) and increasing the number of bits per baud which can be interpreted.

35. Dial-up lines are usually two-wire circuits while leased lines are most often four-wire circuits. Two-wire typically supported half-duplex while four-wire supported full-duplex.

36. With half-duplex, handshaking and turnaround time can take a significant amount of time. In full-duplex, handshaking and turnaround time are cut since there is no "role reversal" necessary, thus no modem turnaround time delays.

37. CSU/DSU - Customer Service Unit/Data Service Unit - are used with DDS (Digital Data Service) over leased lines for all digital transmission. No digital to analog modulation is necessary.

38. When a dial-up line/analog circuit has line problems, a modem can fallback or lower speeds automatically and continue with data transmissions. With a digital line, if problems are encountered with the line, the data transmission ceases. However, digital circuits generally tend to be more error free than analog circuits.

39. ASCII and EBCDIC coding schemes have sufficient capacity to represent letters and characters familiar to people whose alphabets use the letters A, B, C etc. It should be obvious that 128 or 256 possible characters will not suffice when other languages and alphabets are considered. Unicode is a 16 bit code supporting up to 65,536 possible

characters (2^{16}= 65,536). It is backward compatible with ASCII as the first 128 Unicode characters are identical to the ASCII table. In addition, Unicode includes over 2000 Han characters for languages such as Chinese, Japanese, and Korean. It also includes Hebrew, Greek, Russian, and Sanskrit alphabets as well as mathematical and technical symbols, publishing symbols, geometric shapes, and punctuation marks.

40. It is up to the operating systems vendors to include support for particular encoding schemes such as Unicode/ISO 10646. Only Microsoft's Windows NT currently supports Unicode.

41. It is important to note that the designators DB-25, DB-9, and M Block only describe the physical connectors and do not imply anything regarding the transmission protocol which defines the electrical specifications for transmission using one of these physical interfaces. These physical interfaces can be employed using a variety of different transmission protocols.

42. A simple way to represent phase shifts as illustrated in Figure 2-19 is through the use of constellation points. Using a four quadrant representation of the 360 degrees of possible phase shift, individual points represent each different shifted wave. Amplitude changes can also be represented on such a grid. Note that when represented in a constellation diagram, a phase shift of 270 degrees is represented as -90 degrees.

43. As the number of constellation points (symbols) increases and symbols are in closer proximity to each other on the constellation diagram, the chance for a modem to misinterpret constellation points increases. Interference between symbols which can cause misinterpretation is known as intersymbol interference.

44. The data rates theorized by Nyquist's Theorem are not achieved in reality due to the presence of noise on phone lines. Shannon found that the higher the data rate, the more interference is caused by a given amount of noise, thus causing a higher error rate. This should make sense since at higher data rates, more bits are traveling over a circuit in a fixed length of time, and a burst of noise for the same length of time will effect more bits at higher data rates. Obviously, the modems must have a reliable way to know exactly when to sample the line for data. Somehow, the local and remote modems must establish and maintain some type of timing between them so that these detectable events are produced, transmitted, and detected accurately. Modems must find a way to avoid or minimize the impact of interference.

45. Echo cancellation takes advantage of sophisticated technology known as digital signal processors (DSP) which are included in modems that offer echo cancellation. Echo cancellation enables modems to transmit in full-duplex mode over a two-wire circuit.

46. By first testing the echo characteristics of a given phone line at modem initialization time, these DSPs are able to actually distinguish the echoed transmission of the local modem from the intended transmission of the remote modem. By subtracting or canceling the

echoed local transmission from the total data signal received, only the intended transmission from the remote modem remains to be processed by the modem and passed on to the local PC.

47. ISDN and Switched 56K are becoming popular for Internet access.

48. RS-232 is officially limited to 20Kbps for a maximum of 50 ft. Other transmission standards overcome both the speed and distance limitations of RS-232 and are listed in Figure 2-10.

49. RS are EIA/TIA based standards, while V standards are CCITT (ITU-T) based.

50. Accessing an ISDN service from your home computer requires a device which performs the same basic functions as a CSU/DSU but is called a terminal adapter, network termination unit (NTU), or a digital modem.

TEST QUESTIONS

True/False Questions

1. Parallel data transmission is relatively faster than serial data transmission. T/40

2. Serial data transmission can generally be transmitted over a longer distance than parallel data transmission. T/40

3. A leased line is the type of phone line found in most homes. F/59

4. The analog form of data is represented by discrete, digitized 1's and 0's while digital data is represented by continuous wave-like tones. F/49

5. Only one physical characteristic of a carrier wave may be altered or modulated at a time. F/50

6. Baud rate and bps are often used interchangeably and are identical in meaning. F/52

7. Asynchronous transmission is more efficient than synchronous transmission. F/57

8. A transmission rate of 9600 bps can be obtained at 2400 baud. T/54

9. In order to assure proper operation, communicating modems share similar standards and protocols. T/57

10. Generally there is no dial tone on a leased line because it does not go through any switching equipment. T/59

11. Leased lines are charged by the call. F/60

12. Narrowband digital lines have a faster transmission rate than broadband digital lines. F/60

13. Turnaround time is a very important factor in full-duplex transmission. F/58

14. Many CSU/DSU's may use fallback if the line is degraded. F/60

Chapter 2

Multiple Choice Questions

1. Data that is in some type of electrically-based format that the data communications equipment can interpret is said to be
    a. transmitted
p.37 b. encoded
    c. analog
    d. none of the above

2. Which of the following is the type of transmission in which each data bit of a byte, when transmitted, travels simultaneously down its own wire?
    a. demodulation
    b. stop bit
    c. baud
p.40 d. parallel

3. A special computer chip which interfaces the parallel transmission of the CPU and the serial transmission of the serial port is the
    a. DB-25
    b. modem
p.45 c. UART
    d. RS-232-c

4. The device used to monitor RS-232 signals is the
p.45 a. breakout box
    b. RS-232 cable
    c. modem
    d. UART

5. When communicating using the RS-232 standard on a DB-25 cable, the local PC would send a signal (raise voltage) through pin 20 which is abbreviated as
    a. RTS
    b. DSR
    c. CD
p.44 d. DTR

6. The encoding scheme used primarily for IBM mainframes.
    a. ASCII
p.37 b. EBCDIC
    c. Unicode
    d. ISO

7. The data communications equipment which converts digital signals from a PC to analog signals which can then be transmitted over dial-up telephone circuits is called a(n)
   a. CO switch
   b. leased line
p.50 c. modem
   d. RS-232 cable

8. Most of today's voice-grade dial-up circuits (phone lines) were designed to handle a range of frequencies from 300 Hz to 3300 Hz, which is called
   a. analog
   b. digital
p.49 c. bandwidth
   d. I-P-O

9. The new 16 bit encoding scheme which is capable of supporting up to 65,536 possible characters is known as
   a. ASCII
   b. EBCDIC
p.38 c. Unicode
   d. ISO9000

10. All of the following are physical characteristics of an analog wave that can be altered or modulated except
    a. amplitude
    b. frequency
p.50 c. parallel
    d. phase

11. Amplitude modulation of a carrier wave is represented by
    a. a longer or shorter wavelength
p.51 b. an increased or decreased wave height
    c. a shift or departure from the normal continuous pattern
    d. a square wave

12. Frequency modulation of a carrier wave is represented by
p.51 a. a longer or shorter wavelength
    b. an increased or decreased wave height
    c. a shift or departure from the normal continuous pattern
    d. a square wave

13. Phase modulation of a carrier wave is represented by
    a. a longer or shorter wavelength
    b. an increased or decreased wave height
p.52 c. a shift or departure from the normal continuous pattern
    d. a square wave

26   Chapter 2

14. Which of the following is a high speed serial physical connector?
   a. DB-9 connector
   b. DB-25 connector
p.41 c. M block connector
   d. Centronics connector

15. The number of signaling events per second is called
   a. bps
   b. digital transmission
p.52 c. baud rate
   d. byte

16. This type of transmission uses start and stop bits after each character.
p.57 a. asynchronous
   b. synchronous
   c. bps
   d. four-wire

17. This type of transmission uses sync characters after each block of characters.
   a. asynchronous
p.57 b. synchronous
   c. bps
   d. four-wire

18. Varying both phase and amplitude to increase the number of bits/baud which can be interpreted at a time is called
   a. tribit
   b. quadrature phase shift keying
   c. trellis coded modulation
p.54 d. quadrature amplitude modulation

19. Quadrature phase shift would use which of the following to obtain 8 possible detectable events?
   a. dibit
p.54 b. tribit
   c. quadbit
   d. bit

20. For communications purposes, a PC would be classified as
p.45 a. DTE
   b. DCE
   c. Modem
   d. Data Circuit Terminating Equipment

21. The ratio of the strength of the data signal to the strength of the background noise is known as
    a. Nyquist's Theorem
    b. intersymbol interference
p.56 c. signal to noise ratio
    d. crosstalk

22. Most local loops physically connected to the PSTN supply switched, dial-up service over which of the following?
    a. four-wire circuits
    b. eight-wire circuits
    c. leased lines
p.58 d. two-wire circuits

23. Which of the following is used by a modem to provide sophisticated echo cancellation techniques?
    a. handshaking
p.59 b. DSP
    c. half-duplex
    d. QAM

24. Which of the following services offers a broadband digital transmission rate of 44.736Mbps?
    a. POTS
    b. ISDN
    c. T-1
p.60 d. T-3

25. Which of the following services offers a digital dial-up service with a transmission rate of 144Kkbps?
    a. POTS
p.60 b. ISDN
    c. T-1
    d. T-3

26. The process in which two modems initialize themselves and agree to transmit and receive is called
    a. turnaround time
    b. echo cancellation
    c. auto negotiation
p.58 d. handshaking

28   Chapter 2

27. A normal voice-grade line that bypasses the carrier's switching equipment is called a
   a. dial-up line
   b. circuit-switched line
   c. null modem line
p.59 d. none of the above

28. Leased line circuits are usually
p.58 a. four-wire circuits
   b. two-wire circuits
   c. one-wire circuits
   d. found in most homes

29. Two-wire dial-up circuits typically supported
   a. digital data services
p.58 b. half-duplex
   c. full-duplex
   d. bi-polar symmetry

30. Receiving and transmitting simultaneously (signalling in both directions at the same time) over dial-up two-wire circuits is called
   a. digital data services
   b. half-duplex
p.58 c. full-duplex
   d. bi-polar symmetry

31. Digital data service leased lines are terminated with
   a. Modems
   b. POPs
p.60 c. CSU/DSU
   d. analog data

Fill-In the Blank Questions

1. A character's bits transmitted simultaneously is called _____ transmission.

2. DCE stands for _____.

3. _____ is a signaling standard for data transmission over a serial transmission line.

4. The device called a(n) _____ is used to modulate and demodulate data for transmission over phone lines.

5. The normal or neutral wave used as the starting point so an analog wave can change between at least two different states is called a(n) _____.

6. Another name for a signaling event is a(n) _____.

7. A clock provides for timing for _____ transmission.

8. The ordinary phone service is referred to as _____.

9. _____ is the process of converting an analog signal traveling over the PSTN into a digital signal the computer can use.

10. Sending data in either direction, but only one direction at a time is known as _____ transmission.

Answers

1. parallel p.40
2. Data Communications Equipment p.45
3. RS-232 p.41
4. modem p.50
5. carrier wave p.50
6. baud p.51
7. synchronous p.57
8. POTS or PSTN p.49
9. Demodulation p.50
10. half-duplex p.58

CASE STUDY AND ANSWERS

STAMP OF APPROVAL

Activities
1.　Top-down model:

Business	The Detroit District Post Office needed to provide its branch offices with cost-effective, yet high-speed remote LAN access and host access. In other words, they wanted to have high availability of bandwidth at low cost.
Applications	Email, word processing, and printing applications were used at remote sites. Remote access to the District's mainframe was required.
Data	Remote sites needed to send email, files and print jobs to the District office and have access to data on the District office's LANs. Data with mail volume, zip code, budgeting, and other information must be accessed by remote offices from the District headquarter's network. Data from the mainframe must be accessed remotely.
Network	The chattiness of LANs must be overcome for remote access. Adequate bandwidth must be provided to remote sites without the cost of leased lines. Quality of service was an issue.
Technology	Some remote sites had LAN traffic from Novell NetWare and Windows NT based LANs. 64 Kbps ISDN lines from Ameritech were used with Direct-Route-1, and Symplex RemoteOffice-1 routers to do packet-filtering and spoofing in order to keep network traffic and connection time to a minimum.

2.　Unanswered questions:
　　　What type of security was used?
　　　Who managed the remote sites and provided training and maintenance?
　　　Do all remote sites have ISDN availability?
　　　What is the volume of data transferred from the remote sites to the district office?
　　　What is the volume of data transferred from the district office LANs and mainframe to the remote sites?
　　　What is the rest of the U.S. Postal Service using for its network components?

Business
1.　They are prevented from sending in mail volume, zip code, budgeting, and other information.
2.　The monthly costs would have been 100 dedicated lines at about $200 a month.

3. Without spoofing, the user does not realize how active the ISDN links are and may incur a bill in the thousands of dollars for one month per line.

Application
1. Remote branches sent word processing and other documents to the main office using ftp, email, and print jobs, as well as needing access to the mainframe.
2. Keep-alive messages make sure that virtual circuits between two networks are active. They may cause excessive connection time, thus leased lines were often used since they are dedicated lines.
3. Workers at the post office's data center can either send batch jobs running on a host or initiate a mainframe print job over ISDN connections. It gave them high-speed mainframe printing without paying the high-speed cost.

Data
1. The Detroit District Post Office needed to connect its 90-plus branch offices to its central LAN and data center.
2. LAN-to-LAN chattiness was the main characteristic to consider along with fast access from remote sites.

Network
1. ISDN is viable now because routers are able to filter and spoof the chattiness of LAN traffic, minimizing the connect time, making ISDN cost effective.
2. Frame relay provided a steady 56Kbps which worked well for transporting file transfers, email, and print queues from hosts at the central site. However management was a nightmare and cost was prohibitive.
3. Analog lines did not lend themselves well to the chatty LAN traffic that flows from the remote sites to the central LAN and mainframe hosts in Detroit.

Technology
1. High-cost dedicated lines and low-speed analog links were the other connectivity options besides ISDN with packet-filtering and spoofing routers.
2. ISDN was chosen because of its high-speed cost effectiveness when coupled with packet-filtering and spoofing routers.
3. Frame relay provides a steady 56Kbps of throughput to branch offices 24 hours a day, making it a compelling means of transporting file transfers, email, and print queues from hosts at the central site.

CHAPTER 3

Basic Data Communications Technology

ANSWERS TO CHAPTER REVIEW QUESTIONS

1. Business analysis questions yield technical requirements. These resultant technical requirements can then be compared on a technical analysis grid which maps peripheral sharing functionality or whatever functionality you desire against available technology alternatives.

2. Discrete ARQ or ACK/NAK, is also called "Stop and Wait" ARQ. The transmitting device sends a block of data and waits until the remote receiving device sends an ACK or NAK, and transmits the next block of data if an ACK was received or the original block if a NAK was received. With continuous ARQ a Block Sequence Number is appended to each block of data transmitted. The transmitting device continuously transmits blocks of data without waiting for ACK or NAK from the receiving device. The receiving device still checks each block of data for errors. If it detects an error in a block of data, it sends the Block Sequence Number along with the NAK back to the transmitting device in which case retransmission occurs.

3. The transmitting device spends a significant amount of time idly waiting for either an ACK or NAK to be sent by the receiving device.

4. V.34 modems use Quadrature Amplitude Modulation with Trellis coded modulation which is a forward error correction methodology which helps support higher baud rates on dirty phone lines by predicting the location of a given constellation point.

5. A 28.8Kbps (V.34) modem could optimally transfer 115.2Kbps of data across a dial-up phone line. Refer to figure 3-5 for a graphic presentation of this information.

6. Data compressed by the sending modem must be uncompressed by the receiving modem using an identical algorithm or methodology.

7. In the top-down model, each layer may change independently of the others. Thus, while the business demands, applications, data or network design may change, the underlying technology can simply be substituted to meet these changes as the technology evolves.

8. The number of points on a constellation determines the number of different detectable events. Hence, a V.32 constellation has 2 to the 5th power (for 5 bits/baud) or 32

constellation points of which four of the five represent data, yielding the fact that a V.32 modem operating at 2400 baud x 4 bits/baud = 9600 bps.

9. In the case of V.32 modems, Trellis coded modulation adds a redundant fifth bit to each quadbit of data transmitted in order to help the receiving modem determine the correct detectable event by predicting the most likely occurrence of each detectable event (V.32) without the need to request retransmission. V.34 modulation adds more than one redundant bit for TCM.

10. Adaptive protocols are able to adjust transmission session parameters in response to varying line conditions. For instance, if a phone line's echo characteristics change, the receiving modem will adapt the subtracted echo of its own transmitted data accordingly. Other examples are adaptive size packet assembly and dynamic speed shifts.

11. V.32bis has 128 constellation points rather than 32. 7 bits are interpreted with 6 used for data, hence 2400 baud x 6 bits/baud = 14,400 bps over a voice grade dial-up phone line. Also, V.32bis has the ability to re-train or adjust data rates on the fly quickly depending upon the quality of the dial-up circuit.

12. The term "bis" means second version.

13. V.Fast is an extension of the V.32 bis by delivering a maximum data rate of 28,800 bps over dial-up voice grade lines. It is not a CCITT(ITU) standard.

14. V.32terbo will upgrade the 14.4Kbps of V.32bis to 19.2Kbps. It is not a CCITT(ITU) standard.

15. Fully standard compliant means the modem will support use on both dial-up and leased lines or whatever other requirements the full specifications list.

16. The data compression software examines the data, looking for repetitive patterns of characters, before it sends the data onto the circuit. Having spotted a repetitive pattern of up to 32 characters, the two V.42bis modems store this pattern, along with a code or key, in a constantly updated library. The next time this pattern of data comes along to be sent, the sending modem just sends a character or characters which represents the pattern's code or key, rather than the entire data stream itself. The receiving modem, then consults its library to see which uncompressed pattern is represented by the code character(s) received.

17. Some data has more repetitive patterns thus the 4:1 ideal compression ratio may be achieved; however with fewer repetitive patterns, the compression ratio will go down.

18. V.42 provides error control, while V.42bis provides for data compression.

19. A single character may uncompress into many characters, thus the importance of error prevention, detection, and correction should be obvious. An erroneously transmitted character could be referenced in the receiving modem's library of repetitive patterns and incorrectly uncompressed into the wrong data stream.

20. Digital leased lines offering faster transmission rates with fewer errors and line problems.

21. Buy CSU/DSUs from the DDS service provider and make them responsible for the delivery of the service through their DCEs to your DTEs.

22. A CSU/DSU interfaces with a digital leased line, thus there is no modulation/demodulation required.

23. Common uses os switched digital services include connecting LANs (internetworking), backup and disaster recovery for failed leased circuits, and videoconferencing.

24. Handshaking is standardized initial interaction between two modems. It allows two modems to get to know each other and establish the greatest common operating characteristics between themselves.

25. The Hayes AT command set is the de facto standard operating system for modems attached to personal computers. It is supported by nearly all manufacturers' modems, not just Hayes.

26. Error prevention strives to prevent errors from happening in the first place by optimizing the condition of the transmission link. Error detection tries to detect an error if it occurs. Error correction is accomplished when the receiving modem detects an error and requests re-transmission of the incorrect data from the transmitting modem.

27. A repeater is used by a phone company to assure signal quality over the entire length of a digital circuit. An amplifier is used on an analog circuit and a repeater is used on a digital circuit. A repeater just regenerates signal, while amplifier "amplifies" noise as well as signal.

28. With simple parity check, if two bits were changed, 0 to 1 and 1 to 0, then the resulting parity would not change and error detection would not occur.

29. LRC adds a second dimension to Vertical Redundancy Checking adding extra parity bits.

30. A checksum adds up the ASCII decimal face values of several characters rather than just one character, and appends an entire character, rather than just a bit, to a message block. It is a more sophisticated method for error detection. Each bit is assigned a base 2 place value. These place values are then added. An entire block of characters would add each character's total and divided by 255 giving a number and remainder. This remainder is then represented as a single checksum character and the entire set of characters are then

transmitted. The receiving modem would then perform the same algorithm and if the checksums didn't match, an error is detected.

31. A Block Sequence Number is appended to each block of data transmitted. The transmitting device continuously transmits blocks of data without waiting for ACK or NAK from the receiving device. The sliding window block limit prevents a modem from transmitting indefinitely without receiving either an ACK or NAK. The Sliding Window "slides back" to retransmit any blocks received in error.

32. Selective ARQ, a form of Continuous ARQ, allows for retransmission of only those blocks of data received in error.

33. A Block Sequence Number is appended to each block of data as it is transmitted so that when the receiving device detects an error, only the Block Sequence Number and the NAK are sent back to the transmitting device for retransmission.

34. The transmitting device must remember what data was in which block. The data that must be stored and saved in block sequence order is placed in buffer memory.

35. Hardware flow control is done using voltages on Pin #4 Request to Send (RTS) and Pin #5 Clear to Send (CTS). With software flow control actual characters are sent back and forth to tell the transmitting device when to stop (XOFF) and start transmission (XON) of data.

36. Hardware flow control is probably more reliable since software flow control is nothing more than transmitted characters susceptible to the same transmission problems as normal data.

37. Forward Error Correction sends sufficient redundant data to the receiving modem to enable it to not only detect but also correct data transmission errors in some cases, without the need for retransmission. This redundant data adds to the overall traffic but prevents the need for retransmission.

38. A dial backup unit is used to automatically establish a connection via a dial-up line between two points on a failed leased circuit, while a dial back unit receives a call, terminates the call, looks up the User ID and/or Password in a directory, finds the phone number of the valid user in the directory and dials back the valid user and establishes the communication session.

39. Variable callback allows a user to enter both a password as well as a phone number to which the dial back unit should return the call. Might be required for traveling sales reps.

40. Variable callback depends heavily on the secrecy of the passwords and the integrity of the valid users.

41. Software must be easy to use. It must maximize the efficient use of available hardware and circuit technology. The purchase of the software must be cost effective.

42. In order to access the modem attached to the network's communication server, the communications software must send instructions and data out through the PC's network interface card rather than the PC's serial port. The network operating system must support the communications software package also.

43. A UART (Universal Asynchronous Receiver Transmitter) chip is the piece of hardware that actually does the parallel to serial and serial to parallel conversion of data between the PC and its serial port. Some software may not work with Windows. Also Windows 3.0 driver is limited to 19.2 Kbps. Some software packages do not support buffered UART.

44. Error checking techniques, request for retransmit, block size in bytes, batch capability, multiple platforms, and auto-recovery.

45. The Principle of Shifting Bottlenecks states that when one component of a computer system's throughput is improved the slowdown, or bottleneck, shifts to another component which then becomes the bottleneck. With the modem throughput improving to 115.2Kbps with the new V.34 modems, the serial ports of the PCs involved in the end-to-end communications session should be set to 115.2 Kbps. However, most PC serial ports are only able to support transmission speeds of 19.2 Kbps or 38.4Kbps. Thus the bottleneck shifted from the modem to the serial port.

46. A short term solution to the problem would be to increase the speed of serial ports: One example of such an enhanced serial port is the Hayes ESP Communications Accelerator. This serial port replacement supports speeds of up to 921,600 bps by implementing two 1024 byte buffers and minimizing CPU interruption. Such serial port speeds would be necessary if one were to employ Hayes modems on both ends of a transmission which support the Hayes proprietary enhanced V.42bis data compression algorithms with potential compression ratios of 8:1. Another short term solution would be to hook the modem to the parallel port rather than the serial port: The Microcom Deskporte family of modems using Microcom's Advanced Parallel Technology (APT) is an example of modems which communicate with PCs via their parallel port rather than the serial port. Most PC parallel ports are capable of transmitting at 115.2Kbps bi-directionally. One difficulty with this solution is that the PC's communications software must be able to redirect modem output to the parallel rather than serial port. Microcom claims to supply all necessary software and drivers to accomplish PC to modem communication via the PC's parallel port at speeds of up to 300 Kbps. Long term solutions include fundamental changes in PC design may be the ultimate solution to the input/output (I/O) bottleneck. Two of the more significant proposals are:

- Universal Serial Bus (USB) - This external I/O port would supply throughput of up to 8Mbps, can daisy-chain up to 127 devices, and can handle data as well as streaming traffic such as voice and video.
- FireWire (IEEE P1394) - This I/O specification can provide bandwidth of 100Mbps, 200Mbps or 400Mbps and is also being promoted as a standard interface for consumer video products such as VCRs and camcorders.

47. Refer to figure 3-3 which explains several technical innovations introduced as part of the V.34 standard.

48. V.42bis uses a data compression algorithm known as the Lempel Ziv algorithm as described in the previous section . Ideally, it can compress files, and thereby increase throughput by a 4:1 ratio. Proprietary improvements to this algorithm by modem manufacturers can be achieved in two ways: Increase the amount of memory dedicated to the library, also known as the dictionary. (1.5KB standard, some modems use up to 6KB); Increase the size of the pattern of characters, also known as string size, which can be stored in the dictionary. (32 bytes standard, some modems support strings up to 256 bytes). Proprietary improvements to standards such as V.42bis are only effective when both modems involved in a transmission are identical. It should also be noted that most independent modem testing suggests that compression ratios in the range of 2.5:1 are most likely despite higher optimal claims.
MNP Class 5 yields data compression ratios in the range of between 1.3:1 and 2:1. MNP5 uses two data compression algorithms: Huffman encoding is a special character encoding scheme which re-encodes ASCII characters. Frequently used characters such as "a", "e" and "s", are encoded with only 4 bits, while rarely occurring characters such as "x" or "z" are encoded using as many as 11bits. Overall, the effect of Huffman encoding in that more characters are transmitted using fewer bits. Run-length encoding exams a data stream in search of repeating characters. When any character repeats more than three times, the run-length encoding algorithm replaces the entire string of repeated characters with only three repetitions of the character followed by a count field indicating how many times the character is actually repeated.

49. V.42 error correction standards incorporates MNP classes 2, 3, and 4. While MNP 5 is a data compression protocol which can increase throughput by up to 200.

50. One very important point to keep in mind when purchasing pre-standard data communications equipment is the ability of the vendor to upgrade that equipment to meet the specifications of the official standard once it is issued. In some cases, software upgrades are possible, while in other cases, hardware upgrades or chip replacement is required. In some cases, these upgrades may be free and easily accomplished via a toll-free number, while in other cases, the upgrade may involve returning the equipment to the factory involving upgrade fees of several hundred dollars. Be sure to understand all of the details regarding standards compliance upgrades before ever purchasing pre-standards data communications equipment.

TEST QUESTIONS

True/False Questions

1. The V.34 standard provides for 28.8Kbps transmission over dial-up lines or leased lines. T/69

2. The V.34 standard transmission rate is achieved by interpreting 9 data bits per baud at a baud rate of 2400. F/72

3. One modem with only V.42bis data compression will be able to talk with another modem using only MNP Class 5 data compression. F/74

4. Data compressed by the sending modem must be uncompressed by the receiving modem using an identical algorithm. T/71

5. Data compression requires less error prevention, detection, and correction since it speeds transmission rates. F/74

6. The Hayes AT Command Set is a de facto standard operating system for modems which allows for a series of commands that allow the PC to control the set-up and performance of the modem. T/91

7. Error prevention, error detection, and error correction are the same and combine to improve the reliability of the data transmission. F/76

8. Dynamic Speed Shifts is an MNP adaptive protocol which allows two modems to change speeds up or down in the midst of their data transmission in response to varying line conditions. T/77

9. If a transmitted data character had a bit pattern of 1000011 and we were using odd parity, the parity bit would be a 0. T/79

10. Discrete ARQ is more efficient than Continuous ARQ since it stops and waits for either an ACK or ANK before transmission continues. F/82

11. Software flow control uses pins 4 and 5 to send voltages indicating clear to send or request to send. F/83

12. Managing the constant storage and retrieval of blocks of data from a modem's buffer memory is known as flow control. T/83

13. Efficiently and reliably correcting an error once detected is known as error detection. F/82

14. Hardware flow control is more reliable and probably faster than software flow control. T/84

15. V.42 is the first issue of a modem data compression standard, while V.42bis represents the second improved version. F/85

16. Some leased line modems possess sufficient technology to be able to monitor a failed leased line and establish a connection on a dial-up line in a process known as auto-restoral. F/86

17. A cable modem's top transmission speed is 128 Kbps. F/89

18. Making the correct choice of communications software depends more on business analysis questions and requirements than on communications software features. T/93

19. Some file transfer protocols are known as streaming protocols because they do not stop transmitting a file until they reach the end of file indicator. T/96

20. In order to access the modem attached to the network's communication server, the communications software must send instructions and data out the PC's serial port. F/92

Multiple Choice Questions

1. Using the top-down model for data communications analysis, which of the following would be considered business layer demands?
    a. faster
    b. more efficient
    c. more reliable

   p.68 d. all of the above

2. The V series standards are this organization's standards dealing with data communications over the telephone network.

   p.70 a. ITU-T
    b. ANSI
    c. ASCII
    d. IBM

3. V.32 is a standard which supports
    a. 14.4 Kbps transmission
    b. data compression

   p.69 c. 9.6 Kbps
    d. b and c

4. With reference to international modem standards, "bis" refers to
    a. the first update to a given V standard
    b. the second update to a given V standard
p.70 c. the second standard issued by a given standards committee
    d. the third standard issued by a given standards committee

5. This new V series standard will deliver a maximum data rate of 28.8 Kbps over dial-up voice-grade lines.
    a. V.42
p.69 b. V.34
    c. V.42bis
    d. V.32bis

6. This technical innovation of the V.34 modem standard allows increases in transmission rate as line conditions improve.
    a. fallback
    b. handshaking
    c. adaptive line probing
p.72 d. fall forward

7. The V.42bis ITU-T standard is for
p.74 a. data compression
    b. fast retrain
    c. echo cancellation
    d. ASCII to EBCDIC translation

8. Data compression works in part by
    a. stripping out non-significant bits
    b. increasing the baud
    c. digitizing space characters
p.71 d. looking for repetitive patterns of characters

9. The theoretical throughput for a modem configured with V.34 and V.42bis is
    a. 14.4 Kbps
    b. 28.8 Kbps
p.74 c. 115.2 Kbps
    d. 230 Kbps

10. The theoretical transmission rate for a modem configured with V.34 and V.42bis is
    a. 14.4 Kbps
p.74 b. 28.8 Kbps
    c. 115.2 Kbps
    d. 230 Kbps

42   Chapter 3

11. Which of the following standards offers the highest data compression ratio?
p.74
   a. MNP 5
   b. V.42bis
   c. MNP 6
   d. V.8

12. Which of the following solutions eliminates the transmission bottleneck created by the introduction of the V.34 standard?
   a. MNP 5
p.76 b. USB
   c. Dynamic Speed Shifting
   d. CRC

13. Keeping errors from happening in the first place by optimizing the condition of the transmission link is known as
   a. error detection
   b. error correction
p.76 c. error prevention
   d. error protocol deterence

14. A promise from the phone company as to the levels of noise or interference which will occur on a given analog leased line is called
p.76 a. line conditioning
   b. attenuation
   c. amplifier
   d. repeater

15. The loss of signal strength or volume on an analog circuit is known as
   a. line conditioning
p.77 b. attenuation
   c. adaptive protocols
   d. amplifier

16. Which of the following helps prevent errors during data transmission by adjusting transmission session parameters in response to varying line conditions.
   a. line conditioning
   b. amplifier
p.77 c. adaptive protocols
   d. handshaking

17. The simplest of the error detection techniques is
   a. Checksums
   b. Cyclic Redundancy Checks
   c. Longitudinal Redundancy Checks
p.79 d. Parity

18. Longitudinal Redundancy Checks and Cyclic Redundancy Checks are forms of
p.79
    a. error detection
    b. error prevention
    c. error correction
    d. constellation points

19. Which of the following may not be able to detect multiple bit errors within the same character?
    a. CRC
    b. LRC
    c. VRC
p.79   d. Parity

20. Retransmitting data from the transmitting modem to the receiving modem when the receiving modem detects an error is
    a. error detection
    b. error prevention
p.82   c. error correction
    d. none of the above

21. With Continuous ARQ which of the following is **false**?
    a. also called Sliding Window Protocols
p.83   b. transmits blocks of data indefinitely
    c. appends a block sequence number to each block of data transmitted
    d. when an error is detected, receiving device sends the block sequence number and NAK back to the transmitting device

22. Sending a balanced amount of redundant data to avoid retransmission is a form of
    a. discrete ARQ
    b. Continuous ARQ
    c. Sliding Window Protocol
p.84   d. none of the above

23. Name for a form of error correction which only requires retransmission of specific blocks received in error rather than all blocks subsequent to the block in which the error was detected?
    a. discrete ARQ
    b. Continuous ARQ
    c. Sliding Window Protocol
p.83   d. selective ARQ

44   Chapter 3

24. When a leased line fails, which technology is used to automatically re-establish connection over dial-up lines?
    a. V.42
p.86 b. dial backup unit
    c. dial back unit
    d. manual switch

25. Which of the following is a form of software flow control?
    a. RTS/CTS
    b. selective ARQ
    c. continuous ARQ
p.84 d. XON/XOFF

26. Which of the following is a disadvantage of a dial-back unit?
    a. assures only valid user can gain access to the network
    b. network use can be restricted according to time of day or day of the week
    c. reports usage information
p.87 d. none of the above

27. Of the following, which standard assures error free transmission via modems?
    a. MNP 4 and V.42bis
    b. MNP 5 and V.42
p.85 c. MNP 4 and V.42
    d. MNP 5 and V.42bis

28. A technique in which a valid user enters both a password as well as a phone number to which the dial back unit should return the call, is known as
    a. POTS
p.88 b. variable callback
    c. fixed callback
    d. out-of-order callback

29. Which of the following modem trends allows simultaneous voice and data transmission to a single location at 28.8Kbps?
    a. ASDL
    b. ISDN
    c. CSU/DSU
p.88 d. DSVD

30. Which of the following modem trends may replace ISDN with up to 8Mbps one way and 64Kbps return transmission rates?
    a. CSU/DSU
p.89 b. ADSL
    c. DSVD
    d. ASVD

31. The interface between data communications user requests and the data communications hardware is
    a. modem cable
    b. modem
p.91 c. communication software
    d. RJ-11 plugs

32. If the user desired communications software that was cost-effective, which layer of the top-down model would reflect this?
    a. Network
    b. Application
p.93 c. Business
    d. Data

33. Which of the following are a series of commands embedded within the communications software which are understood by the installed operating system?
p.91 a. APIs
    b. CSU/DSU
    c. BIOS
    d. passwords

34. Which of the following is not a valid purpose for business uses of communications software?
    a. connect to a remote mini/mainframe computer and log in as a remote terminal
p.93 b. providing word processing capabilities
    c. transfer of files from PC to PC, or from PC to Mini/Mainframe
    d. connect to value-added information services

35. The sole job of this type of service is to manage modem access and other data communications related tasks.
    a. data server
    b. modem server
    c. application server
p.92 d. remote access server

36. In order to access the modem attached to a network's communication server, the communications software must send instructions through the PC's
    a. keyboard
p.92 b. network interface card
    c. monitor
    d. modem cable

46   Chapter 3

37. A type of file transfer protocol which is great for micro to mainframe file transfers, but is not very fast is
p.97
   a. Kermit
   b. Xmodem
   c. Zmodem
   d. Ymodem

38. This file transfer protocol allows for streaming data.
   a. Kermit
   b. Xmodem
p.96   c. Xmodem-G
   d. Zmodem

39. This file transfer protocol has an auto-recovery feature which allows an aborted file transfer to resume at the point where the transfer aborted rather than starting the transfer over at the beginning of the file.
   a. Kermit
   b. Xmodem
   c. Xmodem-G
p.98   d. Zmodem

Fill-In the Blank Questions

1. The essence of the top-down approach is that _____ solutions meet _____ requirements.

2. A dilemma known as the _____ describes the problem an example of which the serial port now becomes the restrictive piece of the transmission link not the modem, since the modem's speed has increased.

3. In the V.32bis standard, the "bis" stands for the _____ version.

4. The _____ modem standard offers a transmission rate of 28.8Kbps over dial-up lines.

5. _____ classes or groups of protocols are defacto standards for error correction and data compression.

6. The _____ is an external I/O port which will supply throughput of up to 8Mbps, can daisy-chain up to 127 devices, and can handle data as well as streaming traffic such as voice and video.

7. The loss of signal strength or volume is known as _____.

8. Another name for Continuous ARQ is _____.

9. Controlling the flow of data into and out of the buffer memory in order to avoid any loss of data is called _____.

10. Network dial-up access to data can be controlled by password protection and _____ security.

11. The operating system interacts with PC hardware (CPU, memory, serial port, etc.) via a series of commands known as the _____.

Answers

1. lower-layer, upper-layer p.69
2. Principle of Shifting Bottlenecks p.75
3. second p.70
4. V.34 p.70
5. MNP or Microcom Networking Protocols p.71
6. USB or Universal Serial Bus p.76
7. attenuation p.77
8. Sliding Window Protocol p.83
9. flow control p.83
10. dial-back p.87
11. BIOS or Basic Input Output System p.91

48 Chapter 3

CASE STUDY AND ANSWERS

PG&E APPS KEEP LIGHTS ON

Activities

1. Top-down model:

Business	The San Francisco-based utility supplies gas and electric power to over 3 million customers with ever-changing power needs.
	The company must anticipate its customers' fluctuating demand and fine-tune the power generation of its power-plant network to meet that load.
	The business objective is to operate the system at the lowest economic point they can possibly achieve in order to provide the cheapest source of power.
Applications	The Energy Management Systems (EMS) manages real-time systems data.
	Telemetering is used to provide up-to-the-second data.
Data	A data warehouse is used by headquarters and by users.
	Remote data is sent to the company's mainframe at headquarters.
	Data includes information concerning line flows, power output, and circuit-breaker status as well as information on ambient temperature of the remote terminal unit's location.
	The warehouse information can be accessed by over 5000 internal users.
Network	The network consists of over 400 remote terminals reporting information every two seconds over leased lines and microwave communications to the headquarters in San Francisco.
Technology	Hardware consists of 400 remote terminals, CDC mainframes, leased lines, microwave communications, RS/6000's and soon, a Windows NT-based machine with 20GB of disk space for the data warehouse.
	Software consists of the EMS software, Oracle7-based data warehouse, Enabling Tools front end, and soon Windows NT.
	There are 110 hydro-, 70 thermal-, and two nuclear-power generators and thousands of miles of transmission lines making up PG&E's power network.

2. Unanswered questions:
   What will be the cost of upgrading?
   What type of WAN services and protocols are used to connect the remote sites?
   What other applications are run on the mainframes and RS-6000 computers?
   What security measures are in place?
   Are any LANs connected into the system, and if so, how?

What are the bandwidth requirements currently and in the future?

Business
1. The company supplies gas and electric power to over 3 million customers with ever changing power needs.
2. The business needs included the management of power supply and demand, power generation, and querying of the data warehouse.
3. It was important to operate the system at the lowest economic point they can possibly achieve in order to provide the cheapest source of power.
4. Data is used for load forecasting and stability analysis so that the company does not generate more power than needed nor does it lack power when required.

Application
1. Applications are used to provide current and historical data needed for managing the power system to minimize losing money by having to sell excess power or buy power.

Data
1. Real-time data is two-second old data provided by its remote sites.
2. Real-time data allows the business to operate the system at the lowest economic point they can to provide the cheapest source of power.
3. Initially, an awkward reporting procedure that funneled user requests through a power-management group was used. Also, the data warehouse was accessible by 5000 internal users which overwhelmed the RS/6000s running the data warehouse.
4. Telemetering is a process in which every two seconds, more than 400 remote terminals at the company's power-generating plants, sub-stations, and temperature monitors communicate with the mainframe at headquarters over leased lines and microwave communications.
5. Data collected from remote terminals includes information concerning line flows, power output, and circuit-breaker status along with information on ambient temperature of the remote-terminal unit's location.
6. The company can save tens of millions of dollars a year in projects and operational expenditures.
7. A data warehouse is a collection of the company's data, both real-time and historical, which can be queried in order to provide information used to effectively manage the business. In the case of PG&E it was used to make decisions on how much power to generate in order to provide the cheapest power possible to its customers.
8. It replaced an awkward reporting procedure that funneled user requests through a power-management group that included hard-coded reports and Microsoft FoxPro.
9. By giving its 5,000 internal users the ability to run daily and ad hoc reports against the data warehouse, PG&E found it had inadvertently overwhelmed the RS/6000s running the data warehouse.

Network
1. Telemetering is supported by leased lines and microwave communications.

Technology
1. The data warehouse is executing on IBM RS/6000s using Oracle7. The EMS system is running on CDC mainframes.
2. PG&E plans to move the data warehouse to a dedicated Windows NT-based maching with 20GB of disk space, running Oracle7 in synchronous mode with the RS/6000 so that as updates are made to the RS/6000 they will be made simultaneously to the NT machine.

CHAPTER 4

Voice Communications
Concepts & Technology

ANSWERS TO CHAPTER REVIEW QUESTIONS

1. Figure 4-1 in the text provides a graphical representation of how voice actually gets transferred on and off the voice network. The transmitter is a movable diaphragm which is sensitive to changes in voice frequency and amplitude and sends a varying analog, electrical signal out onto the voice network based upon the changes in voice frequency and amplitude. This varying electrical analog wave is transmitted over the voice network to the phone of the receiving person. The receiver or earpiece basically works in the opposite fashion of the mouthpiece. The varying electrical waves are received at the receiver at an electromagnet. Varying levels of electricity produce varying levels of magnetism which cause the movable diaphragm to move in direct proportion with the magnetic variance producing varying sound waves which is what the human ear hears.

2. DTMF, dual Tone Multi-Frequency, is touch tone dialing. The tones generated by DTMF phones can be used for enabling specialized services from PBXs, carriers, banks, information services, and retail establishments.

3. Refer to Figures 4-3 and 4-4 in the text.
   PAM - Pulse Amplitude Modulation, varies the amplitude or voltage of the electrical pulses in relation to the varying characteristics of the voice signal.
   PDM - Pulse Duration Modulation, varies the duration of each electrical pulse in relation to the variances in the analog signal.
   PPM - Pulse Position Modulation, varies the duration between pulses in relation to variances in the analog signal.
   PCM - Pulse Code Modulation, (also includes a variation called Adaptive Differential Pulse Code Modulation or ADPCM) transmits a binary representation of either the approximate difference in amplitude of consecutive amplitude samples (ADPCM), or of the absolute amplitude (PCM).

4. PCM uses 8,000 samples per second with each sample requiring eight bits to represent that sampled bandwidth in binary notation. ADPCM transmits only the approximate difference in amplitude of consecutive amplitude samples, rather than the absolute amplitude. By doing this only 32Kbps as opposed to 64Kbps of PCM are required for each conversation digitized via ADPCM. This allows 48 simultaneous digitized voice conversations per T-1 using ADPCM instead of PCM's 24.

52   Chapter 4

5. Digital Signal Processors, which take the digitized PCM code and further manipulate and compress it, are used. Some voice compression techniques attempt to synthesize the human voice, other techniques attempt to predict the actual voice transmission patterns, while still others attempt to transmit only changes in voice patterns.

6. The business motivation is based around the ability to compress more digitized voice conversations onto less bandwidth, increasing transmission efficiency; however the trade-off is that the quality of compressed voice transmissions does not match the quality of an analog voice transmission over an analog dial-up line or a full 64K of digital line.

7. PBX architecture is made up of a CPU or Common Control, switching matrix, station cards, trunk card and outside trunks. Refer to Figure 4-7 in the text.

8. CTI passes actual information such as incoming or outgoing phone numbers along the switched connections to or from the attached computer for subsequent processing by the computer or PBX.

9. Figure 4-13 describes several practical business applications of CTI. These features can be used in an outbound telemarketing setting, phone numbers can be fed from the computer's database to special auto-dialing equipment which interfaces to the PBX. If the call is answered, the PBX triggers the computer to display the associated data record on the data terminal of the telemarketing agent.

10. Figure 4-15 in the text lists the technology for Interactive Voice Response systems. Among its uses are automated systems to check account balances at banks or to check arrival and departure information at airlines.

11. Figure 4-17 in the text is a graphical representation of the voice network hierarchy. Functionality implied by the hierarchy is that higher levels on the network hierarchy imply greater switching and transmission capacity as well as greater expense. Figure 4-18 in the text more clearly illustrates why higher level offices have greater routing flexibility.

12. It is used with inter-switch signaling methodology for such things as call set-up and termination. The signaling used for intelligent services such as ANI (Automatic Number Identification) should not travel over the same logical channel as the voice conversation itself. This is known as out-of-band signaling.

13. The local loop between the local CO and a residence or place of business may be an analog circuit, but it is very likely that high-capacity digital circuits will be employed to transport that call, especially between COs or carriers.

14. The higher the sampling rate of the analog signal/second the better the digitization and quality of the digital signal.

15. By transmitting only the approximate difference in amplitude of consecutive amplitude samples, rather than the absolute amplitude, only 32Kbps of bandwidth is required for each conversation digitized via ADPCM.

16. A DS-0 circuit is exactly 64Kbps, which is just the right bandwidth to carry a digitized voice conversation using PCM (8,000 samples/sec x 8 bits/sample = 64,000 bits/sec).

17. PCM represents the amplitude of the voice signal by using an 8 bit binary code as opposed to an electrical signal.

18. PCM works very nicely with a DS-0 circuit, which in turn can then combine 24 DS-0 circuits to form a T-1 circuit. Also, PCM's related ADPCM allows twice as many digitized voice conversations via a type of voice compression, which allows for more efficient transmission. As a digital payload, PCM encoded voice can be mixed with other digital payloads such as data, image, fax or video.

19. A CODEC, Coder/Decoder, is the technology employed to sample analog transmissions and transform them into a series of binary digits. Many codecs also multiplex several digitized voice conversations onto a single channel and are an integral part of T-1 multiplexers. It is basically the opposite of a modem.

20. Interoperability issues surrounding CTI include three commonly implemented architectures; PBX-to-Host Interfaces, Desktop CTI, and Client/Server CTI. These differ in their implementation and CTI lack of standardization (two major LAN-based CTI API standards are TAPI and TSAPI).

21. Call Accounting Systems can pay for themselves in a short amount of time by spotting and curtailing abuse as well as by allocating phone usage charges on a departmental basis.

22. In a process known as SMDR (Station Message Detail Recording) an individual detail record is generated for each call and then fed to the call accounting system and stored on disk.

23. Multi-vendor interoperability standards are one issue. Q.Sig seeks to allow PBXs of any manufacturer to interoperate with each other and with ISDN networks. It is an extension of Q.931 ISDN standard which allows PBX features to interoperate with PSTN features. Another issue is the interoperability of PBXs with wireless phones.

24. SS7 is the CCITT approved standard for out-of-band signaling. As an underlying architectural component of ISDN, SS7 delivers the out-of-band signaling over ISDN's D channel. SS7 is nothing more than a suite of protocols which controls the structure and transmission of both circuit-related and non-circuit related information via out-of-band signaling between central office switches.

25. SDN is a major component of AIN (Advanced Intelligent Network). A software defined network implies that the user has some control over the flexible configuration of their telecommunications service and network. By extending SS7 out-of-band signaling to the end users, voice networks can be reconfigured as business activities dictate.

26. Network analysts must be qualified to design networks that are capable of carrying voice as well as data. Before designing such networks, it is essential for the network analyst to understand the nature of voice signals, as well as how voice signals can be processed and integrated into a cohesive network with data transmissions.

27. Figure 4-2 provides a comparison between the bandwidth of the PSTN and that of human hearing.

28. When a bank of codecs are arranged in a modular chassis to not only digitize analog voice conversations but also load them onto a shared high capacity (T-1:1.544Mbps) circuit, the hybrid device is referred to as a channel bank.

29. Using a specialized circuit known as an adaptive predictor, ADPCM calculates the difference between the predicted and actual incoming signals and specifies that difference as one of sixteen different levels using 4 bits (2^4= 16). Since each voice channel can be represented by just 4 bits, ADPCM can support 48 simultaneous voice conversations over a T-1 circuit.
The ITU standard for 32Kbps ADPCM is known as G.721 and is generally used as a reference point for the quality of voice transmission known as toll quality.

30. Following is the mathematical proof:

    8,000 samples/sec x 8 bits/sample = 64,000 bits/sec (bps)
    64,000 bits/sec = 64Kbps   = DS-0 Circuit

    24 DS-0s = 24 x 64Kbps = 1536Kbps = 1.536Mbps

    Plus: 1 framing bit/sample x 8,000 samples/sec. = 8,000 framing bits/sec

    8Kbps   + 1536Kbp = 1544Kbps = 1.544Mbps = Transmission capacity of T-1 transmission service

31. A PBX is really just a privately owned, smaller version of the switch in telephone company central offices that can control circuit switching for the general public. Depending on the requested destination, switched circuits are established, maintained and terminated on a per call basis by a portion of the PBX known as the switching matrix. Figure 4-7 illustrates the physical attributes of a PBX.

32. In many ways, the PBX is becoming nothing more than a specialized communications or voice server that must integrate with all other servers as part of an overall enterprise

network. In order to achieve this transparent integration as part of the enterprise network, PBXs have had to undergo a radical change in their overall design from proprietary, monolithic, devices to more open architectures based on industry standard hardware and software components. Figure 4-7 summarizes some of the transitions involved in the migration to the new open PBX architecture, while Figure 4-8 portrays a logical architecture for an open architecture PBX.

33. With automatic call distribution, incoming calls are routed directly to certain extensions without going through a central switchboard. Calls can be routed according to the incoming trunk or phone number. ACD is often used in customer service organizations in which calls may be distributed to the first available agent

34. Computer telephony integration is commonly implemented in one of the following three architectures: PBX-to-Host Interfaces, Desktop CTI, and Client/Server CTI. Figure 4-14 illustrates the various CTI architectures.

35. Outbound Dialing, also known as Predictive Dialing, is a merger of computing and telephony. Using a database of phone numbers, it automatically dials those numbers, recognizes when calls are answered by people, and quickly passes those calls to available agents.

36. Unified Messaging, is perhaps the most interesting CTI application category for the LAN-based user, and also known as the Universal In-Box. It will allow voice mail, e-mail, faxes, and pager messages to all be displayed on a single graphical screen. Messages can then be forwarded, deleted, or replied to easily in point and click fashion. Waiting calls can also be displayed in the same Universal In-Box.

37. TSAPI or Telephony Services API was jointly developed and sponsored by Novell and AT&T. TAPI or Telephony API was jointly developed and sponsored by Intel and Microsoft. Applications that are written to use either of these APIs should be able to operate transparently in either a NetWare (TSAPI) or Windows (TAPI) environment. Both Novell and Microsoft are developing their own CTI application software as well.

38. Following are some key characteristics of CTI application development tools:
    - Graphical code generators allow easy application development with a minimum of programming background.
    - Debugging tools, also known as test utilities or virtual phone utilities, allow applications to be tested without the need for voice cards or phones. Log files that record all user responses and program interactions can also aid in debugging new programs.
    - Interfaces to FAX software for incoming or outbound FAX control can add FaxBack or FAX-on-Demand capabilities
    - Sound editors are able to edit and translate between .WAV and .VOX sound files

56   Chapter 4

- Pre-recorded sound bites with standard greetings and responses can lend a professional image to developed CTI applications
- CTI applications developed with a given CTI application development tool may or may not need to pay royalties on copies of the finished application
- Among the types of CTI applications that can be developed with such application development tools are: voice mail, interactive voice response, inbound/outbound fax-on-demand, and call center CTI.

39. The key functions of a CTI voice card are as follows:
    - Record and playback digitized video
    - Create and recognize DTMF tones (Dual Tone Multiple Frequency)
    - Answer and place phone calls
    - Recognize and process incoming Caller ID (Automatic Number Identification) information

40. Local calls come into the local central office via a local loop and travel to their local destination via a local loop. Calls which are not local but still within the same LATA are known as intra-LATA calls and are handled by a local carrier, most often an RBOC's operating company. Technically, these are long distance calls and a local CO may not have a direct trunk to the destination CO. In this case, the call is routed through a tandem office that establishes the intra-LATA circuit and also handles billing procedures for the long distance call.

41. Required client hardware and software technology for IP-based voice transmission includes the following:
    - Client software for IP-based voice transmission
    - PC workstation with sufficiently fast CPU to digitize and compress the analog voice signal (25Mhz 486 CPU minimum)
    - Sound card for local playback of received voice transmission
    - Microphone for local input of transmitted voice signals and Speakers for local output of received voice signals

42. Important features of IP-based voice transmission software are detailed in figure 4-21.

43. Although transmission quality has improved thanks to improved voice compression algorithms, the fact remains that shared IP networks were designed to carry data that could tolerate delays. Voice networks are designed with dedicated circuits offering guaranteed bandwidth and delivery times to voice transmissions. Depending on the particular codec algorithm used, voice compression can cause a major difference in required bandwidth . Among the more popular codec standards are: high bandwidth GSM (Global Systems Mobile Communication) that uses 9600 - 11,000 bps and low-bandwidth RT24, 2400 bps.

44. In order to be able to dynamically adapt in order to transmit data as efficiently as possible, frame relay encapsulates segments of a data transfer session into variable length frames. For longer data transfers, longer frames with larger data payloads are used and for short messages, shorter frames are used. These variable length frames introduce varying amounts of delay due to processing by intermediate switches on the frame relay network. This variable length delay introduced by the variable length frames works very well for data but is unacceptable to voice payloads that are very sensitive to delay.

45. More efficient use of ATM network capacity for voice transmission can be achieved in one of the following ways:
    - Voice compression - The ITU standardized voice compression algorithms via the G series of standards. Algorithms vary in the amount of bandwidth required to transmit toll quality voice. (G.726: 48, 32, 24, or 16Kbps; G.728: 16Kbps; G.729: 8Kbps). An important point to remember with voice compression is that the greater the compression ratio achieved, the more complicated and processing intensive the compression process. In such cases, the greatest delay is introduced by the voice compression algorithm with the highest compression ratio, requiring the least bandwidth.
    - Silence suppression - All cells are examined as to contents. Any voice cell that contains silence is not allowed to enter the ATM network. At the destination end, the non-transmitted silence is replaced with synthesized background noise. Silence suppression can reduce the amount of cells transmitted for a given voice conversation by 50%.
    - Use of VBR (Variable Bit Rate) rather than CBR - By combining the positive attributes of voice compression and silence suppression, ATM-based voice conversations are able to be transmitted using variable bit rate bandwidth management. By only using bandwidth when someone is talking, remaining bandwidth is available for data transmission or other voice conversations.

46. ASVD - Analog Simultaneous Voice & Data does not transmit voice and data in a truly simultaneous manner. Instead, it switches quickly between voice and data transmission. Voice transmission always takes priority, so data transfers are paused during voice transmissions. ASVD has been formalized as ITU standard V.61 and is incorporated into VoiceView software from Radish Communications Systems that is included in Windows 95. DSVD- Digital Simultaneous Voice & Data digitizes all voice transmissions and combines the digitized voice and data over the single analog transmission line. The digitized voice is compressed into between 9.6K and 12Kbps leaving between 16.8Kbps and 19.2Kbps for data out of the total 28.8Kbps transmission rate of a V.34 DSVD compliant modem. Such modems are currently available from Boca Research and U.S. Robotics. The DSVD standard has been formalized as ITU V.70.

47. ISDN is not nearly as available as switched analog voice phone service. In addition, pricing policies for ISDN can include both a monthly flat fee as well as an additional usage based tariff. ISDN will be explored further in Chapter 8. Figure 4-25 illustrates the

differences between simultaneous voice and data transmission using DSVD modems on analog services and ISDN data/voice modems over ISDN services.

48. Voice is currently transmitted across ATM networks using a bandwidth reservation scheme known as CBR or Constant Bit Rate which is analogous to a Frame Relay virtual circuit. However, constant bit rate does not make optimal use of available bandwidth since during the course of a given voice conversation, moments of silence intermingle with periods of conversation. By combining the positive attributes of voice compression and silence suppression, ATM-based voice conversations are able to be transmitted using variable bit rate bandwidth management. By only using bandwidth when someone is talking, remaining bandwidth is available for data transmission or other voice conversations.

49. Use of VBR is controlled via two parameters: Peak Voice Bit Rate controls the maximum amount of bandwidth a voice conversation can be given when there is little or no contention for bandwidth. Guaranteed Voice Bit Rate controls the minimum amount of bandwidth that must be available to a voice conversation regardless of how much contention exists for bandwidth.

50. Voice conversations transmitted over Frame Relay networks require 4 -16Kbps of bandwidth each. This dedicated bandwidth is reserved as a end-to-end connection through the frame relay network known as a PVC or permanent virtual circuit. In order for prioritization schemes established by FRADs to be maintained throughout a voice conversation's end-to-end journey, intermediate frame relay switches within the frame relay network must support the same prioritization schemes. At this point, voice conversations can only take place between locations connected directly to a frame relay network. There are currently no interoperability standards or network-network interface standards defined between frame relay networks and the voice-based PSTN. Figure 4-23 illustrates voice transmission over a frame relay network.

TEST QUESTIONS

True/False Questions

1. POTS uses two guardbands to prevent interference from adjacent frequencies from interfering with the voice signal. T/107

2. Although the local loop between the local CO and a residence or place of business may be an analog circuit, it is highly unlikely that the continuously varying analog signal representing a person's voice will stay in analog form all the way to the destination location's phone receiver. T/107

3. Regardless of the voice compression technique or circuit-loading technique employed, the quality of compressed voice transmissions easily matches the quality of an analog voice transmission over an analog dial-up line. F/111

4. In order to increase the capacity of connections to the outside network, cards known as station cards are added to a PBX. F/112

5. A PBX feature known as call pickup allows a user to answer another user's phone without the need to actually forward the call. T/116

6. Call accounting systems can pay for themselves in a short amount of time by spotting and curtailing abuse as well as by allocating phone usage charges on a departmental basis. T/117

7. Signaling system 7 is closely related to ISDN due to SS7's delivery of the out-of-band signaling over ISDN's D channel. T/129

8. The voice response unit is a LAN-based server that stores, processes and delivers voice messages. F/118

9. The CTI application known as automated attendant, allows callers to direct calls to a desired individual at a given business without necessarily knowing their extension number. T/121

10. Client/server CTI, also known as first party call control, is much less expensive than desktop CTI as well as being a simpler alternative to desktop CTI. F/120

11. A major problem with voice conversations transmitted over Frame Relay networks are their inability to reserve the necessary end-to-end bandwidth. F/134

12. ATM is a switch-based WAN service using variable length cells to transmit voice, assuring fixed processing times enabling predictable delay and delivery time. F/135

Multiple Choice Questions

1. 1. This portion of a telephone handset contains a mouthpiece with a movable diaphragm helping to convert sound waves into analog waves.
    a. receiver
p.107 b. transmitter
    c. modem
    d. codec

2. Which portion of a telephone handset contains an earpiece with a movable diaphragm which helps convert analog waves back into sound waves?
p.107 a. receiver
    b. transmitter
    c. modem
    d. codec

3. The bandwidth available for analog voice transmission is
    a. 0-300 Hz
p.107 b. 300-3100 Hz
    c. 3100-3400 Hz
    d. 0-4000 Hz

4. What is the process in which constantly varying analog voice conversation must be sampled frequently enough so that when the digitized version of the voice is converted back to an analog signal, the resultant conversation resembles the voice of the call initiator?
    a. modulation
    b. voice analysis
p.108 c. voice digitization
    d. none of the above

5. Most voice digitization techniques employ a sampling rate of
    a. 1000 samples per second
    b. 2000 samples per second
    c. 4000 samples per second
p.108 d. 8000 samples per second

6. Converting analog waves into digital signals by varying the amplitude or voltage of the electrical pulses in relation to the varying characteristics of the voice signal is known as
    a. PPM
p.108 b. PAM
    c. PDM
    d. PCM

7. Converting analog waves into digital signals by varying the duration of each electrical pulse in relation to the variances in the analog signal is known as
   a. PPM
   b. PAM
   p.108 c. PDM
   d. PCM

8. Converting analog waves into digital signals by varying the duration between pulses in relation to the pulse position in the analog signal is known as
   p.108 a. PPM
   b. PAM
   c. PDM
   d. PCM

9. The most common method used for voice digitization today is
   a. PPM
   b. PAM
   c. PDM
   p.109 d. PCM

10. Using PCM to digitize voice results in a bandwidth requirement of 64Kbps for one conversation. What circuit works just right for this requirement?
    p.110 a. DS-0
    b. DS-1
    c. T-1
    d. T-2

11. This type of voice digitization transmits only the approximate difference in amplitude of consecutive amplitude samples and results in 48 simultaneous digitized voice conversations per T-1.
    p.111 a. ADPCM
    b. PAM
    c. PDM
    d. PCM

12. A privately owned, smaller version of the switched central offices which can control circuit switching for the general public is known as a
    a. POP
    b. CO
    c. LATA
    p.112 d. PBX

62   Chapter 4

13. Phone lines to users' offices for phone connection are terminated in the PBX in slide-in modules or cards known as
    a. RJ-11 cards
p.112 b. station cards
    c. trunk cards
    d. common control CPUs

14. In a PBX, these types of cards allow connections to the outside network and may be specialized to a particular type of network line such as a T-1 or DDS line.
    a. RJ-11 cards
    b. station cards
p.112 c. trunk cards
    d. common control CPUs

15. Which of the following is a voice-based PBX feature in which the PBX chooses the most economical path for any given call?
    a. call pickup
    b. automatic call distribution
    c. hunting
p.116 d. LCR

16. Which of the following is a voice-based PBX service which allows calls to bypass the central switchboard and go directly to a user's phone?
p.116 a. direct inward dialing
    b. hunting
    c. prioritization
    d. call pickup

17. This control and monitoring feature is special software which can provide special reports, sorted billing statements, and exception reports which will spot possible abuses of the PBX.
    a. T-1 support
p.117 b. call accounting system
    c. automated attendant
    d. ISDN support

18. Rather than having an operator answer all calls, this type of PBX auxiliary voice-related service uses a voice processor which first answers and requests callers to press the extension number they wish to reach.
    a. voice mail
    b. voice out
    c. ads on hold
p.118 d. automated attendant

19. This type of PBX auxiliary voice-related service allows messages to be recorded for someone and may even allow forwarding, copying, adding comments to the message, saving and recalling the message.

p.118
a. voice mail
b. voice processor
c. ads on hold
d. automated attendant

20. This important and recent PBX trend uses the CT2 common air interface global standard.
a. multivendor interoperability
b. single user data integration

p.119 c. PBX integration with wireless phones
d. none of the above.

21. Calls which are not local but still within the same LATA are known as
a. inter-LATA calls
b. CO calls
c. POP calls

p.126 d. intra-LATA calls

22. These calls must be turned over from a local carrier to a long-distance carrier.

p.126
a. inter-LATA calls
b. CO calls
c. POP calls
d. intra-LATA calls

23. A long distance switching office, also called a class 4 toll center, is most commonly known as a

p.126
a. POP
b. CO
c. LATA
d. PBX

24. A key requirement to the delivery of intelligent services such as ANI would be
a. inter-switch signaling methodology must be standardized
b. the signal must not travel over the same logical channel as the voice conversation
c. there must be end-to-end signaling between carrier's switches and CPE

p.128 d. all of the above are key requirements

64   Chapter 4

25. A suite of protocols which controls the structure and transmission of both circuit-related and noncircuit-related information via out-of-band signaling between central office switches is known as

p.129
a. SS7
b. TCP/IP
c. IPX/SPX
d. SST

26. Software-defined network (SDN), a major component of the advanced intelligent network, provides flexible configuration of a user's telecommunications service and network. The most common example of SDN is
a. TCP/IP
b. PBX
p.130   c. customer controlled 800 services
d. customer billing

27. Which signaling system 7 protocol is used at the OSI network layer?
a. O&MAP (Operations Maintenance Application Part)
b. TCAP (Transaction Capabilities Application Part)
p.129   c. SCCP (Signaling Connection Control Part)
d. none of the above

28. This technology seeks to integrate the two most common productivity devices, the computer and the telephone.
a. ISDN
p.120   b. CTI
c. PSTN
d. PCS

29. A sub-category of CTI, this application delivers audio information to callers based on responses on the touch-tone keypad to pre-recorded questions.
a. outbound dialing
b. automated attendant
c. automated call distribution
p.121   d. audiotex

30. This sub-category of CTI uses a database of phone numbers, automatically dials those numbers, recognizes when calls are answered by people, and quickly passes those calls to available agents.
p.121   a. outbound dialing
b. automated attendant
c. automated call distribution
d. audiotex

31. This standard provides for interoperability among client software for low bandwidth voice and video for some client IP-based voice transmission software.
p.132
a. ITU H.323
b. T.120
c. RSVP
d. GSM

32. Which of the following is an IP-based protocol enabling routing software to reserve a portion of network bandwidth, known as a virtual circuit, for a particular IP-based voice session?
a. ITU H.323
b. T.120
p.132 c. RSVP
d. GSM

33. Which of the following is a wide area voice transmission service initially deployed for data which encapsulates segments into variable length frames with variable length delay?
a. ATM
b. IP-based voice transmission
c. POTS
p.134 d. Frame Relay

34. Which of the following is a technique used by a FRAD for accommodating voice and data traffic?
a. voice prioritization
b. data frame size limitation
c. separate voice and data queues
p.134 d. all of the above can be used

35. This technique of optimizing voice over ATM by only using bandwidth when someone is talking is known as
p.136 a. VBR
b. CBR
c. voice compression
d. silence suppression

36. Which one of the following transmits voice and data by quickly switching between analog voice and data transmission?
a. VBR
b. ISDN
p.137 c. ASVD
d. DSVD

66   Chapter 4

37. Which of the following transmits voice and data simultaneously over a single analog transmission line by putting compressed digitized voice between 9.6Kbps and 12Kbps, and data between 16.8Kbps and 19.2Kbps?
    a. VBR
    b. ISDN
    c. ASVD
p.138 d. DSVD

38. Of the following, which transmits simultaneous switched digital voice and data over a digital transmission line?
    a. VBR
p.138 b. ISDN
    c. ASVD
    d. DSVD

Fill-In the Blank Questions

1. POTS uses a bandwidth of 4000Hz including two _____ to prevent interference from adjacent frequencies interfering with the voice signal.

2. Specially programmed microprocessors known as _____, take the digitized PCM code and further manipulate and compress it.

3. This device, known as a(n) _____, is the technology used to sample analog transmissions and transform them into a stream of binary digits.

4. Depending on the requested destination, switch circuits are established, maintained and terminated on a per call basis by a portion of the PBX known as the switching _____.

5. A LAN-based server that stores, processes and delivers digitized voice messages is called a(n) _____ server.

6. The _____ market has pushed the need for mini-PBXs for professionals working out of small or home offices.

7. The worldwide, CCITT-approved standard for out-of-band signaling is known as _____.

8. _____ seeks to integrate the two most common productivity devices, the computer and the telephone, to enable increased productivity not otherwise possible by using the two devices in a non-integrated fashion.

9. _____ will allow voice mail, email, faxes, and pager messages to all be displayed on a single graphical screen.

10. Touch-tone dialing is technically known as _____ because the tone associated with each number dialed is really a combination of two tones selected from a matrix of multiple possible frequencies.

11. A key requirement to inter-switch signaling methodology is that the signal must travel out of the voice conversation's band or channel in a process known as _____.

12. A wide area transmission device originally used for data transmission, a(n) _____ is able to accommodate both voice and data traffic by employing voice prioritization, data frame size limitation, and/or separate voice and data queues.

Answers

1. guardbands p.107
2. digital signal processors p.111
3. CODEC p.108
4. matrix p.112
5. voice p.118
6. SOHO p.119
7. signaling system 7 (SS7) p.129
8. CTI p.120
9. Universal In-box or Unified Messaging p.121
10. DTMF p.125
11. out-of-band signaling p.128
12. FRAD or Frame Relay Access Device p.134

68   Chapter 4

CASE STUDY AND ANSWERS

WAN ARCHITECTURE GOES TO SCHOOL

Activities
1. Top-down model:

Business   Educational customers are facing pressure to provide Internet access, remote library access and other new applications while cutting out traditional voice infrastructures, such as tie lines linking PBXs in order to simplify the network and realize cost savings in the management of the overall network.

Applications   A converged voice and data WAN architecture is being used in education to provide Internet access, remote library access and other new applications along with traditional PBX service.

Data   Data consists of voice traffic along with data traffic.
High bandwidth/high speed is required.
Voice traffic must have the ability to be broken out from data traffic in order to allow it to be passed to the PSTN.

Network   The network must support high speeds.
The network must support simultaneous voice and data traffic.
The network must interface with the PSTN for out of district calls.

Technology   Mitel Corp.'s Networked Voice and Data was used to network data and voice traffic for the Stoughton Area School District.
To merge with a distributed data network, the voice control unit is linked to a Madge Networks, Inc. Ethernet switching hub outfitted with a new ATM/Synchronous Optical Network (SONET) module with 155Mbps fiber (single and multi-mode).

2. Unanswered questions:
What other alternatives were researched?
What was the cost savings over the old system?
How much training and maintenance is required?
Did the school district have the manpower to support the network?
How is the network tied into the Internet?

Business
1. They wanted to combine their voice and data traffic over one network for easier management as well as provide Internet access, remote library access and other new applications.

2. They were able to simplify their network and realize cost savings in the management of their overall network.

Application
1. Centrex is a business telephone service offered by a local telephone company from a local central office according to Newton's Telecom Dictionary.
2. NeVaDa (Networked Voice and Data) is a converged voice and data WAN architecture which is an extension of Mitel's existing fiber-distributed PBX in which all telephone calls are handled by a voice control module at the central location. The voice control unit is linked to an Ethernet switching hub outfitted with an ATM/SONET module.
3. According to the district technology director, by combining the two, they were able to simplify their network and realize cost savings in the management of their overall network.
4. New applications include Internet access and remote library access.

Data
1. The new network backbone bandwidth was 155Mbps.
2. Switched Ethernet met the bandwidth requirements of each of the proposed applications.

Network
1. Centrex service was used for voice, and token-ring and Ethernet LANs were used for the data.
2. Media required fiber (18-strand hybrid fiber - 12 single-mode and six multimode) to each site.
3. Telephone calls originating at the remote sites travel over the fiber net through the switching hub to the voice control unit, where they are sent out to carriers.
4. No, voice calls travel through the NeVaDa network via a separate path.
5. Yes, voice calls travel from the remote voice nodes to the voice control unit and then out to the PSTN.

Technology
1. Voice and data networks are merged through Ethernet switching hubs outfitted with a new ATM/SONET module.
2. Ethernet switching modules and ATM/SONET modules were included in the hubs.
3. It differs from other converged voice/data WANs in that an ATM/SONET module within the central Madge hub carves out a separate path for voice traffic rather than interleaving it with data traffic. This difference is significant in that the voice control unit at the central sites acts as the brains of the distributed PBX.
4. The article does not detail what CTI standards, such as TSAPI or TAPI, are supported.

CHAPTER 5

Local Area Networks
Concepts & Architectures

ANSWERS TO CHAPTER REVIEW QUESTIONS

1. A local area network is a combination of hardware and software technology which allows computers to share a variety of resources such as: printers and other peripheral devices, data, application programs, and storage devices.

2. A local area network easily allows computers and their users to interact and to share information, resources, or messages with other users and their computers, which is more difficult with a group of stand-alone PCs.

3. Potential disadvantages of a local area network include the need for more sophisticated technology, extra hardware and software, and in many cases, better trained users as well as highly trained local area network managers.

4. Refer to Figure 5-3 in the text for a generalized listing of business needs and perspectives that may lead to local area networking solutions.

5. The most popular business uses of a local area network include peripheral sharing (printers, modems, etc.), file and data sharing, storage device sharing (hard drives and CD-ROM drives), and sharing of application programs (word processing, spreadsheets, databases, and also business applications such as customer order input, inventory and payroll).

6. The power of the OSI model lies in its openness and flexibility. It can be used to organize and define protocols involved in communicating between two computing devices in the same room as effectively as two devices across the world from each other.

7. A protocol is a set of rules that governs communication between hardware and/or software components.

8. Each layer of the OSI model relies on lower layers to perform more elementary functions and to offer transparency to the intricacies of those functions. A protocol provides the functionality specified by the particular OSI layer.

9. The physical layer is responsible for the establishment, maintenance and termination of physical connections between communicating devices (point-to-point data links).

10. Point-to-point refers to devices physically connected on the same network while end-to-end network links refer to connections between computers which are not physically connected to the same LAN.

11. The data-link layer is the layer which specifies the standards for which network architecture will be used.

12. The MAC (media access control) sub-layer interfaces with the physical layer and is represented by protocols which define how the shared local area network media is to be accessed by the many connected computers. The LLC (logical link control) sub-layer is represented by a single IEEE 802 protocol (802.2).

13. The advantage to splitting the data-link layer into two sub-layers and to having a single, common LLC protocol is that it offers transparency to the upper layers (network and above) while allowing the MAC sub-layer protocol to vary independently.

14. The header is primarily concerned with addressing information, while the trailer is concerned with error checking information.

15. The data-link layer frames are built in the LLC and MAC sub-layers. This is appropriate because the data-link layer provides the required reliability to the physical layer transmission.

16. The network layer is responsible for the establishment, maintenance, and termination of end-to-end network links which are required when computers that are not physically connected to the same LAN must communicate.

17. Just as the data-link layer was responsible for providing reliability for the physical layer, the transport layer protocols are responsible for providing reliability for the end-to-end network layer connections. Transport layer protocols provide end-to-end error recovery and flow control.

18. The session layer is responsible for establishing, maintaining, and terminating sessions between user application programs, which is becoming more important as interactive dialogues between networked computers and distributed computing applications become more and more popular in a client/server environment.

19. One misconception is that the presentation layer is responsible for the protocols which govern graphical user interfaces. Another misconception is that the application layer protocols include end-user application programs. Neither is true. Refer to Figure 5-4 for an explanation of what functionality each layer provides.

20. The purpose of encapsulation/de-encapsulation is for each successive layer of the OSI model to add a header according to the syntax of the protocol which occupies that layer in

order for computers to talk to each other since they are only physically connected by the media and that is the only layer that talks directly between computers.

21. Network architecture is made up of access methodology, logical topology, and physical topology.

22. CSMA/CD listens to the network to see if any other users are "on the line" by trying to sense a neutral electrical signal known as a carrier. If no transmission is sensed, then "multiple access" allows anyone onto the media without further permission. If two user PCs should both sense a free line and access the media at the same instant, a collision occurs and "collision detection" lets the user PCs know that their data were not delivered and controls retransmission. With token passing, the PC must have a free token in order to put data on the network. Token passing assures that each PC user has 100% of the network channel available for their data requests and transfers by insisting that no PC accesses the network without first possessing the free token. Thus there are no collisions with token passing.

23. Propagation delay, which is the time it takes a signal from a source PC to reach a destination PC, is one cause of collisions, while two PCs both sensing a free line and accessing the media at the same instant is the other cause of collisions.

24. With early token release, the token is set to free and released as soon as the transmission of the data frame is completed rather than waiting for the transmitted data frame to return first.

25. A token is actually a 24 bit packet of data.

26. Logical topology refers to how the message will be passed from workstation to workstation until the message ultimately reaches its intended destination workstation. Physical topology refers to the physical layout of the configuration of the network and how clients and servers are physically connected to each other.

27. In sequential logical topology, data are passed from one PC (or node) to another. In broadcast logical topology, a data message is sent simultaneously to all nodes on the network.

28. Refer to Figure 5-7 for a complete description of the bus, star, and ring physical topologies.

29. Figure 5-8 provides a good comparison between the differences of the Ethernet II and IEEE 802.3 frame types. Important to notice is that Ethernet II uses a type field while IEEE 802.3 uses a length field.

30. In order for the IEEE 802.3 compliant network interface card to be able to determine the type of protocols embedded within the data field of an IEEE 802.3 frame, it refers to the header of the IEEE 802.2 LLC data unit.

31. Rendering network protocols to be IEEE 802 compliant was not always an easy task. In order to ease the transition to IEEE 802 compliance, an alternative method of identifying the embedded upper layer protocols was developed, called SNAP.

32. A protocol discriminator follows the control field in a SNAP header and differentiates which particular non-compliant protocol is embedded in the DSAP and SSAP fields.

33. Figure 5-10 lists all the various media-specific alternative configurations of Ethernet.

34. A token ring network architecture consists of token passing as its access methodology, sequential as its logical topology, and ring, but most often star, as its physical topology.

35. The active monitor: removes frames from the ring which have not been removed by their sending workstations; regenerates lost or damaged tokens; provides a special 24 bit buffer if the physical ring is so small that it does not have enough delay or latency to hold the 24 bit token; controls the master clock; and makes sure that there is only one designated active monitor on this ring.

36. Timing is important because the 24 bit token must circulate continuously even if no workstations are in need of transmitting data. Therefore, the entire token ring network must possess enough delay or latency to hold the entire 24 bit token. This calculates into a minimum ring size of 1.062 kilometers. Of course, this is not practical, and is the reason the active monitor must have a 24 bit buffer to ensure that the token will circulate properly, no matter what the actual physical size/length of the ring.

37. Ethernet is a better performer at low usage levels, while token ring is a good performer at high usage networks due to its deterministic nature.

38. FDDI offers reliability and security as well as speed and distance, as advantages over Ethernet and token ring networks.

39. Figure 5-14 provides an excellent graphic of the ability of FDDI to self-heal.

40. FDDI's primary negative feature is its cost. Also, glass cable can break, and connecting, terminating, and splicing fiber optic cables requires special tools and training.

41. The three primary uses of FDDI include its use as a campus backbone, high bandwidth workgroup, and high bandwidth sub-workgroup connection.

42. CDDI still supports 100Mbps and can be run over copper UTP or STP at a savings of about 33% over fiber. Its main detraction is the distance is limited to 100 meters per segment as compared with 2 km per segment of fiber-based FDDI.

43. Dual homing allows a server, for instance, to be connected to two FDDI concentrators for redundancy and increased fault tolerance.

44. 100BaseT is an IEEE standard (802.3u) which uses standard IEEE 802.3 MAC sub-layer frames. Its distance is 210 meters compared to FDDI's 2km. However, it is generally cheaper since it is not fiber based. 100BaseT does not offer the security and redundancy that FDDI does.

45. 100BaseTX - this is the most common of the three standards and the one for which the most technology is available. It specifies 100Mbps performance over 2 pair of Cat 5 UTP or 2 pair of Type 1 STP wiring. 100BaseT4 - physical layer standard for 100Mbps transmission over 4 pair of Cat 3, 4, or 5 UTP. 100BaseFX - physical layer standard for 100Mbps transmission over fiber optic cable.

46. Buying 10/100 NICs means that you are able to support either 10BaseT or 100BaseT, but not simultaneously. It has an advantage as an upgrade strategy.

47. Demand Priority Protocol is an access methodology which replaces the CSMA/CD access methodology. It eliminates collisions and re-transmissions by using a hub-based round robin polling scheme to allow all nodes to transmit in an orderly, sequenced manner.

48. Ports can be designated as high priority; however once lower priority ports have been timed out waiting for access to transmit data, they are boosted to high priority.

49. 100VG-AnyLAN requires compliant NICs, driver software and hubs, while 100BaseT requires the same only if you want each station to operate at 100Mbps. 10Mbps cards will still work with 100BaseT hubs. 100VG-AnyLAN will work with either IEEE 802.3 or 802.5 frames, while 100BaseT only works with IEEE 802.3 frames. Also, 100VG-AnyLAN supports time sensitive data transfer such as voice or video better than 100BaseT since collisions will not occur with 100VG-AnyLAN, which create more delay.

50. Iso-Ethernet can effectively transport voice, video, or multimedia but not at 100Mbps performance. It is closely related to ISDN wide area network services, which makes it a good match to use from your LAN to your WAN services.

51. Iso-Ethernet offers three different service modes: 10BaseT mode, which uses only the 10Mbps P channel for Ethernet traffic; Multi-service mode, which uses both the 10Mbps P channel for Ethernet and the 6.144Mbps C channel for video/multimedia; and all Isochronous mode, which uses all 16.144Mbps for streaming protocols, which support real time video or voice distribution.

52. Isochronous means "same clocking signal", which is the same 8KHz clocking signal as the commercial ISDN WAN services offered by long distance carriers.

53. Iso-Ethernet uses the same 8KHz clocking signal as the commercial ISDN WAN services offered by long distance carriers enabling a transparent interface between the Iso-Ethernet LAN and WAN segments. Also, refer to Figure 5-20.

54. Gigabit Ethernet, also known as 1000Base-X, is a proposed upgrade to Fast Ethernet that is being standardized as the IEEE 802.3z standard. An alternative gigabit ethernet version of 100VG-AnyLAN is being developed by the IEEE 802.12 committee. If the final standard retains Ethernet's CSMA/CD access methodology, then actual throughput could be far less than 1Gbps.

55. Fibre channel is often used to connect high performance storage devices and RAID subsystems to computers. Fibre channel switches and NICs are also available.

TEST QUESTIONS

True/False Questions

1. A Local Area Network (LAN) is comprised of hardware only. F/148

2. The server version of a particular network operating system is more complex and expensive, and is larger than the client version of the same network operating system. T/151

3. Meeting stated business needs is only one of the many reasons local area networks should be implemented. F/152

4. Each layer of the OSI model relies on lower layers to perform more elementary functions and to offer transparency to the intricacies of those functions. T/154

5. Network interface cards (NIC) are given a unique MAC address which is usually assigned by the network administrator when the NIC is placed in the computer. F/154

6. The first three layers of the OSI model are manifested as hardware, while the remaining layers of the OSI model are all installed as software protocols. F/154

7. The advantage of splitting the data link layer into two sub-layers and having a single common LLC protocol is that it offers transparency to the upper layers while allowing the MAC sub-layer protocol to vary independently. T/155

8. The presentation layer is responsible for providing the graphical user interface protocols. F/156

9. The application layer is responsible for protocols which include end-user application programs. F/156

10. CSMA/CD assures that each PC User has 100% of the network channel available for their data requests and transfers by insisting that no PC accesses the network without first possessing a specific packet of data known as a token. F/160

11. Token passing is a more efficient access methodology at higher network utilization rates than CSMA/CD. T/161

12. Strictly speaking, Ethernet and IEEE 802.3 are the same standard. F/163

13. One of the main differences between the Ethernet II frame and the IEEE 802.3 frame is that the destination and source address fields are reversed. F/164

78   Chapter 5

14. One of the major differences between an Ethernet and Token Ring network is that Token Ring guarantees no data collisions with assured data delivery. T/171

15. Under high traffic conditions Token Ring, with its deterministic access methodology, will perform better than Ethernet. T/172

16. Not only is the speed of Fast Ethernet 10 times the speed of regular 10BaseT Ethernet, but it is also capable of 10 times the network diameter of 10BaseT. F/179

17. The major advantage of 100VG-AnyLAN is that both IEEE 802.3 and IEEE 802.5 frame types can be delivered simultaneously by the same 100VG-AnyLAN network. F/181

Multiple Choice Questions

1. Which of the following are required to create a LAN?
   a. networking software
   b. networking hardware
   c. shared media physically connecting computers and peripheral devices
   p.149 d. all of the above

2. Its job is to provide a transparent interface between the shared media of the LAN and the computer into which it is physically installed.
   p.150 a. NIC
   b. hub
   c. network operating system
   d. serial port

3. This device provides a connecting point through which all attached devices are able to converse with one another.
   a. NIC
   p.150 b. hub
   c. network operating system
   d. serial port

4. This software interfaces between applications programs and client hardware.
   a. network operating system
   p.151 b. operating system
   c. file transfer software
   d. file sharing software

5. This software runs on a PC and allows it to log into a LAN and converse with other LAN-attached devices.
p.151
a. network operating system
b. operating system
c. file transfer software
d. file sharing software

6. A LAN-attached computer which provides services to other computers is known as
a. a client
b. a stand-alone PC
p.151 c. a server
d. a network operating system

7. Local area networks are implemented because
p.152 a. they meet the business needs as articulated by management
b. they always solve business needs
c. all business problems can be solved by LANs
d. they provide faster technology

8. A set of rules which governs communication between hardware and/or software components is referred to as a
a. header
b. trailer
p.154 c. protocol
d. frame

9. The OSI layer responsible for the establishment, maintenance and termination of point-to-point data links between communicating devices is the
a. data link layer
b. network layer
c. transport layer
p.154 d. physical layer

10. The OSI layer responsible for providing reliability to upper layers for point-to-point connections is the
p.154 a. data link layer
b. network layer
c. transport layer
d. physical layer

11. Data link layer builds these within the network interface card.
a. protocols
b. standards
p.154 c. frames
d. headers

12. The data link layer is comprised of two sub-layers, the MAC sub-layer and the
    a. network sub-layer
p.155 b. logical link control sub-layer
    c. physical link control sub-layer
    d. logical sub-layer

13. This layer or sub-layer is responsible for interfacing with the physical layer and is represented by protocols which define how the shared local area network media is to be accessed by the many connected computers.
p.155 a. MAC sub-layer
    b. LLC sub-layer
    c. network layer
    d. transport layer

14. The OSI layer responsible for the establishment, maintenance, and termination of end-to-end communication links is the
    a. data link layer
p.155 b. network layer
    c. transport layer
    d. physical layer

15. The OSI layer responsible for providing reliability for the end-to-end communications links as well as end-to-end error recovery and flow control is the
    a. data link layer
    b. network layer
p.155 c. transport layer
    d. session layer

16. This OSI layer is responsible for establishing, maintaining, and terminating sessions between user application programs.
    a. data link layer
    b. network layer
    c. transport layer
p.156 d. session layer

17. A network architecture consists of which of the following?
    a. access methodology
    b. logical topology
    c. physical topology
p.159 d. all of the above

18. CSMA/CD is an example of which of the following?
p.159
a. access methodology
b. logical topology
c. physical topology
d. none of the above

19. Which of the following is a factor contributing to a data collision on a CSMA/CD shared media LAN?
a. only one PC wants to send data
p.160 b. propagation delay
c. one station accepts the free token
d. the free token becomes lost

20. The successful receipt of the data frame in a token ring LAN is indicated by settings in these fields.
a. header fields
b. early token release fields
c. data fields
p.160 d. frame status flags fields

21. The methodology in which the token is set to free and released as soon as the transmission of the data frame is completed is known as
a. CSMA/CD release
p.160 b. early token release mechanism
c. free token release mechanism
d. collapsed ring mechanism

22. How the message is passed through the network until the message ultimately reaches its intended destination workstation is known as
a. access methodology
p.161 b. logical topology
c. physical topology
d. none of the above

23. With this logical topology a data message is sent simultaneously to all nodes on the network.
a. ring
b. sequential
c. simulcast
p.162 d. broadcast

82   Chapter 5

24. This physical topology is in a linear arrangement with terminators on either end and devices connected to it via connectors and/or transceivers.
p.162   a. bus
b. ring
c. star
d. circle

25. This physical topology uses some type of central management device which may be a single point of failure.
a. bus
b. ring
p.162   c. star
d. circle

26. This field in the IEEE 802.3 frame indicates the number of octets in the LLC data field.
a. type field
p.165   b. length field
c. SNAP field
d. FCS field

27. An alternative method of identifying the embedded upper layer protocols in order to ease the transition to IEEE 802 compliance was known as
a. IEEE 802.5
b. Ethernet II
c. IEEE 802.2
p.166   d. SNAP

28. An Ethernet media standard which is 10Mbps over thin coaxial cable.
a. 10Base5
p.167   b. 10Base2
c. 10BaseT
d. 10BaseF

29. An Ethernet media standard which is 10Mbps over UTP.
a. 10Base5
b. 10Base2
p.167   c. 10BaseT
d. 10BaseF

30. Which of the following Ethernet media standards gives you the longest maximum segment length?
a. 10Base5
b. 10Base2
c. 10BaseT
p.167   d. 10BaseF

31. In a Token Ring network, this acts as a kind of caretaker of the token ring network architecture and can even regenerate lost or damaged tokens.
    a. frame status field
    b. free token
p.170 c. active monitor
    d. passive monitor

32. This network architecture is a 100Mbps, modified token passing using dual counter-rotating rings.
    a. Ethernet
p.173 b. FDDI
    c. Token Ring
    d. IEEE 802.3

33. FDDI's reliability is due to which of the following?
p.173 a. It uses fiber optic cabling which is immune to EMI and RFI
    b. It uses copper for better connections
    c. It needs no terminators because is uses a hub
    d. none of the above

34. Multiple concentrators attaching multiple devices to the FDDI rings is known as
    a. dual homing
    b. TP-PMD
    c. dual attachment stations
p.177 d. dual ring of trees

35. Connecting a server to more than one FDDI concentrator to provide redundant connections and increased fault tolerance is known as
p.177 a. dual homing
    b. TP-PMD
    c. dual attachment stations
    d. dual ring of trees

36. A high speed Ethernet standard which uses 2 pair of Cat 5 UTP.
    a. 100BaseT4
    b. 100BaseFX
    c. 100BaseUTP
p.179 d. 100BaseTX

37. Which of the following is the access methodology used by 100VG-AnyLAN?
p.181 a. demand priority access
    b. token passing
    c. CSMA/CD
    d. modified token passing

84   Chapter 5

38. Which of the following is a major difference between 100BaseT and 100VG-AnyLAN?
    a. 100BaseT supports a longer network diameter than 100VG-AnyLAN
    b. 100VG-AnyLAN uses the same CMSA/CD found in 100BaseT
p.182 c. 100BaseT requires only 2 pair of UTP and 100VG-AnyLAN requires 4 pair
    d. 100BaseT supports both IEEE 802.3 and IEEE 802.5 frames

39. This type of high speed Ethernet standard can carry voice, video, or multimedia by using connections which are synchronized using a single common clocking reference.
    a. 100VG-AnyLAN
p.183 b. Isochronous Ethernet
    c. 100BaseT
    d. Full-duplex Ethernet

40. This channel on Iso-Ethernet is used for standard 10Mbps Ethernet traffic.
    a. C channel
    b. B channel
p.184 c. P channel
    d. D channel

41. The Iso-Ethernet service mode which uses both the 10Mbps P channel for Ethernet and the 6.144Mbps C channel for video/multimedia is the
    a. 10BaseT mode
p.184 b. multi-service mode
    c. all isochronous mode
    d. full timing mode

42. Iso-Ethernet is associated most closely with which of the following WAN services?
p.184 a. ISDN
    b. Frame relay
    c. ATM
    d. X.25

43. Which of the following is the proposed IEEE standard for gigabit Ethernet?
    a. IEEE 802.3u
    b. IEEE 802.3x
    c. IEEE 802.5
p.185 d. IEEE 802.3z

Fill-In the Blank Questions

1. A(n) _____ PC would be characterized as a service requester.

2. Mapping business strategic plans to technological strategic plans is the purpose of _____.

3. The _____ can be used to organize and define protocols involved in communicating between two computing devices in the same room as effectively as two devices across the world from each other.

4. The RS232-C specification for serial transmission is an example of a(n) _____ layer protocol.

5. The IEEE 802 committee establishes standards which pertain to the _____ layer of the OSI model.

6. Information added to the front of a data-link layer frame is known as a(n) _____, and contains the addressing information needed to deliver the frame.

7. The IEEE 802.5 standard defines protocols for the _____ sub-layer of the data link layer.

8. The _____ sub-layer is represented by a single IEEE 802.2 protocol.

9. In the network layer, data is usually organized into _____ for transmission between networks.

10. Transport layer protocols also provide mechanisms for sequentially organizing multiple network layer packets into a coherent _____.

11. As data messages emerge from a client front end program and proceed down the protocol stack of the network operating system, they are _____ at each successive layer and finally sent over the physical media which connects computers.

12. A logical topology of delivering data, called _____, is similar to a bucket brigade in which a bucket of water is filled by one PC User and passed to the neighboring PC User until it gets to the PC User with the flames.

13. The _____ field in an Ethernet II frame identifies which network protocols are embedded within the data field.

14. In the IEEE 802.5 network architecture standard, the _____ is actually a 24 bit formatted data packet.

15. FDDI uses _____ as its access methodology which physically removes the token from the ring and transmits a full data frame. Upon completion of transmission, it immediately releases a new token.

16. FDDI over copper is known as _____ or TP-PMD.

17. Using a(n) _____ polling scheme, 100VG-AnyLAN hubs scan each port in sequence to see if the attached workstations have any traffic to transmit.

Answers

1. client p.151
2. LAN analysis and design p.153
3. OSI Model p.154
4. physical p.154
5. data link p.154
6. header p.154
7. MAC (Media Access Control) p.155
8. LLC (Logical Link Control) p.155
9. packets p.155
10. message p.155
11. encapsulated p.157
12. sequential p.161
13. type p.164
14. token p.168
15. modified token passing p.173
16. CDDI p.176
17. round robin p.182

CASE STUDY AND ANSWERS

MEETING BEEFIER BANDWIDTH GOALS

Activities

1. Top-down model:

Business	As the data transfer needs of the DPC for Harmon Consumer Group increased, bandwidth became a problem reducing production by users. A network infrastructure was needed that could support more users with larger files.
Applications	Graphic design applications were used most often with printing, BBS, email and Mac copying.
Data	Data primarily consisted of large graphics files, but also included email and other business office data.
Network	The network bandwidth needs needed to grow in order to support transfer of large graphics files. Simplicity was the major requirement for the network manager. The installed base of Ethernet was to be maintained.
Technology	A combination of fast Ethernet and standard Ethernet were used with a Power Macintosh 7200 file server, and a Macintosh Quadra 950 BBS and email server. The 10Mbps segment was supported by an Asante NetStacker Intelligent Ethernet hub. This was coupled through an Asante Fast 10/100 bridge to an Asante Fast 100 TX hub connected to seven graphics designers and the Power Mac server on a 100Mbps segment. New 10/100 Asante adapters were installed in the graphics designers' machines. 10Mbps connections were used for the printers. Cat 5 cabling was already installed.

2. Unanswered questions:
   What were the costs of upgrading?
   What plans have been built in for future growth?
   Are any remote connections anticipated? Internet connections?
   What security measures are in place?
   What backup procedures have been set up?
   What protocols are in use and may need to be set up for the future?

Business
1. The Harmon Consumer Group has a design and production center (DPC) which use graphics packages to develop brochures, ads, posters, and other promotional materials for the Harmon product lines.
2. Without the information systems and networks the business could not promote their products.

Application
1. Adobe Systems Inc. Photoshop produced a 600MB file which took 30 minutes to move from an Apple Mac file server to a Mac workstation.
2. Core applications included Photoshop, Adobe Illustrator, QuarkXPress, and Home Page graphics packages.

Data
1. Graphics data between 50 and 600MB were being transferred when the network bandwidth proved insufficient.
2. DPC worked mainly with 50MB files.

Network
1. The original network architecture was 10Base-T Ethernet running Appleshare.
2. Appleshare.
3. 10Base-T cat 5.
4. Management simplicity was the key criteria for the upgrade.
5. The printers could only use 10Mbps and swapping adapter cards for the copywriters wasn't worth the investment.
6. In the fall of 1995, AppleShare did not support 100Mbps speeds.
7. Future upgrade options include SCSI-to-SCSI, ATM or gigabit Ethernet.

Technology
1. 100Mbps Ethernet was chose because it provided the bandwidth to transfer the large files and was a simple upgrade.
2. New components included the 10/100 NICs, 10/100 bridge, and 100 TX hub.
3. In the graphics designers' workstations, 10/100 NICs were installed. In the other workstations and the printers no changes were made.

CHAPTER 6

Local Area Network Hardware

ANSWERS TO CHAPTER REVIEW QUESTIONS

1. Major components of the LAN Technology Architecture include:
    - A central wiring concentrator of some type which serves as a connection point for all attached local area network devices. Depending on the particular network architecture involved and the capabilities of the wiring center, this device can be known alternatively as a hub, MAU, CAU, concentrator, LAN switch or a variety of other names.
    - Media such as shielded or unshielded twisted pair, coaxial cable, or fiber optic cable must carry network traffic between attached devices and the wiring center of choice.
    - Network Interface Cards (NIC) are installed either internally or externally to client and server computers in order to provide a connection to the local area network of choice.
    - Finally, network interface card drivers are software programs which bridge the hardware/software interface between the network interface card and the computer's network operating system. Figure 6-1 summarizes the key components of the Local Area Network Technology Architecture.

2. Figure 6-3 provides an excellent description of the differences between a shared-media and switch-based network architecture. The main advantage to the switched-based architecture is that it provides more bandwidth and is an easy alternative to upgrade from a shared-media architecture. It is more costly than the shared-media architecture.

3. One major drawback to moving to a switch is that it becomes very difficult to gather full LAN traffic statistics for LAN management and analysis. The problem exists because unlike a shared-media architecture where an attached monitor can view the entire LAN architecture due to the shared nature of the architecture, in a switch-based architecture, only one point-to-point switched connection can be viewed at any one time. Also, the traffic patterns differ each time the switch makes a new circuit. Traffic analysis must be done first so that busiest devices are given their own switch port.

4. The three implementation scenarios for switched LAN architectures include:
    - Stand-alone Workgroup/Departmental LAN switches - offer dedicated connections to all attached client and server computers via individual switch ports. Such an implementation is appropriate for multimedia or

videoconferencing workstations and servers. In some cases, such as a distributed computing environment, dedicated ports are only necessary for servers, while client workstations share a switch port via a cascaded media-sharing hub. This variation is sometimes referred to as a server front-end LAN switch.
- Backbone-attached Workgroup/Departmental LAN switches - offer all of the local switching capabilities of the stand-alone workgroup/departmental LAN switch plus switched access to higher speed backbone networks. This higher speed backbone connection may be to a higher capacity backbone switch or may be to a higher speed shared-media device such as a backbone router.
- Backbone/Data Center Switches - offer high capacity, fault tolerant, switching capacity with traffic management capabilities. These high-end switches are really a self-contained backbone network which is sometimes referred to as a collapsed backbone network. These backbone switches most often offer switched connectivity to other workgroup switches, media-sharing hubs, and corporate servers which must be accessed by multiple departments/workgroups. They are often modular in design allowing different types of switching modules such as Ethernet, Token Ring, Fast Ethernet, and ATM (Asynchronous Transfer Mode) to share access to a high capacity switching matrix or backplane.

5. These backbone switches most often offer switched connectivity to other workgroup switches, media-sharing hubs, and corporate servers which must be accessed by multiple departments/workgroups. They are often modular in design, allowing different types of switching modules such as Ethernet, Token Ring, Fast Ethernet, and ATM (Asynchronous Transfer Mode) to share access to a high capacity switching matrix or backplane. The primary disadvantage is they are a potential single point of faulure.

6. Disadvantages of full duplex network architectures include the need for a multithreading operating system, new hubs, NICs and NIC drivers. The advantage is double the amount of bandwidth, such as 20Mbps instead of the normal non-full duplexed Ethernet 10Mbps.

7. Full duplex architectures require specialized full duplex Ethernet NICs, NIC drivers, and full duplex Ethernet switches, along with a multithreaded operating system.

8. Full duplex is especially well suited for switch-to-switch connections and switch-to-server connections.

9. The MAC Layer is determined by the adapter card protocol it is designed for, such as Ethernet or Token Ring.

10. The PCI bus offers its own clocking signal and low CPU utilization, making it the bus of choice for high performance NICs.

11. Bus Mastering DMA is the most efficient NIC data transfer method because it leaves the system CPU alone to process other applications.

12. It requires the expansion bus in the PC to support being "mastered" by the CPU on the network adapter card.

13. External adapters cannot draw electricity from the expansion bus like internal adapters and therefore require a power source of their own such as an AC adapter in most cases. Also, throughput is limited to the speed of the parallel port.

14. The functional role of a NIC driver is to link the Network Operating system with the NIC card hardware so that the NOS can work with the NIC.

15. A monolithic driver must be written for each specific NIC and NOS combination possible.

16. Adapter card specific drivers should be developed independently from network operating system specific protocol stack drivers and the two drivers should be bound together to form a unique driver combination. Secondly, driver management software should allow for installation of both multiple network adapter cards and multiple protocol stacks per adapter card.

17. Figures 6-10 and 6-11 show the differences between NDIS and ODI. Both allow users to load several protocol stacks simultaneously for operation with a single network adapter card and support independent development with subsequent linking of protocol drivers and adapter drivers.

18. Binding creates the complete driver using the NOS protocol stack and NDIS-compliant NIC card driver to create the driver allowing the NOS to talk to the NIC card and the NIC card to forward frames to the correct protocol stack.

19. PROTOCOL.INI, PROTMAN.DOS and the particular protocol drivers and MAC drivers are all needed for the binding operation.

20. Protocols are actually directed to the proper protocol stack by a layer of software known as the vector.

21. The Card services sub-layer is hardware independent and interfaces to the client operating system or network operating system driver software. Card services deliver error messages, and enable resource management and configuration. The Socket services sub-layer is written specifically for the type of PCMCIA controller included in a notebook computer. Among the common varieties of controllers are Intel, Cirrus Logic, Databook, Vandem, Toshiba, VLSI, and Ricoh. Socket services are more hardware oriented and provide information concerning insertion and removal of cards from available slots.

22. CSS enables several functions and is relatively self-configuring. If CSS drivers are not available for a particular PC Card/Controller combination, or if the amount of memory CSS drivers require is unacceptable, then lower-level drivers known as direct enablers must be configured and installed. Direct enablers do not support swapping PCMCIA cards in and out of the PCMCIA slot without the re-configuration as is the case with CSS drivers.

23. Refer to Figure 6-12 for the technology and functionality of the three major categories of hubs.

24. Active management MAUs are able to send alerts to management consoles regarding malfunctioning token ring adapters and can also forcibly remove these misbehaving adapters from the ring.

25. Modules depend upon the backplane design within the enterprise hubs, which is a proprietary design.

26. Two layers of management software are most often involved :
First, local hub management software is usually supplied by the hub vendor and runs over either DOS or Windows. This software allows monitoring and management of the hub from a locally attached management console.
Secondly, since these hubs are just a small part of a vast array of networking devices which might have to be managed on an enterprise basis, most hubs are also capable of sharing management information with enterprise network management systems such as HP OpenView, IBM NetView, Sun SunNet Manager, or Novell NMS (Network Management System)

27. Network management information is formatted according to a standard called SNMP or Simple Network Management Protocol.

28. Three methods for LAN switches to process and forward packets are:
Cut-Through Switches read only the address information in the MAC layer header before beginning processing. After reading the destination address, the switch consults an address lookup table in order to determine which port on the switch this frame should be forwarded to. Once the address lookup is completed, the point-to-point connection is created and the frame is immediately forwarded. Cut-through switching is very fast. However, because the Frame Check Sequence on the forwarded frame was not checked, bad frames are forwarded. As a result, the receiving station must send a request for retransmission followed by the sending station retransmitting the original frame leading to overall traffic increases.
Store-and-Forward Switches read the entire frame into a shared memory area in the switch. The contents of the transmitted Frame Check Sequence field is read and compared to the locally recalculated Frame Check Sequence. If the results match, then the switch consults the address lookup table, builds the appropriate point-to-point

connection, and forwards the frame. As a result, store-and-forward switching is slower than cut-through switching but does not forward bad frames.

Error-Free Cut-Through Switches read both the addresses and Frame Check Sequences for every frame. Frames are forwarded immediately to destinations nodes in an identical fashion to cut-through switches. However, should bad frames be forwarded, the error-free cut-through switch is able to reconfigure those individual ports producing the bad frames to use store-and-forward switching. As errors diminish, to pre-set thresholds, the port is set back to cut-through switching for higher performance throughput.

29. Backpressure is liable to be an issue in switches without deep buffers. Also the difficulty with backpressure mechanisms in the case of multiple device LAN segments being linked to a single switch port is that the false collision detection signal stops all traffic on the connected LAN segment, even peer-to-peer traffic which could have been delivered directly without the use of the switch.

30. In a switched LAN architecture, each port is the equivalent of a dedicated LAN which must be individually monitored and managed.

31. Port mirroring copies information from a particular switch port to an attached LAN analyzer. The difficulty with this approach is that it only allows one port to be monitored at a time.

    Roving port mirroring creates a roving RMON (Remote Monitoring) probe which gathers statistics at regular intervals on multiple switch ports. The shortcoming with this approach remains that at any single point in time, only one port is being monitored.

    Simultaneous RMON View allows all network traffic to be monitored simultaneously. Such a monitoring scheme is only possible on those switches which incorporate a shared memory multi-gigabit bus as opposed to a switching matrix internal architecture. Furthermore, unless this monitoring software is executed on a separate CPU, then switch performance is likely to degrade.

32. Multiple workstations per switch port is a good solution to segmenting a LAN provided each workstation does not need a lot of bandwidth. It can also help to localize traffic to the LAN segment and reduce traffic overall on the backbone. The disadvantage results from the application of backpressure. The difficulty with backpressure mechanisms in the case of multiple device LAN segments being linked to a single switch port is that the false collision detection signal stops all traffic on the connected LAN segment, even peer-to-peer traffic which could have been delivered directly without the use of the switch.

33. See Figure 6-16. Token Ring switches need buffering so that outbound messages can be stored until the token arrives at the switch port.

34. Figure 6-18 provides an excellent description of the roles ATM can play in Local Area Network implementation.

35. Legacy LANs can be integrated into an ATM network using IP over ATM or LAN Emulation.

36. ATM's fixed cell length of 53 bytes allows timed, dependable delivery for streaming traffic such as voice and video, and also simplifies troubleshooting, administration, setup and design. Also, ATM is the first single protocol to be supported on all platforms from LAN to WAN.

37. LAN Emulation provides a translation layer which allows ATM to emulate existing Ethernet and token ring LANs and allows all current upper-layer LAN protocols to be transported by the ATM services in an unmodified fashion. With LAN emulation, ATM networks become nothing more than a transparent, high-speed delivery service. LAN emulation is most often implemented by the ATM vendor by the installation of an address resolution server which provides translation between the ATM addressing scheme and the addressing scheme which is native to a particular emulated LAN. It requires absolutely no hardware or software changes at LAN workstations.

38. Twisted pair wiring is twisted to reduce interference both between pairs and from outside sources such as electric motors and fluorescent lights.

39. EIA/TIA 568 established the topology, cable types, and connector types for EIA/TIA 568 compliant wiring schemes and the minimum performance specifications for cabling, connectors and components such as wall plates, punch down blocks and patch panels to be used in an EIA/TIA 568 compliant installation.

40. Cat 5 UTP is the most common type of UTP installed.

41. It is easier to work with than other alternatives as well as being cheaper in most cases. Also, it may already be installed in some buildings, thus not requiring upgrade for higher speed network architectures.

42. Often, the shielding is terminated in a drain wire which must be properly grounded. The bottom line is that improperly installed Shielded Twisted Pair Wiring can actually increase rather than decrease interference and data transmission problems.

TEST QUESTIONS

True/False Questions

1. One disadvantage of switched LAN architecture implementations is that both the NIC and the wiring center need to be changed. F/197

2. The most likely implementation scenarios for Full Duplex Ethernet is in switch-to-switch connections and switch-to-server connections. T/198

3. Since NICs are Network layer interfaces, it is fair to say that they determine the network architecture. F/201

4. Bus Mastering DMA as a feature on adapter cards requires the expansion bus in the PC to support being "mastered" by the CPU on the network adapter card. T/205

5. PCMCIA adapters can transfer data faster than NICs designed to work with an EPP. F/206

6. MIB is an Internet Protocol used to format network management information. F/218

7. Switched LAN media is different from shared LAN media in that in switched media only one workstation at a time can broadcast its message onto the shared 10Mbps backbone. F/221

8. Error-Free Cut-Through Switches read both the addresses and Frame Check Sequences of each frame. T/222

9. The difficulty with deep buffering in the case of multiple device LAN segments being linked to a single switch port is that the false collision detection signal stops all traffic on the connected LAN segment, even peer-to-peer traffic. F/222

10. 4 conductor station wire or RYGB is suitable for data transmission and is the same as UTP. F/226

11. 10Base2, frozen yellow garden hose, and thick Coax are three names for the exact same coaxial cable media. F/229

96   Chapter 6

Multiple Choice Questions

1. The limiting factor in which of the following LAN architectures is the number of simultaneous point-to-point connections which a given wiring center can support?
    a. shared-media network architecture
    b. multiple shared media architecture
    c. shared-bandwidth network architecture

   p.196 d. switched media network architecture

2. Which of the following is not a general guideline for switch port allocation?
    a. Servers and UNIX workstations should have their own switch port

   p.198 b. Each casual or light traffic workstation should have their own switch port
    c. Users with frequent queries to servers should have their own switch port
    d. Casual or light traffic workstations should be placed on a shared LAN segment with its own switch port

3. Offering dedicated connections to all attached client and server computers via individual switch ports is often done with which of the following implementation scenarios?

   p.198 a. Stand-alone Workgroup/Departmental LAN switches
    b. Backbone-attached Workgroup/Departmental LAN switches
    c. Backbone/Data Center switches
    d. ATM WAN switches

4. Offering high capacity, fault tolerant, switching capacity with traffic management capabilities is often done with which of the following implementation scenarios?
    a. Stand-alone Workgroup/Departmental LAN switches
    b. Backbone-attached Workgroup/Departmental LAN switches

   p.199 c. Backbone/Data Center switches
    d. ATM WAN switches

5. Offering all of the local switching capabilities of individual workgroup/departmental LAN switches plus switched access to higher speed backbone networks is often done with which of the following implementation scenarios?
    a. Stand-alone Workgroup/Departmental LAN switches

   p.199 b. Backbone-attached Workgroup/Departmental LAN switches
    c. Backbone/Data Center switches
    d. ATM WAN switches

6. Which of the following components are unique requirements for Full Duplex Ethernet?

   p.200 a. multithreaded operating system
    b. CSMA/CD
    c. data collisions
    d. none of the above

7. Which of the following statements best describes Network Interface Cards?
   a. it is a layer one device only
   b. it is a network layer device capable of routing
   c. it is a MAC layer device capable of routing
p.201 d. it is a MAC layer device which determines the network architecture

8. Which of the following data transfer methods leaves the system CPU alone to process other applications?
   a. Shared Memory
p.205 b. Bus Mastering DMA
   c. DMA
   d. Programmed I/O

9. Which of the following NIC media interfaces is used with thin Ethernet?
p.205 a. BNC connector
   b. AUI connector
   c. RJ45 connector
   d. RJ11 connector

10. This is a type of adapter which is roughly the size of a credit card and can now achieve throughput speeds up to 80Mbps.
   a. EPP
   b. High Performance Parallel Port
   c. BNC connector
p.207 d. PCMCIA/PC Card V3.0

11. This NIC trend allows servers with high traffic demands to have up to four links to the network while using only a single expansion slot.
   a. Integrated NIC
   b. Integrated Repeater Module
   c. Full-Duplex Mode
p.208 d. Multi-port NICs

12. This NIC trend allows the packet of information coming into the NIC to immediately be forwarded as soon as its start of frame is detected.
p.208 a. Fast-packet forwarding
   b. Integrated Repeater Module
   c. Full-Duplex Mode
   d. Multi-port NICs

98   Chapter 6

13. Drivers written for specific adapter card/network operating system combinations are known as
    a. multi-protocol drivers
    b. TCP/IP drivers
p.209 c. monolithic drivers
    d. NDIS drivers

14. Which of the following allows adapter card specific drivers to be developed independently from network operating system specific protocol stack drivers and then bound together to form a unique driver combination?
    a. multi-protocol drivers
    b. TCP/IP drivers
    c. monolithic drivers
p.210 d. NDIS drivers

15. This multiprotocol network interface card driver specification uses a program known as LSL.COM and MLID network interface card drivers.
p.212 a. ODI
    b. TCP/IP
    c. IPX/SPX
    d. NDIS

16. AUI connectors allow Ethernet NICs to be attached to thin or thick coax Ethernet backbone networks via
    a. BNC connectors
    b. RJ-45 connectors
    c. Fiber optic connectors
p.205 d. transceivers

17. This type of shared-media wiring center is used primarily for Token Ring networks.
    a. Repeaters
    b. Hubs
p.214 c. MAUs
    d. AUIs

18. This type of hub, also known as modular concentrators, allows for hot-swapping and has chassis-based design.
    a. Switched hub
p.214 b. Enterprise hub
    c. Stackable hub
    d. Stand-alone hub

19. This type of hub has a fixed number of ports, is not expandable and generally supports only a single network architecture.
    a. Switched hub
    b. Enterprise hub
    c. Stackable hub
p.214 d. Stand-alone hub

20. This device "cleans up" the digital signals by re-timing and re-generating them before passing the data from one attached device or LAN segment to the next.
p.215 a. Repeater
    b. Hub
    c. MAU
    d. Enterprise hub

21. The feature which allows hubs to be stacked by using a specialized port on the hub allowing repeated data to flow out of the special port to the next hub.
    a. concentrator ports
    b. repeater ports
p.216 c. cascading ports
    d. stackable ports

22. These hubs are sometimes known as a "network in a box" and offer a backplane design.
    a. Repeater
    b. Hub
    c. MAU
p.217 d. Enterprise hub

23. Network statistics and information are gathered by specialized software which reside within the monitored network device and are called
    a. SNMP
    b. management information bases
p.218 c. agents
    d. RMON

24. Network management traffic which exits the hub via a separate serial port or along a separate bus within the hub so as not to diminish the amount of bandwidth available for data is called
    a. serial management
    b. virtual management
    c. in-band management
p.219 d. out-of-band management

100   Chapter 6

25. This type of LAN device is actually able to create connections between any two attached Ethernet devices on a packet by packet basis in as little as 40 milliseconds.

p.221
a. LAN switch
b. shared-media hub
c. repeater
d. MAU

26. This method of switching reads only the address information in the MAC layer header before beginning processing.

a. Store-and-Forward
p.221 b. Cut-Through
c. ASIC
d. CPU

27. This method of switching reads the entire frame into a shared memory area in the switch and looks at the FCS field to detect errors, not forwarding bad frames.

p.222
a. Store-and-Forward
b. Cut-Through
c. ASIC
d. CPU

28. This approach to switch flow control is basically hardware-based and expensive.

a. port mirroring
b. backpressure
c. RMON view
p.222 d. deep buffers

29. This approach to switch flow control prevents lost frames during overload conditions by sending out false collision detection signals in order to get transmitting clients and servers to time-out long enough for the switch to forward stored data.

a. port mirroring
p.222 b. backpressure
c. RMON view
d. deep buffers

30. This approach to switch management copies information from a particular switch port to an attached LAN analyzer.

a. Simultaneous RMON View
b. Roving mirroring
c. Switch mirroring
p.223 d. Port mirroring

31. This approach to switch management allows all network traffic to be monitored at the same time and requires the switch to incorporate a shared memory multi-gigabit bus as opposed to a switching matrix internal architecture.
p.223
   a. Simultaneous RMON View
   b. Roving mirroring
   c. Switch mirroring
   d. Port mirroring

32. This ATM standards interface effort defines standards for interoperability between end-user equipment and ATM equipment and networks.
   a. ATM CDDI
p.225 b. UNI
   c. NNI
   d. AUI

33. This ATM standards interface effort defines interoperability standards between various vendors' ATM equipment and network servers, and are not well defined.
   a. ATM CDDI
   b. UNI
p.225 c. NNI
   d. AUI

34. This migration approach for existing LAN network architectures to ATM provides a translation layer which allows ATM to imitate existing Ethernet and token ring LANs and allows upper-layer LAN protocols to be transported by the ATM services in an unmodified fashion.
   a. IP over ATM
   b. WAN emulation
   c. Classical IP
p.225 d. LAN Emulation

35. The term used to mean signal interference caused by a strong signal on one-pair (transmitting) overpowering a weaker signal on an adjacent pair (receiving).
p.228 a. Near-End Crosstalk
   b. Attenuation
   c. degradation
   d. AWG

36. Widely used UTP category capable of transmitting up to 100Mbps and tested for attenuation and NExT to 100MHz.
   a. Category 2 UTP
   b. Category 3 UTP
   c. Category 4 UTP
p.228 d. Category 5 UTP

102   Chapter 6

37. In this type of fiber optic cable, the rays of light will bounce off of the cladding at different angles and continue down the core while others will be absorbed in the cladding.
p.230
   a. multimode graded index fiber
   b. single mode fiber
   c. multimode step index fiber
   d. single mode step index

Fill-In the Blank Questions

1. In a Token Ring architecture, all that needs to be replaced in order to move to a switched environment is the _____.

2. A switch dependent architecture in which no data collisions occur allowing for a dedicated switched connection for both sending and receiving data is known as _____ Ethernet.

3. The _____ bus offers its own clocking signal and low CPU utilization, which makes it the bus of choice for high performance NICs.

4. External adapters called _____ are able to deliver a throughput of up to 2Mbps through the parallel port of a PC.

5. Full interoperability of NICs depends on compatibility between the NIC and the network operating system installed in a given computer and is delivered by a software program called a(n) _____.

6. Using NDIS driver specifications, once bound and operating, packets of a particular protocol are forwarded from the adapter card to the proper protocol stack by a layer of software known as the _____.

7. In a chassis-based architecture, modules can be inserted and/or removed while the hub remains powered-up using a capability known as _____.

8. An Internet Protocol used to format network management information is called _____.

9. _____ is supported by many high-end LAN switches and allows not only LAN network architectures such as Ethernet, Token Ring and FDDI to be switched extremely quickly but can also switch voice, video, and image traffic as well as interface to WAN services.

10. _____ is the decrease in the power or signal over a distance in a particular type of wire or media.

11. The "S" in STP stands for _____.

Answers

1. MAU or Multistation Access Unit p.197
2. Full Duplex p.199
3. PCI p.202
4. EPP or Enhanced Parallel Port p.206
5. driver p.208
6. vector p.211
7. hot-swapping p.214
8. SNMP p.218
9. ATM (or Asynchronous Transfer Mode) p.221
10. Attenuation p.228
11. Shielded p.229

CASE STUDY AND ANSWERS

KODAK DEVELOPS BANDWIDTH

Activities
1. Top-down model:

Business	The Image Science Division of Kodak needed to upgrade their low-bandwidth, shared-medial networks to accommodate more complex information requirements, specifically larger graphics files.
Applications	Image processing was done to very large files which must be transferred from large secondary storage devices across the network to high-powered graphics workstations.
Data	Large image files were stored on optical jukebox and magnet storage devices.
Network	The network shared-media bandwidth was not capable of supporting the transfer of large files from storage device to workstation creating a bottleneck. Switched fast Ethernet would provide the proper bandwidth.
Technology	100Mbps switched fast Ethernet Catalyst 5000 hubs with high port density and hot-swapping capability were used. Intelligent ports and vLANs were used. TrafficDirector used embedded RMON agents to maintain a detailed look into the switched internetwork. Cisco Internetwork Operating System (IOS) software was used on many network devices to provide manageability across the network.

2. Unanswered questions:
   What network operating systems were used on workstations and servers?
   What training was needed by the network staff to support the new technologies?
   What other business data traffic passed through the network?
   What communications protocols needed to be supported?
   What network management software is used?
   What upgrades had to be made at the workstation level for both hardware and software?

Business
1. Kodak wanted to upgrade their low-bandwidth, shared-media networks to accommodate more complex information requirements and increase performance, reduce cost, and enhance manageability.
2. Transfer of large files over the network took too much time and caused bottlenecks for routine activities.

3. The image processing took photographic images and turned them into electronic images for online storage and manipulation.

Application
1. Image processing was the main application supported at this location.
2. Cisco's TrafficDirector leverages embedded RMON agents in the switches to obtain a detailed look into the switched internetwork. Also, IOS was used to provide a cohesive software layer among routers, switches, file servers, multi-service WAN-access switches, and ATM-capable PBXes.

Data
1. Researchers rely on a 1,000GB optical jukebox and 500GB of magnetic storage.
2. Average files sizes were about 200MB, with some files as large as 500MB.

Network
1. Network requirements for data trend and long-term planning were required.
2. Transfer of very large files caused bottlenecks from routine activities.
3. The new technologies had to provide increased performance, reduce cost, and enhance manageability.
4. The switched LAN architecture allowed for better performance with vLAN benefits including more options for port grouping, security, filtering, and broadcast impression.
5. Traditional network management tools may no longer work. With a vLAN, an IP view is no longer sufficient to view the network's virtual topology making it difficult to discern traffic patterns.
6. Kodak is using TrafficDirector to help manage its network.
7. TrafficDirector runs on the switch along with IOS in order to provide a cohesive software layer between networked devices.
8. High speed connections were given to key hubs and file servers.
9. ATM could be one upgrade used if additional bandwidth is needed.
10. Depending upon how they want to upgrade, according to the article, the company is well-positioned to move to and ATM-backbone access through its Cisco 5000 switches using LAN Emulation.

Technology
1. 100Mbps fast Ethernet switching was chosen because of the large file transfer needs.
2. TrafficDirector manages the switches.
3. The backplane operates at 1.2Gbps, using a distributed buffering and prioritization scheme to provide nonblocking performance for switched-Ethernet interfaces. Tri-level priority on the backplane ensures that delay-sensitive applications receive the necessary priority on a port-by-port basis. A 192KB buffer provides adequate port buffering for workgroup applications without dropping information during peak traffic periods.
4. Port density can be doubled by adding a couple of cards, and hot-swapping capabilities are available.
5. Fiber or Cat 5 cabling is required.

6. They met the high level requirements by providing rock-solid stability, high-performance bandwidth, and network-management efficiencies with growth potential for the future.

CHAPTER 7

Local Area Network Operating Systems

ANSWERS TO CHAPTER REVIEW QUESTIONS

1. Network operating systems architectures are in a state of transition from closed environments, in which only clients and servers running the same network operating system could interact, to open environments, in which universal clients are able to interoperate with servers running any network operating system.

2. Peer-to-peer network operating systems, also known as DOS-based LANs or Low-cost LANs, offered easy to install and use file and print services for workgroup and departmental networking needs. Client/Server network operating systems offered more powerful capabilities including the ability to support hundreds of users, and the ability to interact with other network operating systems via gateways. These client/server network operating systems were both considerably more expensive and considerably more complicated to install and administer than peer-to-peer network operating systems. Also, refer to Figure 7-3 for graphical representation of differences.

3. Client network operating systems, as illustrated in Figure 7-5, integrate traditional operating system functionality with advanced network operating system features to enable communication with a variety of different types of network operating system servers. This client workstation's ability to interoperate transparently with a number of different network operating system servers without the need for additional products or configurations is described as a universal client capability. The client portion of client/server network operating systems does not necessarily work with any other server-side network operating system other than the same vendor's product.

4. Figure 7-5 provides an excellent comparison of client/server network operating systems versus client and server network operating systems.

5. Client network operating systems that are able to connect to a great many different server operating systems are sometimes referred to as a universal client. This client workstation's ability to interoperate transparently with a number of different network operating system servers without the need for additional products or configurations is described as a universal client capability.

6. Because of the universal client's ability to communicate with any server, and the server network operating system's ability to communicate with a variety of different client

network operating systems, the choice of server network operating system can be based more on optimizing functional performance than on delivering required communication protocols.

7. The new or emerging demands being put on network operating systems are application services, directory services and integration/migration services. Refer to Figure 7-4 for more details.

8. Refer to Figure 7-4 for details and importance of the three service categories.

9. Peer-to-peer networking functionality such as file sharing, printer sharing, chat and e-mail, is now included in most client network operating systems. Architecturally, rather than remaining as closed, identically configured, peer-to-peer environments, today's small business network operating systems offer interoperability with server network operating systems via universal client capabilities. In addition, they offer their own 32-bit server software to offer greater performance than the 16-bit peer software merely configured as a server. One important characteristic of the latest small business network operating systems is that they continue to exhibit all of the positive attributes of the peer-to-peer network operating systems from which they evolved such as: DOS-based, low memory and disk requirements, easy installation, configuration, and management, high quality file and print services. Additionally, small business network operating systems have had to differentiate themselves from client network operating systems by offering more advanced features such as: dedicated 32-bit server software; bundled workgroup software; and easy migration path to server-based network operating systems.

10. Small business network operating systems have had to offer more advanced features such as: dedicated 32-bit server software; bundled workgroup software; and easy migration path to server-based network operating systems. This was caused by the fact that traditional peer-to-peer networking functionality was being bundled in the client NOS.

11. Three major categories of functionality include: Operating system capabilities, Peer-to-peer networking capabilities, Client software for communicating with a variety of different server network operating systems. Also, refer to Figure 7-8.

12. Object-Oriented User Interfaces present the user with a graphical desktop on which objects such as files, directories, folders, disk drives, programs, or devices can be arranged according to the user's whim. More importantly, as objects are moved around the desktop, they retain their characteristic properties. As a result, when a desktop object is clicked upon, only legitimate actions such as associated programs presented in context-sensitive menus appropriate for that class of objects can be executed. Unlike object-oriented user interfaces, Windows-based user interfaces, although graphical, do not allow icons representing directories, files, disk drives, etc. to be broken out of their particular Window and placed directly on the desktop. Figure 7-9 contrasts Windows-based User Interfaces and Object-Oriented User Interfaces.

13. When it comes to 32 bit applications, client network operating systems may execute these applications in their own address space, otherwise known as protected memory mode. However, all of these protected mode 32-bit applications may execute over a single 32-bit sub-system, in which case a single misbehaving 32-bit application can crash the entire 32-bit sub-system and all other associated 32-bit applications. Many legacy applications are 16 bit applications that try to control hardware devices directly. This is not allowed in protected mode 32 bit systems.

14. Programs or sub-routines which write directly to computer hardware are sometimes referred to as employing real-mode device drivers. Applications that communicate with hardware via APIs use virtual device drivers.

15. Many computer games, in order to gain speed and efficiency, must access and control hardware and memory directly, rather than going through the operating system's memory management system.

16. Many 32 bit network operating systems do not allow application programs to address or control hardware directly in the interest of security and protecting applications from using each other's assigned memory spaces and causing system crashes.

17. All of these protected mode 32-bit applications may execute over a single 32-bit sub-system, in which case a single misbehaving 32-bit application can crash the entire 32-bit sub-system and all other associated 32-bit applications.

18. The goal of plug-n-play is to free users from having to understand and worry about such things as IRQs (Interrupt Requests), DMA (Direct Memory Access) channels, memory addresses, COM ports, and editing CONFIG.SYS whenever they want to add a device to their computer.

19. A PnP BIOS (Basic Input Output System) is required to interface directly to both PnP and non-PnP compliant hardware. PnP capabilities must be supported by the client network operating system through interaction with the PnP BIOS. The devices which are to be installed must be PnP compliant. This basically means that the manufacturers of these devices must add some additional software and processing power so that these devices can converse transparently with the PnP operating system and BIOS. In some cases, PnP compliant device drivers may also need to be supplied.

20. Windows 95 possesses the most PnP capability among currently available client network operating systems.

21. Interoperability solutions cannot be assumed to be two-way or reversible. For example, as illustrated in Figure 7-11, although NetWare clients are able to connect to a Windows 95 client running File and Print Services for NetWare, the converse is not true. Windows 95 clients are not able to log into, or share the disks and files of, the NetWare clients.

22. The three elements are: (1.) Client software and network drivers which allow a particular client to communicate with a compatible server. These are MAC (Media Access Control) protocol specifications such as NDIS and ODI. (2.) Network transport protocols which package and transport messages between clients and servers. These protocols correspond to the network and transport layers of the OSI model. (3.) Network re-directors which trap API (application program interface) calls and process them appropriately. Redirectors are concerned with providing file system related services in support of application programs.

23. It is important for a client network operating system to be able to support more than one transport protocol to allow client platforms to automatically find and connect to reachable, compatible servers.

24. As mobile computing on laptop and notebook computers has grown exponentially, a need to synchronize versions of files on laptops and desktop workstations became quickly apparent.

25. Global and domain directory services differ primarily in the organization of information concerning network users and resources. Global directory services organize all network user and resource data into a single hierarchical database, providing a single point of user and resource management. In contrast, domain directory services see the network as a series of linked sub-divisions known as domains. Domain directory services associate network users and resources with a primary server known as a PDC or Primary Domain Controller. Each domain's directory must be individually established and maintained. Domains can be individually maintained and controlled in terms of how much of other domains can be seen.

26. This global directory database may well be distributed, implying that different portions of the data are physically stored on multiple distributed servers linked via the network. In addition, this global directory database may be replicated, implying that multiple copies of identical data may also be stored on multiple servers for redundancy and fault tolerance purposes. In terms of a logical view of the network, global directory services provide a view of a single, enterprise network.

27. The remote or foreign server receives the user authentication from the user's primary domain controller (local server) in a process known as Interdomain Trust (IT). By having servers act on behalf of their local users when verifying authenticity with remote and foreign servers, every user ID does not have to be entered and maintained in every domain's directory service.

28. Once the interdomain trust has been established for a particular user, the remote domain server does not repeat the request for authentication.

29. The need will arise for different network operating systems to share each other's directory services information. A directory services specification known as X.500 offers the potential for this directory services interoperability.

30. Applications programs are stored in a particular file system format. In addition, when these application programs execute, they may request additional services from the resident file system via API calls. Server network operating systems vary in the types and number of supported file systems. Some network operating systems, such as Windows NT, can have multiple partitions on a disk drive, with one partition supporting FAT (File Allocation Table) file system and another partition supporting the NTFS (NT file system) file system.

31. Supporting more than one file system would allow the network operating system to work in a heterogeneous environment. Ultimately, this would provide more accessibility to network resources.

32. Figures 7-12 and 7-13 provide a good description of the role NCP and SMB redirectors play in support of application services across many different network operating systems.

33. In these cases, because the previously listed operating systems possess no native networking functionality, the server network operating system must possess the ability to generate diskettes with the necessary operating system-specific network communications capabilities. These diskettes are then loaded on the intended networking client, and the required network communication capabilities are merged with the native operating system. However clients running a network operating system such as Windows 95 have all required functionality included.

34. This multiprotocol routing software may be either included, optional, or not available, depending on the server network operating system in question. Multiprotocol routing provides the functionality necessary to actually process and understand multiple network protocols as well as translate between them. Without multiprotocol routing software, clients speaking multiple different network protocols cannot be supported.

35. In some cases, it may be necessary for either clients or servers to access IBM mainframe computers or AS/400s which are linked on IBM's proprietary network architecture known as SNA (Systems Network Architecture). In such cases, it makes more sense for the translation software necessary to access the SNA network to reside on a single server rather than on multiple clients. In this scenario, the server with the SNA translation software installed becomes a gateway to the SNA network.

36. Reviews of server network operating systems consistently list auto-detection & configuration of installed controllers, interface cards and peripherals as the most important installation-related feature. The ability of a server network operating system to automatically configure a controller, adapter, or peripheral is dependent on the network operating system possessing a compatible driver for that device. It should stand to reason

that the greater the number of drivers supported by a given network operating system, the greater the probability that auto-configuration will be successful. Another hardware compatibility issue related to installation is the number of different CPUs on which a given server network operating can operate.

37. Integration and migration features of next-generation network operating systems are clearly aimed at one audience: the 60+% of servers currently running NetWare 3.12. Migration features are aimed at easing the transition from NetWare 3.12 to either NetWare 4.1 or Windows NT. Key among the migration concerns is the conversion of the directory services information stored in the NetWare 3.12 bindery into either NetWare 4.1 NDS or Windows NT domain directory services. Utilities are available from third-party software vendors as well as from Novell and Microsoft to at least partially automate the bindery conversion. Integration refers to that transitional period of time in the migration process when both network operating systems must be running simultaneously and interacting to some degree. Integration utilities or strategies include the following:
    - NetWare File and Print Services for NT - which allows a Windows NT server to appear to be a NetWare server by offering native file and print services to NetWare clients.
    - NW-Link - which allows Windows NT Workstation clients and Windows '95 clients to communicate with NetWare 3.12 servers.
    - File Access Protocols for NCP (NetWare Core Protocol) and SMB (Server Message Block) can be loaded simultaneously as redirectors allowing either NetWare or Windows compatible programs to be executed.

38. Although not distributed as a ready-to-run single product Unix as an operating system, combined with the TCP/IP family of protocols for network communications, and NFS for a network aware file system, comprise a very common combination of elements which offer all the functionality of commercially available single-product network operating systems. Figure 7-17 conceptually illustrates how Unix, the Internet Suite of Protocols (TCP/IP), and NFS can be combined to offer full network operating system functionality to network-attached clients and servers.

39. Refer to Figure 7-18 for the relationship between Unix systems programs, Unix system kernels, Unix shells, and Unix applications programs.

40. Unix implements a hierarchical, multi-level tree file system starting with the root directory as illustrated in Figure 7-19. In fact, Unix is able to support multiple file systems simultaneously on a single disk. In Unix, files are treated by the kernel as just a sequence of bytes. The basic job of the file system in Unix is to offer file services as a consistent interface without requiring user application programs to worry about the particulars of the physical storage hardware used.

41. NFS, Network File System, was developed by Sun Microsystems as part of their Open Network Computing environment. NFS allows multiple, different computing platforms

to share files. NFS does not replace local file systems but acts as a tranparent extension across multiple platforms.

42. TCP/IP (Transmission Control Protocol/Internet Protocol) is the term generally used to refer to an entire suite of protocols used to provide communication on a variety of layers between widely distributed different types of computers. Strictly speaking, TCP and IP are just two of the protocols contained within the family of protocols more properly known as the Internet Suite of Protocols. TCP/IP and the entire family of related protocols are organized into a protocol model. As can be seen in Figure 7-20, the OSI Model and TCP/IP Model are functionally equivalent, although not identical, up through the transport layer.

43. Strictly speaking, NFS is only the API portion of a collection of programs and utilities which offer the transparent file management interoperability typically associated with the NFS suite of protocols. XDR (External Data Representation) is a presentation layer protocol responsible for formatting data in a consistent manner so that all NFS clients and servers can process it, regardless of the computing platform or operating system on which the NFS suite may be executing. RPC (Remote Procedure Call) is a session layer protocol responsible for establishing, maintaining, and terminating communications sessions between distributed applications in an NFS environment. NFS protocols may use either UDP or TCP for transport layer services. The architectural relationship between the NFS suite of protocols and the TCP/IP suite of protocols is illustrated in Figure 7-21.

44. Vertical software compatibility is concerned with making sure that all necessary compatible protocols are in place in order for all of the software and hardware within a single client or server to operate harmoniously and transparently. Horizontal software compatibility is most often concerned with getting different software of the same category to interoperate transparently between clients, between clients and servers, or between servers. Vertical software compatibility is achieved by adjacent software layers each supporting a common compatibility protocol. Horizontal software compatibility is most often delivered by a category of software known as middleware.

45. Middleware is an actual additional installed software program which is often specialized by software layer: database middleware, network operating system middleware, operating systems middleware, or distributed application middleware.

46. The role of the enterprise network is to deliver the integration and transparent interoperability enabled by the client/server architecture. It also incorporates host-terminal traffic, voice traffic, and videoconferencing traffic in an integrated and well-managed fashion.

47. It is most often the combination of network devices and connections of the following categories: Local Area Network (LAN), LAN-to-LAN (Internetwork), and Wide Area Network (WAN).

48. It incorporates host-terminal traffic, LAN to LAN traffic, voice traffic, and videoconferencing traffic in an integrated and well-managed fashion.

49. An Enterprise Network Management System manages a multi-vendor enterprise network, while an Integrated Client/Server Management System must also be able to supply the following management capabilities: enterprise database management, enterprise desktop management, enterprise transaction processing management, and enterprise distributed processing management.

50. NetWare 4.1 SFT III offers a unique fault tolerant feature known as server duplexing. In such a case, not only are the contents of the disks synchronized, but the contents of the servers' memory and CPUs are also synchronized. In case of the failure of the primary server, the duplexed server takes over transparently. The major drawback to server duplexing is the cost.

TEST QUESTIONS

True/False Questions

1. Horizontal software compatibility is achieved by adjacent software layers each supporting a common compatibility protocol, while vertical software compatibility is most often delivered by a category of software known as middleware. F/242

2. Traditional peer-to-peer network operating systems are characterized as excellent with regard to interoperability and scalability. F/244

3. Because of the universal client's ability to communicate with any server, and the server NOS's ability to communicate with a variety of different client NOSs, the choice of server NOS can be based more on optimizing functional performance than on delivering required communication protocols. T/247

4. By their very nature, interoperability solutions are assumed to be two-way or reversible. F/257

5. The client software does not have to be pre-configured with any information about the servers because the server discovery and access is all handled transparently by the client network operating system. T/259

6. As client/server information systems have boomed in popularity, data base services have become the criteria by which server network operating systems are judged. F/263

7. One of the most significant characteristic of the Unix operating system is the availability of the source code, allowing individual programmers to enhance and modify Unix over the years. T/266

8. Unix is able to support multiple file systems simultaneously on a single disk. T/267

9. The TCP/IP and OSI models have basically identical layers from layer 1 through layer 5. F/269

10. The greater the number of drivers supported by a given network operating system, the greater the probability that auto-configuration will be successful. T/275

Multiple Choice Questions

1. Which of the following are concerned with providing an interface between LAN hardware, such as NICs, and the application software installed on a particular client or server?
   a. operating systems
   b. LAN application software
   c. LAN productivity software
   p.239 d. network operating systems

2. Which of the following is a type of application software which is concerned with providing access to shared network resources and services?
   a. operating systems
   b. LAN productivity software
   p.240 c. LAN resource management software
   d. network operating systems

3. Which of the following would be considered LAN productivity software?
   p.239 a. e-mail
   b. peer-to-peer network operating systems
   c. client/server network operating systems
   d. client-side security software

4. This type of LAN software provides a single, consolidated view of all networked resources, both hardware and software.
   a. LAN security software
   b. network operating systems
   c. LAN productivity software
   p.240 d. LAN management software

5. Software compatibility which is concerned with making sure that all necessary compatible protocols are in place in order for all of the software and hardware within a single client or server to operate harmoniously and transparently is known as
   p.241 a. vertical software compatibility
   b. diagonal software compatibility
   c. horizontal software compatibility
   d. distributed software compatibility

6. Software compatibility which is concerned with transparency between similar software layers between different clients and servers is known as
   a. vertical software compatibility
   b. diagonal software compatibility
   p.242 c. horizontal software compatibility
   d. distributed software compatibility

7. In addition to managing a multi-vendor enterprise network, an integrated client/server management system must also be able to supply which of the following management capabilities?
   a. enterprise database management
   b. enterprise desktop management
   c. enterprise distributed processing management
p.244 d. all of the above

8. This type of network operating system is also known as a DOS-based LAN.
   a. client/server NOS
   b. gateway NOS
   c. high-end NOS
p.244 d. peer-to-peer NOS

9. Which of the following NOSs offers powerful capabilities, is the most expensive, and is complicated to install?
   a. DOS-based LAN
p.245 b. Client/server NOS
   c. Peer-to-peer NOS
   d. client-to-client NOS

10. Which of the following is **not** an advantage of client/server network operating systems?
    a. provide fast service
    b. offer reliable performance
p.245 c. are easy to install and configure
    d. offer good security capabilities

11. This is an emerging service requirement for network operating systems which will allow all network objects to be defined in a single location and shared by all applications.
    a. file services
p.247 b. directory services
    c. application services
    d. printer services

12. Allowing for multiple different client network operating systems to transparently interoperate with multiple, different server network operating systems would fall under which of the following emerging service requirements?
    a. file services
    b. directory services
    c. application services
p.247 d. integration/migration services

13. "Independently installed client and server network operating systems provide transparent client to server interoperability" describes which of the following?
p.248
   a. client and server network operating systems
   b. client/server network operating systems
   c. peer-to-peer network operating systems
   d. DOS-based network operating systems

14. Which of the following has been a method that small business network operating systems have used to differentiate themselves from peer-to-peer network operating systems?
   a. DOS-based, low memory and disk requirements
p.249
   b. bundled workgroup software
   c. easy installation, configuration, and management
   d. high quality file and print services

15. Which of the following prevents misbehaving programs from monopolizing systems resources at the expense of the performance of other applications?
   a. multithreading
   b. symmetrical multiprocessing
   c. protected memory space
p.252
   d. preemptive multitasking

16. Which of the following prevents application programs from causing general protection faults and/or system crashes?
   a. multithreading
   b. symmetrical multiprocessing
p.252
   c. protected memory space
   d. preemptive multitasking

17. Another term for legacy application support is
   a. multithreading
p.252
   b. backward compatibility
   c. symmetrical multiprocessing
   d. forward compatibility

18. Programs or sub-routines which write directly to computer hardware are sometimes referred to as containing
   a. protected memory mode drivers
   b. APIs
   c. virtual device drivers
p.252
   d. real-mode device drivers

19. 32-bit network operating systems which do not allow application programs to address or control hardware directly use
    a. protected memory mode drivers
    b. APIs
p.254 c. virtual device drivers
    d. real-mode device drivers

20. In which of the following would a single misbehaving program crash the entire sub-system?
p.254 a. shared 16-bit sub-system
    b. individual 16-bit sub-system
    c. virtual machine sub-system
    d. protected memory mode sub-system

21. Which of the following is a PnP functionality?
    a. automatically detect the addition or removal of PnP devices
    b. pre-set settings so that they do not conflict with other devices
    c. automatically load necessary drivers to enable the particular device
p.255 d. all of the above

22. Which of the following is not a PnP element needed to support PnP standards?
    a. PnP BIOS
p.255 b. PnP application software
    c. PnP capabilities must be supported by the client network operating system
    d. devices which are installed must be PnP compliant.

23. Client software and network drivers which allow a particular client to communicate with a compatible server belongs to which category of client networking functionality?
    a. application redirectors
    b. network transport protocol
p.258 c. MAC sub-layer specifications
    d. physical layer specifications

24. Rules for packaging and sending messages between clients and servers correspond to which category of client networking functionality?
    a. application redirectors
p.258 b. network transport protocol
    c. MAC sub-layer specifications
    d. physical layer specifications

25. This category of client networking functionality traps API calls and processes them appropriately.
p.258
    a. application redirectors
    b. network transport protocol
    c. MAC sub-layer specifications
    d. physical layer specifications

26. Software which deals with the problems of file version differences on laptops and desktop workstations is known as
    a. remote node software
    b. file access software
p.260   c. file or directory synchronization software
    d. all of the above

27. Of the following client network operating systems, which is based on a 16-bit architecture?
    a. Windows NT workstation
    b. OS/2 Warp Connect
    c. Windows 95
p.262   d. Windows for Workgroups

28. Of the following client network operating systems, which supports SMP?
p.262
    a. Windows NT workstation
    b. OS/2 Warp Connect
    c. Windows 95
    d. Windows for Workgroups

29. The portion of a distributed application which runs on the server is known as the
    a. front-end engine
p.264   b. back-end engine
    c. front-side application
    d. GUI

30. Which of the following Unix architectural components delivers requested functionality to users by issuing system calls to the Unix system kernel?
    a. Unix user interface
p.265   b. Unix system programs
    c. Unix system kernel
    d. Unix system kernel calls to hardware

31. Which of the following Unix architectural components fulfills user requests by interacting with the hardware layer and returning requested functionality to the systems programs and utilities?
    a. Unix user interface
    b. Unix system programs
- p.265 c. Unix system kernel
    d. Unix shells

32. This Unix attribute allows application programs written for Unix to be theoretically used across all Unix platforms.
    a. modularity
    b. shells
- p.266 c. portability
    d. hardware dependence

33. This Unix attribute allows Unix to be a viable, dynamic operating system to which functionality can be added in the form of new system utilities or system programs.
- p.266 a. modularity
    b. shells
    c. portability
    d. hardware dependence

34. In a Unix file system, the top level of the hierarchical, multi-level tree file system is called the
    a. slice
    b. path
    c. link
- p.267 d. root

35. Which of the following is used in a Unix file system to identify the specific route through which the hierarchical file structure follows to a particular destination file?
    a. slice
- p.267 b. path
    c. link
    d. root

36. Which of the following is used in a Unix file system to allow a given file to be known by, and accessed by, more than one name?
    a. slice
    b. path
- p.268 c. link
    d. root

122   Chapter 7

37. The suite of communications protocols originally developed by DARPA and used by the Unix operating system.
    a. IPX/SPX
p.268 b. TCP/IP
    c. NetBIOS
    d. NetBEUI

38. A system which organizes all network user and resource data into a single hierarchical database, providing a single point of user and resource management is a
    a. bindery
    b. local directory service
p.270 c. global directory service
    d. domain directory service

39. A process used by Windows NT 3.51 in which the remote or foreign server receives the user authentication from the user's primary domain controller (local server) is a(n)
    a. NDS
p.271 b. Interdomain Trust
    c. Bindery
    d. X.500

40. This NOS software provides the functionality necessary to actually process and understand multiple network protocols as well as translate between them.
    a. global directory software
    b. Interdomain Trust software
p.274 c. multiprotocol routing software
    d. multi-NIC software

41. Security in which every packet transmitted from a particular client workstation can have a unique encrypted digital signature attached to it which can only be authenticated by the server is known as
    a. authentication
    b. auditing
p.278 c. packet signing
    d. file authentication

42. This component of the Windows NT security model accompanies every process or program launched by the user and is used as a means to reference whether or not the user and their spawned processes have sufficient permissions to perform requested services or access requested resources.
    a. logon process
    b. security account manager
p.279 c. security access token
    d. user accounts database

43. Which of the following is an important process in symmetric multiprocessing?
p.283 a. load balancing
b. processor loads can be unbalanced
c. each CPU is generally assigned their own memory and sub-systems
d. an entire applications process is assigned to one CPU

44. NetWare uses this product to run NetWare in a symmetrical multiprocessing mode.
a. NetWare 4.1 SFT
b. NetWare 4.1 Mirrored Server Link
c. NetWare 4.1 NLSP
p.283 d. NetWare 4.1 SMP

45. A form of fault tolerance for NetWare 4.1 in which not only the servers' disks are synchronized, but the contents of the servers' memory and CPUs are also synchronized.
a. disk block sub-allocation
b. disk duplexing
p.283 c. server duplexing
d. disk mirroring

46. The term used when a client NOS let's a 32 bit application operate in it's own address space.
a. application program interfaces
p.254 b. protected memory mode
c. real-mode memory
d. virtual mode memory

47. Applications are able to issue commands and requests for network-based services using a pre-defined format called
p.254 a. application program interfaces
b. protected memory mode
c. real-mode memory
d. virtual mode memory

48. This directory interoperability protocol is a simplification of X.500's directory access protocol and utilizes TCP/IP as a transport protocol.
a. ODSI
b. X.400
c. Cell Directory Services
p.271 d. LDAP

49. SNMP formatted performance statistics are gathered and stored in
a. agents
b. monitors
p.276 c. MIBs
d. CPUs

124   Chapter 7

50. A system architecture in which multiple CPU's are controlled by the operating system and individual threads of application processes are assigned to particular CPUs on a first-available basis.

p.282
a. SMP
b. ASMP
c. MMP
d. DMP

Fill-In the Blank Questions

1. The _____ connects the client and server and acts as the transportation system of the client/server architecture.

2. In a(n) _____ LAN, individual workstations can be configured as a service requester (client), a service provider (server) or a combination of the two.

3. A client workstation's ability to interoperate transparently with a number of different network operating system servers without the need for additional products or configurations is described as a(n) _____ capability.

4. The goal of _____ is to free users from having to understand and worry about such things as IRQs, DMA channels, memory addresses, COM ports, and editing CONFIG.SYS whenever they want to add a device to their computer.

5. How finely access can be controlled (by disk, directory, or file level) is sometimes referred to as the _____ of the access control scheme.

6. An alternative to server-based remote access software is a standalone device known as a(n) _____.

7. Rather than sending entire files across the dial-up or LAN link, _____ only transfers the changes to those files.

8. _____ is a characteristic of Unix which allows it to be used across numerous hardware platforms.

9. In Unix, the command interpreter with which a user interfaces is a specialized user process known as a(n) _____.

10. Developed by Sun Microsystems, _____ allows multiple, different computing platforms to share files.

11. When a global directory database is _____, it implies that multiple copies of identical data may also be stored on multiple servers for redundancy and fault tolerance purposes.

12. _____ implies using the CPU power of multiple CPUs located in separate computing platforms to produce a single, more powerful, virtual computer.

Answers

1. enterprise network p.242
2. peer-to-peer p.245
3. universal client p.247
4. Plug-n-Play (PnP) p.255
5. granularity p.256
6. dial-up server or remote node server p.260
7. delta file synchronization p.262
8. Portability p.266
9. shell p.266
10. NFS p.268
11. replicated p.270
12. Clustering p.284

CASE STUDY AND ANSWERS

HOSPITAL WEIGHS NT MOVE

Activities
1. Top-down model:

Business	A very old and heterogeneous mix of LANs exists across six buildings and eight satellite clinics at Harlem Hospital with little or no internetworking capabilities.
	Management of the many diverse networks is very difficult with many needing upgrades in order to provide better email, groupware and document-management capabilities.
	The hospital doesn't have the staff or the budget to maintain all of the NetWare servers.
Applications	Upgrades to better software utilizing newer GUIs cannot be done without first upgrading the network operating systems.
	Many users have no email and can perform only DOS-based word processing.
	The networks can not talk to one another.
Data	Sharing of data is not currently available.
	Email and documents need to be shared among all users.
Network	A diversity of protocols and network operating systems has kept Harlem Hospital from being able to establish and enterprise network.
	User of a standardize NOS such as Windows NT would solve the protocol and interconnectivity issues.
Technology	Windows NT will be introduced throughout the enterprise because it can support all the current protocols in use.
	Windows 95 will be integrated into the network.
	Applications such as Microsoft BackOffice suite, SQL Server, Exchange, Systems Management Server, and Visual Basic will be introduced because they provide the necessary development environment and work well with Windows NT.

2. Unanswered questions:
   - How will overall management of the network be accomplished?
   - What will the cost be to begin the integration of Windows NT into the enterprise?
   - What other data must be shared across the enterprise?
   - What network architecture will be used for each LAN? For the enterprise backbone?
   - Who will provide the necessary training to move away from legacy LAN environments to Windows NT?
   - What is the typical client hardware needing support?
   - What hardware and software will be used to interconnect LANs across the backbone?

Business
1. Health care is provided by Harlem Hospital across its six building on the main campus and eight satellite clinics.
2. Since there was basically no budget to support the many different LANs and very few trained personnel, the hospital had to find a way to standardize its network operating systems.
3. Only one user per group will initially be entrusted with all other relevant domains because of users relative inexperience with shared services beyond their departments.
4. NT seems to be a good choice because it supports all the protocols mentioned. It can then be gradually introduced into each department as training and experience grow.

Application
1. Some email, DOS-based word processing and specialized applications by the radiology department are currently being used.
2. Microsoft BackOffice suite, including SQL Server, Exchange, Systems Management Server, and Visual Basic will be used in the new enterprise network.
3. The radiology department might use picture-archiving and -retrieval systems.
4. It was one of the major criteria for selection of Windows NT.

Data
1. Sharing email, imaging information, documents, and possibly billing are just a few of the possible data sharing needs.
2. There is probably a wide range of network protocols and operating systems in use, thus by using Windows NT the hospital will be able to interconnect with them, since NT supports most of the major network protocols.

Network
1. NetWare 3.x and lower, DEC LAT, AppleTalk, Virtual Operating System, and MPE/iX are some of the NOSs currently serving the hospital.
2. IPX/SPX, TCP/IP and probably AppleShare are in use.
3. No backbone exists.
4. Since no common standard is used and no backbone exists, users between departments are unable to share data or transfer information, files, or email each other. Many of the systems are dated and provide only DOS-based applications.
5. The new enterprise backbone will have to support TCP/IP in order to connect all the different LANS.
6. TCP/IP was chosen since it can generally be supported by most NOSs.
7. The client platform will be a Windows 95 machine because it integrates tightly with Windows NT.

Technology
1. It was easy to configure, worked well with Windows 95, and integrates well with most other NOSs.
2. They needed to take advantage of 4.11's IPX-to-IP gateway.
3. It will allow IPX networks to connect to the TCP/IP backbone.
4. As people use Windows 95 on NetWare they will become familiar with the NT-like environment of 95 and be able to transition with less help.

CHAPTER 8

Wide Area Networking Concepts, Architectures, & Services

ANSWERS TO CHAPTER REVIEW QUESTIONS

1. Frequency Division Multiplexing - Figure 8-3 in the text describes it as:
   (mechanics) multiple input signals are modulated to different frequencies within the available output bandwidth of a single composite circuit.
   (technology) uses a composite bandwidth (often 3000Hz) over a dial-up line. Space provided between frequency channels (guardbands) used to prevent crosstalk.
   (application) used in data over voice units. As terminal speeds and demand for more bandwidth per terminal have risen, FDM is no longer the most practical multiplexing method employed.

   Time Division Multiplexing - Figure 8-4 in the text describes it as:
   (mechanics) the total bandwidth of the composite channel is divided into equal time access slots.
   (technology) from a connected terminal's point of view, 100% of the total bandwidth is available a portion of the time. A fixed portion of time is reserved for each attached input device.
   (application) transmit over composite links of 9600bps to 38.4Kbps and can handle up to 4 input devices with the programming allowing the channels to be assigned fixed percentages of the total time allotment in multiples of 25%.

   Statistical Time Division Multiplexing - Figure 8-5 in the text describes it as
   (mechanics) allocation time is allotted to input devices dynamically; as terminals become more active they get more time to send data directly to the Stat Mux.
   (technology) uses buffer memory, sophisticated programming, and an integral microprocessor producing increased efficiency in time slot allocation and composite bandwidth usage.
   (application) can interfere with any timing which might have been previously set-up between the remote device and the central processor. This is particularly important in manufacturing or process control operations.

2. The time allocation protocols and composite message frame building protocols are proprietary and vary from one manufacturer to the next, making multiplexers from different manufacturers non-interoperable. If any devices are expecting certain timing signals, the muxes may not maintain the correct timing.

3. The cost for buying one mux must be doubled since it would be important to have the same mux at the other end of the line in order to break down the signal correctly. This is a particularly difficult problem when trying to build enterprise networks among numerous trading partners who have installed muxes from different manufacturers.

4. When X.25 was developed, long distance circuits connecting the X.25 packet switches were not nearly as error free as they are today. An X.25 switch will send either a positive ACK or negative NAK acknowledgment upon the receipt of each packet and will not forward additional packets until it receives an ACK or NAK. This error checking is done on a point-to-point or hop-by-hop basis at every X.25 packet switch in the network. If a Frame Relay switch detects an error when it compares the computed vs. transmitted FCSs, the bad frame is simply discarded. Frame relay uses point-to-point error detection with end-to-end error correction while X.25 is point-to-point error detection and correction.

5. In terms of the OSI model, the difference between X.25 Packet Switching and Frame Relay is simple. Frame Relay is a two layer protocol stack (Physical and Data Link) while X.25 is a three layer protocol stack (Physical, Data Link and Network). There is no network layer processing in Frame Relay, accounting for the decreased processing time and increased throughput rate.

6. Frame Relay assumes fast and reliable transmission media and services, a relatively safe assumption given the abundance of relatively error free fiber optic transmission employed today.

7. Figure 8-29 in the text shows an excellent description of what makes up a packet besides the data message.

8. The output of a DOV unit has two wires. The voice call is routed through a PBX to any destination and the data portion is connected directly to a computer or terminal server of some type.

9. TDM uses a fixed portion of time for each attached input device whether the device is active or not (efficiency is sacrificed for the sake of simplicity). STDM overcomes this by eliminating idle time allocations to inactive terminals and by eliminating padded blanks or null characters in the composite message blocks.

10. Polling is done by the mux when it checks on each connected terminal in order to see if any data is ready to be sent. If a mux (STDM) doesn't have to poll inactive devices then it can be more efficient.

11. Without switching, every possible source of data in the world would have to be directly connected to every possible destination of data in the world. Switching allows temporary connections to be established. The data is then transmitted through these switches.

12. Circuit Switching - a switched dedicated circuit is created to connect the two or more parties, eliminating the need for source and destination address information such as that provided by packetizing techniques. All data or voice travels from source to destination over the same physical path. Packet Switching - packets travel one at a time from the message source through the packet switched network to the message destination. Packets may take different physical paths within packet-switched networks. Circuit switched connections are billed according to time connected to the circuit. Packet switched networks usually charge according to packet transfer volume. Refer to Figure 8-8 in the text for more details.

13. PADs take data from a computer or to a computer and assemble or disassemble the data into packets for transmission. Packet switches pass packets among themselves as the packets are routed from source to destination.

14. There are no error-detection or flow-control techniques. Because datagrams are sent along multiple paths to the destination address there is no guarantee of their safe arrival. (This is also known as unreliable packet network.) Packets can travel over different circuits should some circuits become unavailable (down). On the positive side, because no virtual circuit needs to be set up, there is less overhead with datagram delivery.

15. Connectionless services do not use error detection or flow-control and are sometimes known as unreliable packet networks. Connection-oriented or reliable packet networks use virtual circuits in which packets follow one another, in sequence, down the same connection. Before a connection-oriented circuit can be set up, a type of explorer packet must be sent out to find the path from source to destination incurring some overhead. It can also offer check sum error-detection with ACK/NAK re-transmission control and flow-control. Connection-oriented networks do not require the full global addressing on each packet as in the case of connectionless datagram networks.

16. Connection-oriented or reliable packet networks use virtual circuits in which packets follow one another, in sequence, down the same path or logical channel. Packets are addressed with a logical channel number.

17. Overhead items for each packet include an abbreviated logical channel number, or LCN, connection set-up, including establishing and maintaining the virtual circuit table and network-based, point-to-point error detection, and flow control.

18. The SVC connection is terminated when the complete message has been sent and a special clear request packet causes all switched virtual circuit tables related to this connection to be erased. The virtual circuit table of the PVC is not erased, making the PVC the equivalent of a "virtual" circuit-switched leased line.

19. X.25 defines the interface between terminal equipment (DTE) and any packet switched network (the cloud). It does not define standards for what goes on inside the cloud.

20. It is bursts of data followed by variable length pauses due to users reading screen prompts or pauses between transactions. It must be delivered as quickly and reliably as the network can possibly perform. Bursty data requires variable and sometimes unpredictable amounts of bandwidth in order to handle bursts.

21. Transaction oriented processes produce interactive data which is bursty like an ATM machine. LAN to LAN communication such as database transfers can also be very bursty.

22. Refer to Figure 8-7 in the text. User demands are the driving force behind the WAN services. Interface specifications must be developed to insure interoperability. Network services can be offered if the infrastructure is in place. The network architecture really depends upon the integration of switching and transmission architectures which assure proper routing over the circuits.

23. Transmission architecture - copper, fiber, microwave, and satellite, SONET, T-1, T-3. Switching architecture - central office switches and packet switches, X.25, Frame Relay, ATM.

24. An X.25 switch will always send either a positive ACK or negative NAK acknowledgment upon the receipt of each packet and will not forward additional packets until it receives an ACK or NAK. If a NAK is received, the packet received in error will be retransmitted. Packets are stored in X.25 switches in case a NAK is received, necessitating re-transmission. Frame relay says that given the quality of the transmission system (high quality), stop all point-to-point error correction and flow control within the network itself and let the end-nodes worry about it. Error detection is still done on a point-to-point basis but frames with detected errors are simply discarded.

25. End nodes can only manage flow control between themselves and whatever frame relay network access device they are linked to. In the frame relay structure the BECN (Backward Explicit Congestion Notification), FECN (Forward Explicit Congestion Notification) and DE (Discard Eligibility) bits are the elements of a scheme to allow frame relay devices to dynamically adjust flow control. However, how these bits are used has not necessarily been standardized or implemented in all frame relay networks.

26. They are variable in length with the maximum frame transporting nearly 8000 characters at once. Figure 8-29 in the text illustrates the frame definition in more detail. The significance is that a variable length frame implies variable processing and delay times as a result, traffic that requires predictable delivery times such as voice and video may not be well suited to frame relay.

27. Dynamic allocation of bandwidth is important in order to handle bursts of data. Also, in terms of charges, billing is by bandwidth used (frames sent).

28. Frame Relay transmission rates are commonly as high as 1.544 Mbps and occasionally as high as 44.736Mbps. Remembering that multiple PVCs can exist within the Frame Relay Network cloud, another key advantage of frame relay over circuit-switched options such as leased lines is the ability to have multiple PVCs supported from only one access line. From a cost justification standpoint, this would allow a Frame Relay user to replace multiple leased line connections with a single access line to a Frame Relay Network. Remember also, that Frame Relay Network charges are based on usage, whereas circuit-switched leased lines charges are based on flat monthly fees whether they are used or not. Figure 8-30 illustrates the concept of multiple PVCs per single access line.

29. Cell relay has fixed length frames or cells. These cells allow the switches to perform faster which lead to a predictable and dependable processing rate and forwarding or delivery rate which was a weakness of frame relay. What this really means is that voice or video can be transmitted reliably over cell relay.

30. ATM (Asynchronous Transfer Mode) is a key standard developed for the cell relay switching methodology.

31. CBR or Constant Bit Rate provides a guaranteed amount of bandwidth to a given virtual path, thereby producing the equivalent of leased T-1 or T-3 line. The negative side of CBR is that if this guaranteed amount of bandwidth is not required 100% of the time, no other applications can use the unused bandwidth.
VBR or Variable Bit Rate provides a guaranteed minimum threshold amount of constant bandwidth below which the available bandwidth will not drop. However, as bursty traffic requires more bandwidth than this constant minimum, that required bandwidth will be provided.
ABR or Available Bit Rate takes advantage of leftover bandwidth whenever it is not required by the variable bit rate traffic.

32. ATM Adaptation Layer protocols are designed to optimize the delivery of a wide variety of possible types of user inputs or traffic by adapting those various types of traffic into standardized ATM cells.

33. B-ISDN operates at 155Mbps or about ten times Narrowband ISDN. The B-ISDN underlying network is formed by ATM and SONET and should provide bandwidth on demand transparently, and hopefully affordably. ISDN consists of 2 Bearer channels (64Kbps each) and one Delta channel (16Kbps) combined into a 144Kbps interface. The bearer channels are intended to carry services such as voice, video, or data, while the delta channel is intended for network management data for call set-up and teardown, calling number identification and other ISDN specific network signals.

34. POTS (Plain old telephone service) was introduced in chapter 4 as the default local loop technology. Users employ V.34 (28.8Kbps) or V.34+ (33.6Kbps) modems for transmitting data over the analog POTS network. Due to line impairments and interference on analog transmission lines, research indicates that optimal transmission

rates are seldom achieved and rarely maintained. POTS architecture and technology was detailed in Chapter 4, Voice Communications Concepts and Technology.
ISDN is somewhat of a phenomena in the telecommunications industry. A constant topic of discussion, opinions on it range from consideration of it as a revolutionary breakthrough to absolute conviction that it won't ever materialize. ISDN is a digital dial-up service.

35. ISDN has brought more humor to telecommunications than nearly any other topic with the various interpretations of the ISDN acronym such as: **I**t **S**till **D**oes **N**othing of **I** **S**till **D**on't **N**eed it. ISDN has been described as a solution in search of an application. The need for dial-up access to Internet services at transmission rates greater than those available via POTS has significantly increased the interest in ISDN as a local loop transmission alternative. A lack of national standards and resultant interoperability problems may be solved by the N-ISDN standards.

36. SONET is an optical transmission service delivering multiple channels of data from various sources. It is a service independent transport function which can carry the services of the future such as B-ISDN, FDDI, or HDTV. Together with ATM, it will bring B-ISDN and bandwidth on demand in an affordable manner.

37. SONET is a service independent transport function which can carry the services of the future such as B-ISDN (Broadband ISDN) or HDTV (High Definition Television), as easily as it can carry the circuit-switched traffic of today such as DS-1, and DS-3. It has extensive performance monitoring and fault location capabilities. For instance, if SONET senses a transmission problem, it can switch traffic to an alternate path in as little as 50 msec. (1000ths of a sec.) This network survivability is due to SONET's redundant or dual ring physical architecture. Based on the OC hierarchy of standard optical interfaces, SONET has the potential to deliver multi-gigabyte bandwidth transmission capabilities to end-users.

38. A T-1 line has a bandwidth of 1.544Mbps and is a standard for North America while an E-1 has a transmission rate of 2.048Mbps and is a CCITT standard.

39. In a technique known as periodic framing or synchronous TDM, twenty-four channels of eight bits each (192 bits total) are arranged in a frame. Each group of eight bits represents one sampling of voice or data traffic to be transmitted on its associated channel. Each group of eight bits is known as a time slot. Twenty-four time slots are grouped into a frame, sometimes also known as a D-4 frame. Each frame is terminated with a framing bit in the 193rd position. Such a frame, sometimes known as a D-4 frame, is illustrated in Figure 8-17. Rather than just using the 193rd bit as a simple frame marker, techniques have been developed to combine the values of sequential framing bits into meaningful arrangements that provide management and error control capabilities for the T-1 transmission service. A group of 12 frames is known as a superframe and a group of 24 frames is known as an ESF or Extended Superframe. Superframes and extended superframes are illustrated in Figure 8-18.

40. NISDN-1 defines a national standard for ISDN switches as well as inter-switch communication. It seeks to overcome the interoperability problems of the past.

41. DS-1 is a digital service standard and is independent of the transmission services which may deliver the required bandwidth of the standard. T-1 is a line which can deliver DS-1 equivalent bandwidth.

42. Fractional T-1 allows a business to only use a certain number of the 64Kbps channels offered over a T-1 line. The business only pays for whatever fraction of the T-1 line it uses.

43. Unlike ISDN, ADSL works along with POTS for traditional voice services. In fact, ADSL works over POTS, at higher frequencies, on the same copper pair that currently carries voice transmission. Unlike using a modem on a voice line, ADSL does not interfere with voice services. That is to say, one could be connected to the Internet via ADSL and still make and receive voice phone calls on the same line. The term "asymmetric" in ADSL refers to the service's differing upstream (away from the user) and downstream (toward the user) bandwidths. The bandwidths and associated distance limitations from the carrier's central office of two of the most common ADSL implementations are listed in Figure 8-14. Other transmission speeds and distance limitations are possible.

44. ADSL is an attractive alternative from a carrier perspective because it does not require carriers to upgrade switching technology.

45. At least three other DSL solutions are currently in various stages of development. All DSL solutions support simultaneous POTS service :
    - VDSL (Very High Speed DSL) - provides 52Mbps downstream and between 1.6-2.3Mbps upstream over distances of up to only 1,000 ft. It is being explored primarily as a means to bring video on demand services to the home.
    - RADSL (Rate Adaptive Digital Subscriber Line) - is able to adapt it's data rate to the level of noise and interference on a given line. Currently, it is not able to support this adaptive rate on a dynamic basis, however.
    - SDSL (Symmetric Digital Subscriber Line) differs from ADSL in that it offers upstream and downstream channels of equal bandwidth.

46. Providing upstream bandwidth is only one of the architectural obstacles that cable providers must overcome. While phone carriers provide voice service via a switched media architecture (circuit-switching), cable companies provide cable service via a shared media architecture in which an entire neighborhood may be served by the same shared coaxial cable. Therefore, although 30Mbps downstream bandwidth may sound impressive, one needs to really know among how many users will that 30Mbps be shared. The access methodologies for sharing cable bandwidth are being standardized as IEEE

802.14 cable network specifications. Cable companies, like voice-service carriers, must either develop their own Internet access services or buy these services from an existing Internet service provider in order to provide transparent Internet access to their customers.

47. VTs are flexibly defined channels within the payload area of SONET. They allow circuit switched services to be delivered over cell-switched network architectures.

48. SONET is the optical transmission interface and mechanism which will deliver Broadband ISDN services. ATM is the switching architecture which will assure that video, voice, data, and image packets delivered by B-ISDN services are delivered to the proper destination. Together, ATM and SONET form the underlying network architecture of the B-ISDN of the future.

49. B-ISDN services include Interactive Services and Broadcast or distributed services.

50. The D-channel is intended for network management data for call set-up and teardown, calling number identification and other ISDN specific network signals. Some D-channel bandwidth (9600bps) has been used for X.25 packet transmission.

51. BRI - Basic Rate Interface - 2B+D = 2x64Kbps, 1x16Kbps = 144Kbps
PRI - Primary Rate Interface - 23B+D = 24x64Kbps = 1.544Mbps

52. An inverse mux combines two or more network circuits to satisfy the transmission needs of a single local application such as videoconferencing. By accumulating multiple circuits on demand, the inverse mux offers the videoconference just the bandwidth it needs to maintain desired video and audio quality without requiring payment for unused or unnecessary bandwidth and has become known as a "Bandwidth on Demand" device.

53. SMDS, Switched Multimegabit Data Service is a connectionless network service delivering switched LAN internetworking and data dial tone in a Metropolitan Area Network deployment while adhering to the IEEE 802.6 and DQDB (Distributed Queue Dual Bus) protocols by delivering fixed length cells of data to their destinations via a SONET transmission system at speeds up to T-3 (45Mbps). Architecturally, it differs from frame relay primarily in the fact that it is a connectionless service and does not support virtual circuits. Practically speaking, SMDS is losing the WAN services battle to frame relay. In 1996, 27% of WAN services customers purchased frame relay services while only 1% purchased SMDS. Projections for 1999 call for frame relay usage to increase to 47% while SMDS is projected to increase to only 6% of WAN services customers, although some studies predict no market growth whatsoever. Part of the reason for the small market share has to do with a lack of support from carriers. Among the local service providers, only Ameritech, Bell Atlantic, Bell South, PacTel, GTE and Southwestern Bell offer SMDS services while MCI is the only long distance carrier offering SMDS.

TEST QUESTIONS

True/False Questions

1. By knowing exactly which bits within a packet represent a destination address and which bits represent data to be forwarded, the data communications device can process incoming data packets more quickly and efficiently. T/296

2. FDM is a type of multiplexing in which multiple input signals are sent over the composite channel by dividing the channel into multiple subchannels by time. F/297

3. Although FDM is no longer the most practical multiplexing method employed, it is still used in DOV units. T/297

4. With TDM, the portion of time available to each connected input device is not constant and cannot be controlled by the TDM. F/298

5. The insertion of blanks, or null characters, into composite message links when a terminal is inactive is one of TDM's inefficiencies. T/299

6. In a stat mux, time is allotted to input devices dynamically. T/300

7. In a connectionless packet-switched network, data travels through the network one packet at a time, traveling over a single, dedicated path within the network. F/304

8. X.25 is a standard which defines the specifications for a packet switching network. F/323

9. The switched virtual circuit connection is terminated when the complete message has been sent and a special clear request packet causes all switched virtual circuit tables related to this connection to be erased. T/306

10. Circuit switched connections are billed according to time connected to the circuit, while packet-switched networks usually charge according to packet transfer volume. T/308

11. DS-1 and T-1 are not the same although the terms are often used interchangeably. T/317

12. Both frame relay and X.25 perform point-to-point error detection, however frame relay does not perform error correction. T/327

13. A key advantage of frame relay over circuit-switched options is the ability to have multiple PVCs supported from only one access line, allowing a frame relay user to replace multiple leased-line connections. T/330

138   Chapter 8

14. An unpredictable delivery time for each and every cell makes cell relay a poor choice for transmission of voice or video applications. F/333

15. X.25 is a three layer protocol stack corresponding to the first three layers of the OSI model. T/323

16. An ISDN Terminal Adapter must be used in order to get voice or data onto the ISDN network, and is the equivalent of an ISDN modem. T/312

Multiple Choice Questions

1. Which of the following is the term for segmenting of data transmissions between devices into structured blocks of data which contain enough "overhead" or management information in addition to the transmitted data itself to assure delivery of the block of data to its intended destinations?
    a. multiplexing
    b. switching
p.294 c. packetizing
    d. integrating

2. Taking structured blocks of data and sending it over a shared wide area connection along with other structured blocks of data from other sources is called
p.294 a. multiplexing
    b. switching
    c. packetizing
    d. integrating

3. With this type of multiplexing, multiple input signals are modulated to different frequencies within available output bandwidth of a single composite circuit and subsequently demodulated back into individual signals on the output end of the composite circuit or channel.
p.297 a. FDM
    b. TDM
    c. STDM
    d. DTM

4. DOV units (Data Over Voice) cannot be used over which type of phone network?
    a. local PBX
p.298 b. PSTN
    c. private branch exchange
    d. none of the above

5. With this type of multiplexing, each of the multiple input signals is allocated 100 percent of the total bandwidth for a portion of the time, yielding the appearance of a dedicated circuit whether the attached device is active or not.
    a. FDM
p.298   b. TDM
    c. STDM
    d. DTM

6. In TDM, the process of checking each connected terminal in order to see if any data is ready to be sent is known as
    a. checking
    b. flow control
    c. framing
p.299   d. polling

7. This type of multiplexing eliminates idle time allocations to inactive terminals.
    a. FDM
    b. TDM
p.299   c. STDM
    d. DTM

8. With this type of multiplexer, dynamic allocation of time afforded to individual terminals or devices can interfere with any timing that might have been previously set up between the remote device and the central processor.
    a. FDM
    b. TDM
p.300   c. STDM
    d. DTM

9. The STDM's increased costs are due to
    a. increased buffer memory
    b. more sophisticated programming
    c. an integral microprocessor
p.301   d. all of the above

10. This type of network is often represented by a "cloud."
p.304   a. packet switched network
    b. circuit switched network
    c. PBX
    d. DOV

140   Chapter 8

11. Which type of network uses a dedicated circuit to connect the two or more parties, eliminating the need for source and destination address information?
    a. packet switched network
p.304 b. circuit switched network
    c. PBX
    d. DOV

12. The assembly and disassembly of a packet is done by a device known as a(n)
    a. analog modem
p.304 b. PAD
    c. modem
    d. DOV

13. Self-sufficient packets containing full source and destination address information plus a message segment are know as
    a. PADs
    b. global addresses
p.305 c. datagrams
    d. muxes

14. In this type of packet-switched network, packets do not follow one another in order down an actual or virtual circuit or connection.
    a. reliable
    b. connection-oriented
    c. global
p.305 d. connectionless

15. In a connectionless packet network, flow-control and error-detection are provided by
    a. the cloud
p.305 b. end-user devices
    c. circuits
    d. datagrams

16. In this type of packet-switched network, virtual circuits enabling message packets to follow one another, in sequence, down the same connection or physical circuit, is known as
    a. unreliable
p.305 b. connection-oriented
    c. global
    d. connectionless

17. In a connection-oriented packet switching network, an LCN reduces overhead while _____ adds to the overhead.
    a. flow control
    b. connection set-up
    c. point-to-point error detection
p.306 d. all of the above

18. Which is a switched digital network service offering both voice and nonvoice connectivity to other users of the same service?
    a. SONET
    b. frame relay
p.309 c. ISDN
    d. X.25

19. Narrowband ISDN consists of bearer channels and a channel intended to carry network management data called a
    a. voice channel
p.310 b. delta channel
    c. video channel
    d. broadband channel

20. A second ISDN service level known as 23B+D has enough channel for a combined bandwidth which fits nicely on which circuit?
    a. T-3
    b. T-2
p.310 c. T-1
    d. OC-1

21. Which of the following digital service levels offers 24 voice channels at a total transmission rate of 1.544Mbps?
    a. DS-0
p.318 b. DS-1
    c. DS-2
    d. DS-3

22. A single SONET frame containing nine 90 octet rows grouped together is known as a
p.321 a. SONET superframe
    b. synchronous payload envelope
    c. megaframe
    d. none of the above

23. SONET's flexibly defined channels within the payload area are known as
    a. virtual paths
    b. tributaries
p.321 c. virtual tributaries
    d. paths

24. HDLC is which OSI layer protocol for the X.25 protocol stack?
    a. physical layer
p.324 b. data-link layer
    c. network layer
    d. transport layer

25. The network layer protocol for an X.25 protocol stack is known as
    a. RS-232
    b. SDLC
    c. HDLC
p.324 d. PLP

26. An X.25 related standard which provides a global addressing scheme is
p.325 a. X.121
    b. X.28
    c. X.32
    d. X.75

27. An X.25 related standard which provides synchronous dial-up access directly into PADs is
    a. X.121
    b. X.28
p.325 c. X.32
    d. X.75

28. An X.25 related standard which provides for internetworking packet switched networks is
    a. X.121
    b. X.28
    c. X.32
p.325 d. X.75

29. This packet switching methodology takes advantage of today's more reliable transmission systems and relying on end-to-end error correction instead of hop-by-hop error correction.
    a. X.25
    b. X.135
p.327 c. frame relay
    d. PBX

30. In a frame relay frame structure which of the following are the elements of a scheme to allow frame relay devices to adjust flow control dynamically?
    a. BECN
    b. FECN
    c. DE
p.328 d. all of the above

31. Frame relay is often described as a data only service because
    a. only data bits work with a frame
    b. options do not exist to transport digitized, compressed voice transmissions
p.329 c. framed voice and video may not arrive in a predictable timed fashion for conversion back to understandable voice and video
    d. voice may become intermixed with video

32. Which term refers to the minimum bandwidth guaranteed to users for "normal" transmission?
p.331 a. CIR
    b. CBS
    c. BIR
    d. SVC

33. The extent to which a user can exceed their committed information rate over a period of time is known as
    a. CIR
p.331 b. CBS
    c. BIR
    d. SVC

34. In a frame relay network, this device allows computers to access the frame relay network.
    a. FRDA
p.321 b. FRAD
    c. PAD
    d. NAK

35. Frame relay can be categorized as
    a. an interface specification
    b. a network service
    c. a switching architecture
p.332 d. all of the above

144   Chapter 8

36. A connectionless network service delivering switched LAN internetworking and data dial tone in a MAN deployment while adhering to the IEEE 802.6 and DQDB protocols.
    a. Ethernet
    b. Token Ring
p.332 c. SMDS
    d. FDDI

37. The key standard developed for the cell relay switching methodology is known as
p.332 a. ATM
    b. VTAM
    c. BRI
    d. FRAD

38. The key physical difference between frame relay and cell relay is
    a. cell relay is slower
    b. frame relay has fixed length frames
p.332 c. cell relay has fixed length cells
    d. cell relay has variable length cells

39. Because ATM can carry multiple types of information, this field is included in the ATM cell structure.
    a. virtual path identifier
    b. payload type
    c. header error control
p.335 d. virtual channel identifier

40. Using this type of network to connect two or more parties, eliminates the need for source and destination address information.
p.307 a.   circuit switched
    b.   packet switched
    c.   frame switched
    d.   none of the above

41. This type of WAN transmission technology provides bandwidth to users' residences and businesses, generally offering connectivity between these end-points and the carrier network service of choice.
    a. broadband transmission
    b. T-1 circuit
    c. T-3 circuit
p.309 d. local loop transmission

42. Term used for assuring interoperability standards among inverse multiplexing devices supported by most ISDN inverse multiplexers.
    a. NISDN-1
    b. PRI-ISDN
p.311 c. BONDING
    d. BRI-ISDN

43. Which of the following flavors of DSL offers upstream and downstream channels of equal bandwidth?
    a. ADSL
p.314 b. SDSL
    c. RADSL
    d. VDSL

44. This ATM cell format carries information between the user and the ATM network.
p.333 a. UNI
    b. INU
    c. NNI
    d. OSI

45. What ATM layer is the processing done to change user inputs of data, video, or voice into fixed length ATM cells?
    a. TCS
    b. Signaling
p.333 c. AAL
    d. PMD

46. This ATM category of bandwidth management provides a guaranteed amount of bandwidth to a given virtual path.
    a. VBR
p.334 b. CBR
    c. ABR
    d. RBR

47. This ATM category of bandwidth management provides leftover bandwidth whenever it is not required by the variable bit rate traffic.
    a. VBR
    b. CBR
p.335 c. ABR
    d. RBR

146   Chapter 8

Fill-In the Blank Questions

1. In order to understand the basic technical principles of wide area networking, one must really start by looking at the basic _____ principles of wide area networking.

2. In FDM, sufficient space in between the separate frequency subchannels is reserved in _____ in order to prevent interference.

3. In TDM, each input channel has a fixed amount of buffer memory into which it can load data. _____ tells the terminal to stop transmitting to the buffer memory when the buffer memory fills.

4. _____ allows temporary connections to be established, maintained, and terminated between message sources and message destinations.

5. A(n) _____ is a specially structured group of data that includes control and address information in addition to the data itself.

6. _____ is an international CCITT standard which defines the interface between terminal equipment (DTE) and any packet-switched network (the Cloud).

7. A connectionless packet-switched network is also know as a(n) _____ network because of the lack of inherent error-detection or flow-control.

8. A connection-oriented packet-switched network is also known as a(n) _____ network because error-detection and flow control are offered.

9. Use of the D channel in ISDN for carrying signal data is know as _____ signaling.

10. Using multiple 64K channels within a T-1 transport circuit on an individual basis is a service known as _____.

11. X.25 packet switching is sometimes called a _____ switching methodology because packets are stored in X.25 switches in case a NAK is received, necessitating retransmission.

12. In a frame relay network, _____ are used to forward frames from source to destination through the frame relay cloud.

13. SONET + ATM = _____

14. _____ is a digital local loop transmission technology which works along with POTS for traditional voice services unlike ISDN.

15. The standard high capacity digital transmission circuit in North America is known as a _____ with a bandwidth of 1.544Mbps.

16. A(n) _____ LAN refers to a group of workstations that appear to be all locally connected to each other but that, in fact, are geographically dispersed.

Answers

1. business p.294
2. guardbands p.297
3. Flow control p.299
4. Switching p.303
5. packet p.304
6. X.25 p.323
7. unreliable p.305
8. reliable p.305
9. out-of-band p.310
10. fractional T-1 p.319
11. store-and-forward p.327
12. PVCs p.330
13. B-ISDN p.338
14. ADSL p.313
15. T-1 p.316
16. virtual p.337

CASE STUDY AND ANSWERS

LEASED LINES TRADED IN

Activities

1. Top-down model:

Business	J.W. Charles, a brokerage company, needed a flexible, reliable and easily managed way to accommodate its rapid growth while reducing WAN costs. The company needed to avoid the expense of leased lines. An easy method to add new affiliate sites was needed.
Applications	Stock quotes and back-office applications such as accounting, payroll, and billing were needed.
Data	Real-time stock data, portfolio data, and buy/sell orders were made. Data would be aggregated and sent over a carrier's frame relay WAN.
Network	The network designed must be flexible yet easy to manage. The network must allow for the headquarters to connect to a disaster recovery site, branch offices and independent brokers. A public frame relay network was chosen.
Technology	Frame relay with 56Kbps connections to branch offices and independent brokers was chosen. Develcon Electronics Ltd. Athena frame relay switches are used to connect to MCI's frame relay WAN and Develcon's 4000 routers. T-1, 56Kbps, and fractional T-1's are used to connect frame relay devices, routers and switches.

2. Unanswered questions:
   What LAN NOSs and protocols are currently used?
   Are leased lines available to all possible sites?
   What is the estimated growth that will cause 100 percent load and when might it be reached?
   What security procedures are in place?
   What are typical client hardware and software configurations?
   Are Internet connections anticipated?

Business

1. J.W. Charles Group Inc., is a brokerage company which manages portfolios and buys and sells stocks.
2. The individual broker would need back-office quotes to buy and sell stock.

3. 16 branch offices and 50 affiliate sites are connected to the WAN.
4. Monthly costs were $1,200 per leased line and $450 for a 28.8Kbps dial-up connection.
5. The motivating factor for looking at switched frame relay was to avoid expensive leased line costs.
6. Costs were reduced to between $250 and $350 for dedicated 56Kbps connections.
7. WAN migration saved thousands of dollars per month.
8. They add five remote sites per month.

Application
1. Applications to check stock prices, update portfolios, and buy and sell stocks are the primary applications with other back-office applications such as accounting, payroll, and billing.
2. Back-office applications such as accounting, payroll, and billing, were also run at each location.

Data
1. The original leased lines were 9,600-baud.
2. Two leased lines were run to each location, one for stock quotes and the other for back-office applications.

Network
1. They migrated to frame relay to avoid the costs of leased lines.
2. The bandwidth was 56Kbps.
3. The bandwidth was 1.544Mbps (T-1).
4. The bandwidth was 768Kbps.

Technology
1. The overall benefits were easier manageability, flexibility, and cost savings.
2. An Athena enterprise switch was used to interface to the frame relay service because it provided scaleability, letting them quickly connect remote LANs and PCs to J.W. Charles' network.
3. It give the company greater scaleability.
4. Each affiliate occupies only one port on the router, which itself occupies only on of the switches 18 ports.
5. The routers are connected to the switch which is connected to the carrier's frame relay WAN.
6. Management has become easier, providing flexibility for J.W. Charles' rapidly growing WAN.
7. The design allows them to troubleshoot their network and determine if the problem is with the equipment or with the telephone company by allowing them to switch port connections easily and create point-to-point connections to determine the trouble spot.

CHAPTER 9

Internetworking

ANSWERS TO CHAPTER REVIEW QUESTIONS

1. Internetworking is overall LAN-to-LAN or LAN-to-mainframe transparent interoperability.

2. Local area networks tend to grow by a natural process until the shared media network architecture (Ethernet, Token Ring, FDDI, etc.) becomes too congested and network performance begins to suffer. This scenario is one of the two primary reasons for investigating internetworking solutions. The other situation which often leads to internetworking design is when independently established and operated LANs wish to begin sharing information.

3. Segmentation is usually the first approach to reducing shared media congestion. By having fewer workstations per segment, there is less contention for the shared bandwidth. Segmentation improves performance for both CSMA/CD (Ethernet) and Token Passing (Token Ring) access methodologies. Some type of internetworking device, such as a bridge or router, will be required to link the LAN segments. When segmentation is taken to the extreme of limiting each LAN segment to only a single workstation, the design strategy is known as micro-segmentation. A micro-segmented internetwork requires a LAN switch which is compatible with the NICs installed in the attached workstations. Both Ethernet and Token Ring switches are readily available. Instead of assigning all workstations to their own LAN segment as in micro-segmentation, only selected high-performance devices such as servers can be assigned to their own segment in a design strategy known as server isolation. By isolating servers on their own segments, guaranteed access to network bandwidth is assured. Hierarchical networking isolates local LAN traffic on a local network architecture such as Ethernet or Token Ring while transmitting internetwork traffic over a higher speed network architecture such as FDDI or Fast Ethernet. Servers are often directly connected to the backbone network while individual workstations access the backbone network only as needed through routers. Figure 9-1 illustrates these overall internetworking design strategies.

4. A bridge reads the destination address (MAC layer address of destination NIC) of each data frame on a LAN, decides whether the destination is local or remote (on the other side of the bridge), and only allows those data frames with non-local destination addresses to cross the bridge to the remote LAN.

152   Chapter 9

5. Since only frames with destination addresses not found in the known local nodes table are forwarded across the bridge, bridges are sometimes known as a "Forward-if-not-local" devices.

6. The primary limitation of bridges is also one of their strengths. Because bridges learn and do not require on-going configuration, they only know to forward all packets which are addressed to non-local nodes. In the case of a destination node which is many LANs and connecting bridges away from its source workstation, all workstations on all LANs between the source and destination workstation will be broadcast with the frame bound for the distant destination. Forwarding messages to all workstations on all intermittent LANs is known as propagation. In the case of improperly addressed frames or frames destined for non-existent addresses, frames can be infinitely perpetuated or flooded onto all bridged LANs in a condition known as a broadcast storm. Bridges are generally not able to support networks containing redundant paths since the multiple active loops between LANs can lead to the propagation of broadcast storms.

7. Although a bridge reads the destination address of every data packet on the LAN to which it is attached, a router only examines those data packets which are specifically addressed to it. Rather than just merely allowing the data packet access to the internetwork in a manner similar to a bridge, a router is both more cautious as well as more helpful. Routers only forward packets directly to other routers and not all intermediate LAN attached workstations.

8. The router itself is a datalink layer destination address, available to receive, examine, and forward data packets from anywhere on any network to which it is either directly or indirectly internetworked. How do data packets arrive at a router? The destination address on an Ethernet or Token Ring packet must be the MAC address of the router which will handle further internetwork forwarding. Thus, a router is addressed in the data link layer destination address field. The router then discards this MAC sub-layer "envelope" which contained its address, and proceeds to read the contents of the data field of the Ethernet or Token Ring frame. Data link layer addressing is functionally referred to as point-to-point addressing.

9. Routers make their forwarding decisions based on the contents of the network layer addresses embedded within the data field of the data link layer frame. Network layer protocols dictate a bit-by-bit data frame structure which the router understands. What looked like just "data" and was ignored by the data link layer internetworking device, the bridge, is "unwrapped" by the router and examined thoroughly in order to determine further processing.

10. Unlike the bridge which merely allows access to the internetwork (forward-if-not-local logic), the router specifically addresses the data packet to a distant router. However, before a router actually releases a data packet onto the internetwork it confirms the existence of the destination address to which this data packet is bound. Only once the router is satisfied with both the viability of the destination address as well as with the

quality of the intended path will it release the carefully packaged data packet. This meticulous processing activity on the part of the router is known as forward-if-proven-remote.

11. Routers provide the following services to the internetwork:
    - Create firewalls to protect connected LANs
    - Filter unwanted broadcast packets from the internetwork
    - Discriminate and prioritize processing of packets according to network layer protocol
    - Provide security by filtering packets by either datalink or network layer addresses
    - Provide transparent interconnection between LANs

12. Switching, otherwise known as LAN switching, is very similar in function to bridging. The key difference between switching and bridging is that switching is done in hardware, or ASIC (Application Specific Integrated Circuit) chips and is extremely fast in comparison to bridging.

13. A LAN switch's limitations are largely a result of its bridging heritage. Switching cannot perform sophisticated filtering or security based on network layer protocols because LAN switches are unable to read network layer protocols. Switches are not able to discriminate between multiple paths and make best path decisions. Management information offered to enterprise network management systems by LAN switches is minimal in comparison to that available from routers.

14. A few characteristics are true of all internetworking devices in relation to the protocols of the OSI layer with which they are associated.
    - Any given network device can translate or convert protocols associated with OSI layers lower than or equal to the OSI layer of the internetworking device.
    - Any given network device is unable to process protocols associated with OSI layers higher than the OSI layer of the internetworking device.

    The relationship between the OSI model and internetworking devices is illustrated in Figure 9-5.

15. The primary reasons for employing a repeater are:
    - Increase the overall length of the network media by repeating signals across multiple LAN segments. In a Token Ring LAN, several MAUs can be linked together by repeaters in order to increase the size of the LAN.
    - Isolate key network resources onto different LAN segments in order to assure greater survivability.
    - Translate between different media types supported for a given network architecture.

16. Auto-partitioning is an important feature which prevents failure of one connected segment from affecting other segments. Auto-restoral upon segment re-establishment is often also included.

17. Token Ring repeaters can extend either the overall Ring length as measured by the distance between MAUs, or the Lobe length which is the distance from the workstation to the MAU.

18. Filtering Rate: Measured in Packets/sec or Frames/sec. When a bridge reads the destination address on an Ethernet frame or Token Ring packet and decides whether or not that packet should be allowed access to the internetwork through the bridge, that process is known as filtering. Filtering rates for bridges range from 7,000 to 60,000 frames per second. Forwarding Rate: Also measured in Packets/sec or Frames/sec. Having decided whether or not to grant a packet access to the internetwork in the filtering process, the bridge now must perform a separate operation of forwarding the packet onto the internetwork media whether local or remote. Forwarding rates range from as little as 700 packets per second for some remote bridges to as much as 30,000 packets per second for RISC based high speed local bridges.

19. The Spanning Tree Algorithm (IEEE 802.1), which is implemented as software installed on STA compliant bridges, can sense multiple paths and can disable all but one. In addition, should the primary path between two LANs become disabled, the Spanning Tree Algorithm can re-enable the previously disabled redundant link, thereby preserving the inter-LAN link.

20. Data messages arrive at a source routing bridge with a detailed map of how they plan to reach their destination. One very important limitation of source routing bridges as applied to large internetworks is known as the 7 Hop Limit. Because of the limited space in the RIF (Router Information Field) of the explorer packet, only 7 hop locations can be included in the path to any remote destination. In order to avoid constantly flooding the network with explorer packets seeking destinations, source routing bridges may employ some type of address caching or RIF caching, so that previously determined routes to known destinations are saved and re-used.

21. Bridges that connect LANs of similar data link format are known as transparent bridges. Transparent bridges exhibit the following characteristics:
    - Promiscuous listen, meaning that transparent bridges receive all data packets transmitted on the LANs to which they are connected.
    - Store-and-forward bridging between LANs means that messages which are not destined for local workstations are forwarded through the bridge as soon as the target LAN is available.
    - Learning is achieved by examining all MAC source addresses on data link frames received in order to understand which workstations are locally attached to which LANs through which ports on the bridge.
    - The IEEE 802.1 spanning tree algorithm is implemented in order to manage path connectivity between LANs.

22. A special type of bridge which includes a format converter can bridge between Ethernet and Token Ring. These special bridges may also be called multi-protocol bridges or translating bridges. A third type of bridge, somewhat like a translating bridge, is used to bridge between Ethernet and FDDI networks. Unlike the translating bridge which must actually manipulate and re-write the data link layer frame, the encapsulating bridge merely takes the entire Ethernet data link layer frame and stuffs it in an "envelope" (data frame) which conforms to the FDDI data link layer protocol.

23. Source routing bridges are specifically designed for connecting Token Ring LANs which have source routing enabled. Not all Token Ring LANs are source routing LANs but only Token Ring LANs can be source routing LANs. Bridges which can support links between source routing Token Ring LANs or transparent LANs are known as Source Routing Transparent (SRT) bridges. These bridges are able to identify whether frames are to be bridged transparently or source routed by reading the flags setting in the data link frame header.

24. An increasingly popular alternative for bridging remote LANs within 3 miles of each other are wireless bridges.

25. Other protocols processed by some routers are actually data link layer protocols without network layer addressing schemes. These protocols are considered non-routable.

26. Routing tables must be kept up-to-date in order to reflect any changes in the network. The key problem with distance vector routing protocols is that changes in the network are not always known by all routers immediately due to the delays in having routers recalculate their own routing tables prior to re-transmitting updated information to neighboring routers. This phenomenon is referred to as slow convergence.

27. A major distinction between routing protocols has to do with the method or algorithm by which up-to-date routing information is gathered by the router. For instance, RIP uses a distance vector algorithm which only measures the number of hops to a distant router, to a maximum of 16, while the OSPF protocol uses a more comprehensive link state algorithm which can decide between multiple paths to a given router based upon variables other than number of hops such as delay, and capacity, throughput, and reliability of the circuits connecting the routers. Perhaps more importantly, OSPF uses much less bandwidth in its efforts to keep routing tables up to date.

28. Boundary or branch office routers are employed at remote corporate locations with less routing requirements and fewer technical support personnel. For branch offices whose amount of internetwork traffic does not warrant the constant bandwidth and higher cost of leased lines, dial-up routers are often employed.

29. In the case of boundary or branch office routers, all routing information is kept at the central site router. This allows the boundary router to require less technical configuration and to be available for a lower cost than central site routers. Boundary routers generally

have just two interfaces: one WAN link and one LAN link. The ability to be remotely configured is particularly important.

30. In those cases where the amount of inter-LAN traffic from a remote site does not justify the cost of a leased line, dial-up routers may be the appropriate choice of internetworking equipment. This is especially true if the dial-up digital WAN service known as ISDN (Integrated Services Digital Network) is available at the two ends of the LANs to be linked. ISDN BRI (Basic Rate Interface) provides up to 144Kbps of bandwidth on demand, and ISDN PRI (Primary Rate Interface) provides up to 1.536Mbps of usable digital bandwidth on demand. There are currently no interoperability standards for dial-up routers. As a result, dial-up routers should always be bought in pairs from the same manufacturer. The ability to spoof chatty protocols is particularly important to dial-up routers so that connections are not dialed-up unnecessarily.

31. Spoofing is a method of filtering chatty or unwanted protocols from the WAN link while assuring that remote programs which require on-going communication from these filtered protocols are still re-assured via emulation of these protocols by the local dial-up router. It prevents dial-up links from being dial-up unnecessarily.

32. Three primary methods for efficient updating are as follows:
    - Timed Updates - are performed at regular pre-determined intervals.
    - Triggered Updates - are performed whenever a certain programmable event, such as a change in available services, occurs.
    - Piggyback Updates - are performed only when the dial-up link has already been established for the purposes of exchanging user data.

33. Three different possible internetwork design evolutionary scenarios are as follows:
    - Distinct Layer 2 Switching & Layer 3 Routing in which separate Layer 2 switches and Layer 3 routers cooperatively contribute what each does best in order to deliver internetwork traffic as efficiently as possible.
    - Distributed Routing in which layer 2 switching and layer 3 routing functionality are combined into a single device sometimes referred to as a multi-layer switch.
    - Route Servers will provide a centralized repository of routing information while edge switches deployed within the LANs will be programmed with minimal routing information. Edge switches will consult distributed route servers for "directory assistance" when they encounter routing situations which they are not equipped to handle. In this scenario, routing information and processing overhead is kept to a minimum at the switches which are primarily responsible for providing local bandwidth.

34. In micro-mainframe connectivity, the micro (Standalone or LAN-attached PC) pretends to be or "emulates" a mainframe terminal such as an IBM 3270 attached and logged into the mainframe. Presentation may be controlled by the micro; however, data management and application processing take place on the mainframe. Although file transfer utilities

may allow more capability than mere remote login, this is not the peer to peer networking implied by the term internetworking. With full peer to peer internetworking, the PC can exchange data with any mainframe or any other PC on a host-to-host level rather than acting like a "dumb" terminal as in the case of micro-mainframe connectivity. Presentation, data management, and application processing may be shared among the peer computers.

35. A hierarchical network structure such as the "classic" SNA (Systems Network Architecture) centers around the mainframe. If two devices other than the mainframe on an SNA network wanted to communicate, they would have to establish, maintain, and terminate that communication through the mainframe. This model is in direct contrast to a peer to peer network structure, typical of most LANs, in which any device may communicate directly with any other LAN attached device.

36. A front end processor is a computer which offloads the communications processing from the mainframe, allowing the mainframe to be dedicated to processing activities. A high speed data channel connects the FEP to the mainframe locally, although FEPs can be deployed remotely as well. The FEP, also known as a communications controller, can have devices such as terminals or printers connected directly to it, or these end user devices may be concentrated by another device known as a cluster controller. A cluster controller is a device which allows connection of both 3270 terminals as well as LANs with possible wide area links to packet switched networks (X.25) or high speed leased lines. A cluster controller concentrates the transmissions of its numerous input devices and directs this concentrated data stream to the FEP either locally or remotely.

37. It would be wise to take advantage of the shared resource capabilities of the LAN to share a protocol conversion attachment to the mainframe. Such a LAN server-based, shared protocol converted access to a mainframe is known as a gateway. As an alternative to LAN-based gateways, channel-attached gateways are able to interface directly to the mainframe's high speed data channel, thereby bypassing the FEP entirely. Physically, the channel attached gateways are often modules which are added to enterprise routers. Depending upon the amount of actual 3270 terminal traffic required in a given network, the use of channel attached gateways may either preclude the need for additional FEP purchases or may allow FEPs to be replaced altogether. The price difference between channel-attached gateways and FEPs is significant. An ESCON-attached IBM 3745 FEP costs approximately $225,000 while an equivalent router-based Cisco Channel Interface Processor costs approximately $69,000.

38. Figure 9-20 illustrates the structure of the SDLC (Synchronous Data Link) protocol which is an IBM mainframe datalink layer protocol.

39. Although the protocol structure itself does not look all that unusual, it is the fact that the information block of the SLDC frame does not contain anything equivalent to the OSI network layer addressing information for use by routers which makes SDLC a non-

routable protocol. SDLC is non-routable because there is simply no network layer address information available for the routers to process.

40. Given that SDLC cannot be routed, network managers had no choice but to implement multiple networks between corporate enterprises. One network would carry SDLC traffic between remote cluster controllers and FEPs to local cluster controllers, FEPs and mainframes; a second network would support remote bridged/routed LANs linking with local LANs between the same corporate locations. Such an implementation is sometimes referred to as a parallel networks model.

41. The first characteristic of SNA which can cause trouble on a LAN is the great amount of acknowledgment and polling traffic between SNA processors and SNA end-user devices. This constant chatter could quickly monopolize the better part of the LAN bandwidth. The second SNA characteristic which can cause problems when run over a shared LAN backbone is that SNA has timing limitations for transmission duration between SNA hosts and end-user devices. Thus on wide area, internetworked LANs over shared network media, SNA sessions can "time-out", effectively terminating the session. Another traffic contributor which can easily monopolize internetwork bandwidth comes from the LAN side of the house. As described earlier in this chapter, Token Ring LANs use an internetworking device known as a source routing bridge. In order to define their source routed internetworking paths, source PCs send out numerous explorer packets as a means of gaining a sense of the best route from source to destination. All of these discovery packets mean only one thing - significantly more network traffic. As previously stated, SDLC is a non-routable protocol. In order to maximize the efficiency of the integrated SNA/LAN network, some way must be found to route SDLC or otherwise transparently incorporate it with LAN traffic.

42. Several major categories of SNA/LAN Integration Solutions are currently possible. Each varies in both approach and the extent to which SNA/LAN incompatibilities are overcome:
    - Add a token ring adapter to a compatible cluster controller - least expensive
    - TCP/IP Encapsulation - no actual SNA/LAN integration
    - SDLC Conversion - eliminates FEP, saving several thousand dollars
    - APPN - Advanced Peer-to-Peer Networking - provides multiprotocol networking on a peer to peer basis

43. IBM's version of TCP/IP encapsulation is known as Data Link Switching or DLSw and has been proposed as a standard to the IETF (Internet Engineering Task Force) as RFC (Request for Comment) 1434. DLSw does not propose anything radically new but incorporates many vendor-specific TCP/IP encapsulation features into a single standard which will hopefully be widely supported. DLSw is implemented as a software feature on supported routers.

44. Poll Spoofing is the ability of an internetworking device, such as an SDLC converter or router, to respond directly to, or acknowledge, the FEP's constant polling messages to the remote cluster controller. By answering these status check messages locally, the inquiry and its answer never enter the wide area link portion of the internetwork. Proxy polling, on the other hand, emulates the FEP's polling messages on the remote side of the network, thereby assuring the remote cluster controller that it is still in touch with an FEP.

45. This IP passthrough methodology for SDLC transport is a common feature or option on internetworking routers. In this methodology IP is supplying the network layer addressing which was lacking from the native SDLC protocol. Figure 9-23 illustrates a Passthrough architecture. Upon close examination of Figure 9-23, it may become obvious that, in fact, there is no SNA/LAN integration. What the SNA and LAN traffic share is the T-1 wide area network between routers. The SNA traffic never travels over shared LAN media. Cost savings as compared to the parallel networks model (Figure 9-21) includes eliminating one wide area link and associated internetworking hardware. The third possible solution to SNA/LAN traffic integration is known as SDLC Conversion and is characterized by SDLC frames actually being converted to Token Ring Frames by a specialized internetworking device known as a SDLC Converter. The SDLC converter may be a standalone device or may be integrated into a bridge/router. As can be seen in Figure 9-24, in the SDLC Conversion configuration, the cluster controller is attached to the Token Ring LAN via a standalone or integrated SDLC converter. SDLC frames are converted to Token Ring frames, transported across the Token Ring internetwork, and routed to a gateway which transforms the token ring frames back into SDLC frames and forwards them to the mainframe. Also notice the absence of the FEP from the illustration, a potential savings of several thousand dollars. Eliminating the FEP assumes that all 3270 traffic could be routed through attached LANs and gateways.

46. Simply put, attached computers, whether PC's, AS/400's or mainframes, are welcome to talk directly with each other without having the communications session established, maintained and terminated by the almighty mainframe as was required in the classic SNA architecture. Recent enhancements to APPN known as HPR (High Performance Routing) /AnyNET now allow multiple transport protocols such as IP and IPX to travel over the APPN network simultaneously with SNA traffic. In such an implementation, HPR serves as the single backbone protocol able to transport multiple LAN protocols simultaneously. Alternatively stated, rather than running SNA over a TCP/IP based LAN internetwork, APPN runs TCP/IP, and other protocols, over an SNA mainframe-based internetwork.

47. By implementing IP routing software directly on ATM switching hardware, IP switching combines switching and routing capabilities into a single device and discriminates between which traffic should be switched and which should be routed.. For streaming data such as file transfers or multimedia sessions, ATM switched virtual circuits are established and the traffic is allowed to flow through the virtual circuit without the typical packet-by-packet processing associated with routers. For connectionless datagrams and shorter transmissions, IP routing software is implemented.

TEST QUESTIONS

True/False Questions

1. The goal when using a bridge should be that 80% of all LAN traffic should stay local with no more than 20% of overall traffic requiring processing and forwarding by the bridge. T/347

2. Routers make their forwarding decisions based on the contents of the network layer addresses. T/350

3. Routers are considerably easier to configure and manage than bridges due to their inherent intelligence. F/353

4. Switching is more similar in function to routing than to bridging. F/353

5. Switches work best when traffic does not have to leave the LAN segments linked to a particular LAN switch. T/354

6. In general, switch for filtering and internetwork segmentation; route for bandwidth. F/354

7. Source route bridges and routers work in essentially the same manner by capturing the routing information from the bridge or router. F/359

8. Multiprotocol routers have the capability to interpret, process and forward data packets of multiple protocols. T/361

9. Non-routable protocols can not be processed by routers. F/363

10. Poll spoofing emulates the FEP's polling messages on the remote side of the network, thereby assuring the remote cluster controller that it is still in touch with an FEP. F/378

Multiple Choice Questions

1. Operational characteristics of LANs are defined by which of the following?
    a. physical interfaces
p.346 b. protocols
    c. server CPUs
    d. none of the above

162   Chapter 9

2. This design strategy for overburdened shared media LANs is usually the first approach to reducing shared media congestion.
p.346
   a. segmentation
   b. server isolation
   c. microsegmentation
   d. hierarchical networking

3. This design strategy for overburdened shared media LANs puts one workstation on each individual portion of the LAN by using a LAN switch.
   a. segmentation
   b. server isolation
p.347 c. microsegmentation
   d. hierarchical networking

4. This design strategy for overburdened shared media LANs places selected high-performance devices on their own segment.
   a. segmentation
p.347 b. server isolation
   c. microsegmentation
   d. hierarchical networking

5. This design strategy for overburdened shared media LANs isolates local LAN traffic on a local network architecture while transmitting internetwork traffic over a higher speed network architecture.
   a. segmentation
   b. server isolation
   c. microsegmentation
p.347 d. hierarchical networking

6. Bridging uses which OSI layer addressing process to internetwork LANs?
   a. network layer
   b. session layer
p.347 c. data link layer
   d. physical layer

7. Since only frames with destination addresses not found in the known local nodes table are forwarded across the bridge, bridges are sometimes called
   a. forward-if-local devices
p.349 b. forward-if-not-local devices
   c. forward-if not-remote devices
   d. routing devices

8. Which of the following devices is easy to install and configure, providing quick, cost-effective relief for overburdened network segments?
   a. router
   b. boundary router
   c. switch
p.349 d. bridge

9. Improperly addressed frames or frames destined for non-existent addresses can be infinitely perpetuated or flooded onto all bridged LANs in a process called
   a. propagation
   b. load balancing
p.349 c. broadcast storm
   d. routing

10. Forwarding messages to all workstations on all intermittent LANs is known as
p.349 a. propagation
   b. load balancing
   c. broadcast storm
   d. routing

11. Data link layer addressing is functionally referred to as which of the following types of addressing?
   a. end-to-end addressing
p.350 b. point-to-point addressing
   c. end-to-point addressing
   d. point-to-end addressing

12. Network layer addressing is functionally referred to as which of the following types of addressing?
p.351 a. end-to-end addressing
   b. point-to-point addressing
   c. end-to-point addressing
   d. point-to-end addressing

13. Before a router actually releases a data packet onto the internetwork it confirms the existence of the destination address to which this data packet is bound in a process known as
   a. forward-if-local
   b. forward-if-not-local
   c. forward-if not-remote
p.351 d. forward-if-proven-remote

14. Routers are able to make effective use of a network's redundant paths by distributing network traffic across two or more links between two given locations in a process called
   a. propagation
   b. firewall
p.351 c. load balancing
   d. switching

15. A router process which can filter misbehaving or mis-addressed traffic off of the network through filtering of network layer addresses.
   a. propagation
p.352 b. firewall
   c. load balancing
   d. switching

16. Which of the following is the most significant advantage of routers.
   a. creating firewalls to protect connected LANs
   b. filtering unwanted broadcast packets from the internetwork
   c. providing security by filtering packets by either data link or network layer addresses
p.353 d. being able to process multiple network layer protocols simultaneously

17. LAN switches read which address on incoming frames and then quickly build a switched connection to the switched LAN segment which contains the destination workstation?
p.353 a. MAC layer address
   b. network layer address
   c. IP address
   d. IPX address

18. These internetworking devices are considered a physical layer device.
   a. switches
   b. routers
p.355 c. repeaters
   d. bridges

19. Which of the following is not part of a repeater's job?
   a. repeat the digital signal by regenerating and retiming the incoming signal
   b. pass all signals between all attached segments
   c. allow for the connection of and translation between different type of media
p.356 d. route packets to the least busy segment

20. The distance from the workstation to the MAU in a Token Ring LAN is called the
p.358 a. lobe length
   b. ring length
   c. segment length
   d. network length

21. A feature of a repeater which prevents failure of one connected segment from affecting other segments.
    a. auto-restoral
p.358 b. auto-partitioning
    c. auto-pilot
    d. load balancing

22. This feature in bridges enables the positive aspects of redundant paths while eliminating the negative aspects such as broadcast storms.
p.359 a. Spanning Tree Algorithm
    b. RIF protocol
    c. address caching
    d. transparent bridging

23. Bridges that connect LANs of similar data link format are known as
    a. translating bridges
    b. source routing bridges
p.359 c. transparent bridges
    d. routing bridges

24. Bridges which include format conversion in order to bridge between Ethernet and Token Ring LANs are known as
p.360 a. translating bridges
    b. source routing bridges
    c. transparent bridges
    d. encapsulating bridges

25. Bridges which take the entire Ethernet data link frame and stuff it into and FDDI envelope (data frame) are known as
    a. translating bridges
    b. source routing bridges
    c. transparent bridges
p.360 d. encapsulating bridges

26. Which of the following is a non-routable protocol?
p.364 a. NetBIOS
    b. IPX
    c. IP
    d. OSI

27. Which router-to-router protocol is used by XNS and NetWare?
    a. OSPF
    b. IS-IS
p.364 c. RIP
    d. RTP

28. This type of routing protocol can only measure the number of hops to a distant router as a means of determining the route for internetwork traffic.
    a. OSPF
p.364 b. distance vector
    c. link state
    d. none of the above

29. Which of the following routing protocols is able to maintain a complete and more current view of the total internetwork?
    a. RIP
    b. distance vector
p.364 c. link state
    d. none of the above

30. For branch offices whose amount of internetwork traffic does not warrant the constant bandwidth and higher cost of leased lines, which type of router would be employed?
    a. backbone router
    b. central site router
    c. boundary router
p.365 d. dial-up router

31. This dial-up router update method is performed whenever a certain programmable event occurs.
    a. timed update
p.368 b. triggered update
    c. piggyback update
    d. interval update

32. This dial-up router update method is performed at regular pre-determined intervals.
p.368 a. timed update
    b. triggered update
    c. piggyback update
    d. interval update

33. This dial-up router update method is performed only when the dial-up link has already been established for the purposes of exchanging user data.
    a. timed update
    b. triggered update
p.368 c. piggyback update
    d. interval update

34. In LAN-to-mainframe internetworking, this device is a computer which offloads the communications processing from the mainframe, allowing the mainframe to be dedicated to processing activities.
    a. cluster controller
p.370 b. front end processor
    c. 3270 protocol conversion card
    d. LAN-based SNA gateway

35. In LAN-to-mainframe internetworking this, this device allows connection of both 3270 terminals as well as LANs with possible wide area links to packet switched networks or high speed leased lines.
p.371 a. cluster controller
    b. front end processor
    c. 3270 protocol conversion card
    d. LAN-based SNA gateway

36. This is the data link layer protocol used by IBM mainframe computers in an SNA environment.
    a. TCP/IP
    b. SPX
    c. NLSP
p.375 d. SDLC

37. Which of the following SNA/LAN integration solutions listed below is the least expensive and also the least effective in terms of meeting the SNA/LAN integration challenges?
    a. APPN
    b. SDLC conversion
    c. TCP/IP encapsulation
p.377 d. add a token ring adapter to a compatible cluster controller

38. The ability of an internetworking device to respond directly to, or acknowledge, the FEP's constant polling messages to the remote cluster controller is called
    a. proxy polling
p.378 b. poll spoofing
    c. TCP/IP encapsulation
    d. broadcast filtering

39. Which of the following SNA/LAN integration solutions listed below is IBM's answer to multiprotocol networking on a peer-to-peer basis using the SNA architecture, rather than a LAN-based network architecture?
p.379 a. APPN
    b. SDLC conversion
    c. TCP/IP encapsulation
    d. add a token ring adapter to a compatible cluster controller

168   Chapter 9

40. Which of the following combines switching and routing in a single device allowing the device to discriminate between which traffic should be switched and which should be routed?
p.370
    a. IP switching
    b. link state routing
    c. source route bridging
    d. SNA

Fill-In the Blank Questions

1. Transparent interoperability between LAN-to-LAN and LAN-to-mainframe communication is known as _____.

2. A device called a(n) _____ reads the destination address of each frame on a LAN, decides whether the destination is local or remote, and only allows those data frames with non-local destination addresses to cross the device to the remote LAN.

3. The difference between a bridge and a router is that a(n) _____ only examines those data packets which are specifically addressed to it.

4. A router consults its _____ in order to determine the best path on which to forward a data packet.

5. The key difference between switching and bridging is that switching is done in hardware, or _____ chips, and is extremely fast in comparison to bridging.

6. A process called _____ is performed by bridges when they decide whether or not a packet should be allowed access to the internetwork.

7. One major limitation of source route bridging as applied to large internetworks is called the _____.

8. _____ is a method of filtering chatty or unwanted protocols from the WAN link while assuring that remote programs which require on-going communication from these filtered protocols are still re-assured via emulation of these protocols by the local dial-up router.

9. IBM's version of TCP/IP encapsulation is known as _____ and is implemented as a software feature on supported routers.

Answers

1. internetworking p.346
2. bridge p.347
3. router p.350
4. routing table p.350
5. ASIC p.353
6. filtering p.357
7. 7 hop limit p.359
8. spoofing p.366
9. DLSw or Data Link Switching p.378

170   Chapter 9

CASE STUDY AND ANSWERS

TAKING STANDARDS TO HEART

Activities
1. Top-down model:

Business	Rockwell's Switching Systems Division needed to simplify its network infrastructure by standardizing. A way for employees in the field, engineers and sales representatives, was needed to quickly access customer and product information. Scattered data in disparate systems had created a large number of problems for Rockwell- the most important being flow of information between people who needed to be working together.
Applications	Access to data repositories was needed. Many different applications were used including: financial, engineering, human resources, order entry and inventory systems.
Data	Databases were used throughout the company. Data had to be accessed by traveling sales representatives between flights, roughly about a half-hour.
Network	The network was made up of Unix, mainframe, and NetWare-based information. TCP/IP was used as the standard communications protocol. Network access was both through the backbone and from remote connections.
Technology	Sun SPARC servers and workstations, an IBM mainframe, Sun Solaris 2.5 data repository, Oracle 7, and PC-NFSpro 2.0 were used. Unix, Windows, TCP/IP and Novell Netware 4.1 were also in use across the company. Various client configurations exist, but they are standardizing the configuration for the future.

2. Unanswered questions:
   How much is it going to cost to complete the standardization process across the company?
   How was legacy mainframe data networked to the new system?
   Will all applications used on the NetWare network be available on the new standardized network?
   How will Internet access be provided?
   What security measures are in place?

Business
1. The primary business activity was selling and servicing Rockwell products.
2. Employees needed easy and quick access to information no matter what platform they were on, remote or local.
3. A single vendor approach allowed the company to provide the right information to the right person at the right time.
4. Customer and product information could not be accessed quickly by traveling representatives in order to better service their customers.

Application
1. A common communication's protocol was needed to support engineering, financial, human resources, order entry and inventory systems.
2. Personnel and non-engineering applications ran on a Novell NetWare 4.1 network, engineering applications ran on Sun SPARC servers and workstations, and legacy business and financial applications ran on an IBM mainframe.
3. A TCP/IP-based Sun Solaris system using Oracle7 with Sun's PC-NFSpro 2.0 for Windows users was chosen because of its cost savings and benefits.
4. Future applications include converting the rest of the financial, sales, marketing, and human resources divisions. Also, Internet access will be considered.

Data
1. Field employees needed to access customer and product information.
2. Data needed to be accessed between flights - approximately within one-half hour.
3. Windows clients were able to access the Unix server data by using Sun's PC-NFSpro 2.0.

Network
1. The original network consisted of a NetWare 4.1 network, Sun SPARC network, and IBM mainframe.
2. The original remote access was by dial in to the Novell network to gain remote access to local information.
3. The original network design did not allow for exchange of information as needed.
4. Frame relay is used.

Technology
1. TCP/IP-based network solutions will be used to provide seamless access to a central Sun Solaris 2.5-based data repository, a large Oracl7 7.1 database to store financial, engineering, human resources, order-entry, and inventory data and SPARC servers will be used for engineering. Sun's PC-NFSpro will allow access to Unix resources from Windows-based clients. PCs will be standardized, but the hardware and software configuration was not listed, only that they will run dual stacks for a while until IPX goes away.
2. Desktop PCs will be standardized for easier technical support. NICs and other bells and whistles users have on their systems will be restricted.

3. The migration was done by converting one division at a time, maintaining the data structure that the groups have grown accustomed to until they could migrate off of the Novell NetWare network.

CHAPTER 10

Remote Access & Wireless Networking

ANSWERS TO CHAPTER REVIEW QUESTIONS

1. Key business trends include telecommuting, mobile computing and technical support.

2. As dictated by the Top Down model, before designing network topologies and choosing technology, it is essential to first determine what is to be accomplished in terms of LAN - based applications and use of other LAN-attached resources.

3. Refer to Figure 10-2 for a graphic description of the differences between remote node and remote control. Remote node or remote client computing implies that, in theory, the remote client PC should be able to operate as if it were locally attached to network resources. In other words, the geographic separation between the remote client and the local LAN resources should be transparent. Client/server applications which require large transfers of data between client and server will not run well in remote node mode. Remote node mode requires a full client network operating system protocol stack to be installed on the remote client. In addition, wide area network communication software must be incorporated with the remote client NOS protocol stack. Remote node software often also includes optional support of remote control functionality. Remote control mode requires only remote control software to be installed at the remote PC rather than a full NOS client protocol stack which is compatible with the NOS installed at the local LAN. The purpose of the remote control software is only to extend the input/output capabilities of the local client out to the keyboard and monitor attached to the remote PC. The host version of the same remote control package must be installed at the host or local PC. There are no interoperability standards for remote control software. One of the most significant difficulties with remote control software is confusion by end-users as to logical disk assignments.

4. One of the most important things to understand about LAN remote access is the relatively limited bandwidth of the wide area network links which individuals will use to connect to corporate information resources. Although the goal of LAN remote access may be to offer transparent remote LAN connectivity, decreases in bandwidth by a factor of 100 on WAN links as compared to LAN links cannot be ignored.

5. Figure 10-3 illustrates the protocol related issue of typical remote control and remote node links as well as TCP/IP based links. An advantage would be that a single product offers both functionalities.

6. Password assignment and management- Change passwords frequently, even considering single-use passwords. Passwords should not be actual words found in a dictionary, but should ideally be a random or meaningless combination of letters and numbers. Intrusion responses - User accounts should be locked after a pre-set number of unsuccessful logins. These accounts should only be able to be unlocked by a system administrator. Logical/Physical Partitioning of Data - Separate public, private, and confidential data onto separate physical servers to avoid users with minimum security clearances gaining unauthorized access to sensitive or confidential data. Encryption - Although it is important for any sensitive or proprietary corporate data to be encrypted, it is especially important that passwords be encrypted to avoid interception and unauthorized re-use. Dial-back systems - After remote users enter proper UserID and passwords, these systems terminate the call and dial the authorized user back at pre-programmed phone numbers. Remote Client Software Authentication Protocols - Remote client protocol stacks often include software-based authentication protocols such as PAP (Password Authentication Protocol) or CHAP (Challenge Handshake Authentication Protocol).

7. All token authentication systems include server components linked to the communications server, and client components which are used with the remote access clients. Physically, the token authentication device employed at the remote client location may be a hand-held device resembling a calculator, a floppy disk, or it may be an in-line device linked to either the remote client's serial or parallel port. An added capability is high level of certainty that a person logging in is authentic.

8. A communications server offers both management advantages as well as financial payback when large numbers of users wish to gain remote access to/from a LAN. Besides the cost savings of a reduced number of modems, phone lines and software licenses, perhaps more important are the gains in control over the remote access to the LAN and its attached resources. By monitoring the use of the phone lines connected to the communications server, it is easier to determine exactly how many phone lines are required to service those users requiring remote LAN access. Communications servers may be expensive and require expertise to administer and manage.

9. Communications servers include several CPU boards inside a single enclosure. These servers combine both applications server functionality and remote node server functionality. Applications are physically loaded and executed on the communications server. Communications servers are often used for remote control functionality as an alternative to having several separate desktop PCs available for remote control. Consolidating the CPUs into a single enclosure provides additional fault tolerance and management capabilities over the separate PCs model. Remote node servers are strictly concerned with controlling remote access to LAN attached resources and acting as a gateway to those resources. Applications services are supplied by the same LAN-attached applications servers that are accessed by locally attached clients.

10. Currently, remote node server solutions fall into three major categories:
    - Software-only solutions in which the user supplies a sufficiently powerful server and adds a remote node server software package such as Windows NT RAS or NetWare Connect or other third party remote node software package. In some cases, a multiport serial board may be included with the software in order to add sufficient serial ports to the user's server. More information about software-only solutions is offered in the section on remote node software.
    - Turnkey or Hardware/software solutions in which fully configured remote node servers are compatible with existing network architectures and operating systems. Integrated modems may or may not be included. The remote node server software included on these turnkey systems must be compatible with the installed network operating system.
    - LAN modems, also occasionally known as Dial-up Servers, could be thought of as a remote node server with one or more integrated modems. Included security and management software are also installed on the LAN Modem. Given the rapid increase in modem transmission speeds due to evolving modem transmission standards, integrating a modem which cannot be upgraded within a remote node server may be less beneficial than using external modems which can be more easily upgraded. Perhaps in a response to this need for convenient modem upgrades, some remote node servers now come with four or eight PC Card (PCMCIA) slots into which the latest modem technology can be easily inserted. LAN modems are generally included in reviews of remote node servers rather than being looked upon as a distinct product category.

11. Normally, when a modem is connected directly to a PC, the communications software expects to direct information to the local serial port to which the modem is attached. However, in the case of a pool of modems attached to a remote node server, the communications software on the local clients must redirect all information for modems through the locally attached network interface card, across the local LAN, to the remote node server, and ultimately to an attached modem. This ability to re-direct information for dial-out modem applications from LAN-attached PCs is a cooperative task accomplished by the software of the remote node server and its corresponding remote client software. Not all remote node servers support dial-out functionality.

12. The required dial-out redirection is accomplished through the use of industry standard software re-direction interrupts. Refer to Figure 10-9 which illustrates some of the issues involved in dialing out from the LAN.

13. As can be seen in Figure 10-10, direct sequence spread spectrum is more commonly employed in wireless LAN technology, and in general is capable of delivering higher data throughput rates than frequency hopping spread spectrum. Direct sequence spread spectrum (DSSS) transmits at a particular frequency within the allowable range. In order to distinguish between transmissions from multiple wireless workstations, DSSS adds at

least ten bits to the data message in order to uniquely identify a particular transmission. DSSS receivers must be able to differentiate between these bits, known as chips, in order to properly distinguish transmissions. The addition, removal, and interpretation of chips in DSS adds complexity, cost, and processing overhead. Nonetheless, DSSS generally delivers superior throughput to FHSS. Frequency Hop spread spectrum (FHSS) hops from one frequency to another throughout the allowable frequency range. The pattern of frequency hopping must be known by the wireless receiver so that the message can be reconstructed correctly. A given wireless transceiver's signal is on a given frequency for less than 1 second. Another desirable effect of all of the hopping from one frequency to another is that the transmission tends to be less effected by interference, an especially desirable characteristic for mobile computing applications.

14. Since wireless LAN technology seems to be shifting towards an emphasis on mobile computing via laptops and portables, it should come as no surprise that most wireless LAN network interface cards are available as PC Cards (PCMCIA).

15. CSMA/CA (Carrier Sense Multiple Access with Collision Avoidance) is similar to CSMA/CD except that collisions cannot be detected in wireless environments as they can in wire-based environments. CSMA/CA avoids collisions by listening to the network prior to transmission and not transmitting if other workstations on the same network are transmitting. Before transmitting, workstations wait a pre-determined amount of time in order to avoid collisions, and set up a point-to-point wireless circuit to the destination workstation. Data link layer header and information fields such as Ethernet or Token Ring are sent to the destination workstation. It is the responsibility of the wireless LAN access device to convert IEEE 802.3 or 802.5 frames into IEEE 802.11 frames. The wireless point to point circuit remains in place until the sending workstation receives an acknowledgment that the message was received error-free.

16. One important issue not included in the IEEE 802.11 standard is roaming capability which allows a user to transparently move between the transmission ranges of wireless LANs without interruption.

17. Mobile IP, limited to TCP/IP networks, employs two pieces of software in order to support roaming:
    - A mobile IP client is installed on the roaming wireless client workstation.
    - A mobile IP home agent is installed on a server or router on the roaming user's home network.

    The mobile IP client keeps the mobile IP home agent informed of its changing location as it travels from network to network. The mobile IP home agent forwards any transmissions it receives for the roaming client to its last reported location.

18. The terms remote and local are often replaced by guest (remote) and host (local), when referring to Remote Control Software. They must be compatible. No interoperability standards exist across different remote control products.

19. Operating Remote Control software requires installation of software programs on both the guest and host PCs. Various remote control software packages do not interoperate. Interaction between guest and host is proprietary.

20. In the case of remote control, the fact that proprietary protocols are used between the guest and host remote control software is the reason that remote control software from various vendors is not interoperable. In the case of remote node, redirector software in the protocol stack must take LAN based messages from the NDIS or ODI protocols and convert them into proper format for transmission over asynchronous serial WAN links.

21. The Remote Control Software loaded onto a communications server for use by multiple simultaneous users is not the same as the remote control software loaded onto single remote (guest) and local (host) PCs. Communications Servers' remote control software has the ability to handle multiple users, and in some cases, multiple protocols. Because of this, it is considerably more expensive than the single PC variety.

22. Software should possess features to address the following situations unique to its role:
    - Avoid lockups of host PCs
    - Allow the guest PC to disable the keyboard and monitor of the host PC
    - Additional security precautions to prevent unauthorized access
    - Virus detection software

23. Refer to Figure 10-13 for unique functional requirements of remote node server software.

24. In general, they can link to network operating systems which support IP, IPX, NetBEUI, or XNS as transport protocols. Those that support IPX are generally installable as either NetWare VLMs (Virtual Loadable Modules) or NLMs (NetWare Loadable Modules). In addition, these PPP client packages include sophisticated authentication procedures to insure secure communications, compression to insure optimal use of the WAN link, as well as most of the important features of remote control software. The inclusion of remote control software allows users to choose between remote node and remote control for optimal performance.

25. Unique functional requirements of mobile-aware operating systems include:
    - Auto-detection of multiple configurations
    - Built-in multi-protocol remote node client
    - Direct cable connection
    - File transfer and file/directory synchronizations
    - Deferred printing
    - Power management
    - Infrared connection

26. Figure 10-14 provides an illustration of the differences between the client-agent-server and client/server architectures.

27. The overall objective of mobile-aware applications is to reduce the amount of client to server network traffic by building as much intelligence as possible into the server-based agent so that it can act on behalf of the client application.

28. The client/agent/server architecture consists of three cooperating components:
    - The message manager executes on the mobile client and acts as an interface between client applications requesting services and the wireless link over which the requests must be forwarded. It keeps track of requests pending on various servers which are being handled by intelligent agents. Oracle Mobile Agents also operates over LAN links or PPP based dial-up links.
    - The message gateway can execute on the local server or on a dedicated Unix or Windows workstation, and acts as an interface between the client's message manager and the intelligent agent on the local server. The gateway also acts as a holding station for messages to and from mobile clients which are temporarily unreachable. The client-based message manager and the message gateway communicate with each other via a communications protocol developed by Oracle which provides reliable message delivery over wireless transmission services while minimizing acknowledgment overhead.
    - The agent event manager is combined with a customer written transaction handler to form an entity known as the intelligent agent which resides on the local server. Once the agent event manager receives a request from a mobile client, it acts on behalf of that client in all communications with the local server until the original client request is totally fulfilled. During this processing time in which the intelligent agent is representing the mobile client, the wireless connection can be dropped. Once the original client request has been fulfilled, the entire response is sent from the intelligent agent to the client-based message manager in a single packet, thereby conserving bandwidth and transmission time. Having received the response to a pending request, the client-based message manager deletes the original request from its pending request queue.

29. Mobile middleware products transcend multiple wireless services (and their APIs) and middleware APIs between mobile middleware and the applications.

30. As can be seen in Figure 10-15, the primary purpose of mobile middleware is to consolidate client/server traffic from multiple applications for transmission over a variety of potential wireless (or wire-based) transmission services.

31. In an effort to standardize wireless APIs for mobile middleware, two standardization efforts are currently underway: The Winsock 2 Forum is developing standardized Winsock 2 APIs for linking mobile middleware with Windows-based applications, and

The PCCA is developing the standardized API for linking mobile middleware to a variety of wireless transmission services.

32. The Winsock 2 Forum is developing standardized Winsock 2 APIs for linking mobile middleware with Windows-based applications. This API would be able to deliver transmission related information such as signal strength and transmission characteristics to the applications themselves. Such information could make the applications more intelligent and responsive to changing transmission quality. The PCCA (Portable Computer and Communications Association) is developing the standardized API for linking mobile middleware to a variety of wireless transmission services. This API will provide extensions to existing multi-protocol data link layer device specifications such as NDIS and ODI.

33. Optimization techniques include:
    - Use V.34 modems
    - Use ISDN
    - Use 16550 UARTs and matching serial port drivers
    - Use data compression software/hardware
    - Support screen caching, network/LAN caching

34. Screen caching allows only changes to screens, rather than entire screens, to be transmitted over the limited bandwidth WAN links. Screen caching will reduce the amount of actual traffic transmitted over the WAN link. Not to be confused with screen caching software, network caching or LAN caching software is able to improve overall remote node performance up to five times by caching repetitive applications commands and systems calls.

35. Among the fields of information included in the proposed mobile MIB are the following:
    - Current user location
    - Type and speed of connection device
    - Type of remote client or remote control software installed on remote device
    - Battery power Memory

36. In order to integrate the management of mobile computing users into an overall enterprise network management system such as HP Openview or IBM Systemview, a specialized MIB was required in order to store configuration and location information specific to remote users. The Mobile Management Task Force (MMTF) has proposed a mobile MIB capable of feeding configuration and location information to enterprise network management systems via SNMP. A key to the design of the mobile MIB was to balance the amount of information required in order to effectively manage remote clients while taking into account the limited bandwidth and expense of the remote links over which the management data must be transmitted. From the enterprise network management system's side, controls will need to be installed as to how often remote clients are to be

polled via dial-up or wireless transmission for the purpose of gathering up-to-date management information.

37. CDPD offers fast call setup and is inexpensive for short messages, and can provide a service which uses idle capacity in the circuit-switched analog cellular network to transmit IP-based data packets.

38. LSM (Limited Size Messaging) will be important to someone purchasing a "cellular-ready" modem in order for CDPD to be able to transport two-way messaging. Cable from wireless modems must be compatible with cellular phones.

39. Transaction processing and database queries: CDPD Advantages: Fast call setup, inexpensive for short messages Disadvantages: Limited availability but growing, expensive for large file transfers
Large file transfers and faxes: Circuit-switched cellular Advantages: Widely available, call duration pricing is more reasonable for longer transmissions than per kilopacket pricing Disadvantages: Longer call setup time than CDPD (up to 30 secs. vs. less than 5 secs), expensive for short messages
Short bursty messages and e-mail: Private packet radio Advantages: Wide coverage area and links to commercial e-mail systems. Disadvantage: Proprietary networks, expensive for larger file transfers.

40. Two-way messaging will offer the following key services beyond simple paging:
    - Guaranteed delivery to destination mobile users even if those devices are unreachable at the time the message was originally sent.
    - Return receipt acknowledgments to the party who originated the message.

41. Digital cellular transmission standards are not interoperable, thereby precluding the possibility of transparent global access to digital cellular services. Digital cellular systems will be deployed on an as-needed basis in the most congested metropolitan areas. As a result, existing analog cellular networks will be required to co-exist and interoperate with newer digital cellular networks. Transmission protocols such as TDMA and CDMA must be compatible with analog transmission protocols and next-generation cellular phones must be able to support both analog and digital transmission. Transmitting digital data from a notebook computer over digital cellular networks will not require modulation as was required with analog cellular networks. As a result, notebook computers should be able to interface directly to TDMA or CDMA-based digital cellular phones via serial ports. Figure 10-22 illustrates data transmission over a digital cellular network.

42. A single person has a phone number for their home phone, a voice and fax number for their office, a cellular phone number for their automobile, a pager phone number for their pager, and perhaps even another phone number for their satellite service phone for use outside of cellular phone areas. The premise of PCS is rather straightforward: one person, one phone number. This Personal Phone Number or PPN would become the user's

interface to PCS and the vast array of transparently available telecommunications services. This personal phone number is a key concept to PCS. It changes the entire focus of the interface to the telecommunications environment from the current orientation of a number being associated with a particular location regardless of the individual using the facility to a number being associated with particular individual regardless of the location, even globally, of the accessed facility. Figure 10-20 illustrates the basic elements of PCS.

43. TDMA (Time Division Multiple Access) and CDMA (Code Division Multiple Access) are the two methodologies currently being researched in PCS field trials. TDMA-based digital cellular may be able to support three times (some tests indicate six or seven times) the transmission capacity of analog cellular while CDMA could offer as much as a tenfold increase. Note that the names of each of these techniques end in the words "multiple access" rather than "multiplexing". The "multiple access" refers to multiple phone conversations having access to the same bandwidth and yet not interfering with each other. TDMA achieves more than one conversation per frequency by assigning timeslots to individual conversations. Ten timeslots per frequency are often assigned, with a given cellular device transmitting its digitized voice only during its assigned timeslot. Receiving devices must be in synch with the time slots of the sending device in order to receive the digitized voice packets and re-assemble them into a natural sounding analog signal. TDMA should be able to transmit data at 9.6Kbps. CDMA is the newest and most advanced technique for maximizing the number of calls transmitted within a limited bandwidth by using a spread spectrum transmission technique. Rather than allocate specific frequency channels within the allocated bandwidth to specific conversations as is the case with TDMA, CDMA transmits digitized voice packets from numerous calls at different frequencies spread all over the entire allocated bandwidth spectrum. The "code" part of CDMA lies in the fact that in order to keep track of these various digitized voice packets from various conversations spread over the entire spectrum of allocated bandwidth, a code is appended to each packet indicating which voice conversation it belongs to. This technique is not unlike the datagram connectionless service used by packet switched networks to send packetized data over numerous switched virtual circuits within the packet switched network. By identifying the source and sequence of each packet, the original message integrity is maintained while maximizing the overall performance of the network. CDMA should be able to transmit data at up to 14.4Kbps.

44. Universal PCS is the integration of a number of existing telecommunications environments. PCS seeks to combine the capabilities of the PSTN, otherwise known as the Landline Telephone Network, with a new all digital cellular network, along with paging networks, and satellite communications networks. The need for seamless delivery of a combination of all of the above services is easily illustrated by the plight of today's mobile professional. A single person has a phone number for their home phone, a voice and fax number for their office, a cellular phone number for their automobile, a pager phone number for their pager, and perhaps even another phone number for their satellite service phone for use outside of cellular phone areas. The premise of PCS is rather straightforward: one person, one phone number.

TEST QUESTIONS

True/False Questions

1. Although the goal of LAN remote access may be to offer transparent remote LAN connectivity, decreases in bandwidth by a factor of 100 on WAN links as compared to LAN links cannot be ignored. T/388

2. Redirector hardware/software is required for remote control PC operation. F/391

3. The WAN link traffic of remote control computing consists primarily of keystrokes and screen images, while the traffic for remote node computing consists of all client/server traffic. T/391

4. In the case of remote node computing, redirector software in the protocol stack must take LAN based messages from the NDIS or ODI protocols and convert them into proper format for transmission over asynchronous serial WAN links. T/393

5. In the case of remote node computing, the fact that proprietary protocols are used between the guest and host remote node software is the reason that remote node software from various vendors is not interoperable. F/393

6. Fortunately, microwave ovens can not produce interference for a wireless LAN. F/406

7. Most wireless LAN solutions are designed to work over the Ethernet network architecture. T/405

8. Operating remote control software requires installation of software programs on both the guest and host PCs. T/408

9. Mobile middleware is characterized by standardized APIs and, as a result, full interoperability. F/416

10. CDPD is IP based and uses idle capacity in the circuit-switched cellular network to transmit IP-based data packets. T/422

11. With PCS, numbers are associated with people, not with equipment and phone lines. T/424

184   Chapter 10

Multiple Choice Questions

1. Which of the following remote LAN access categories is often referred to as SOHO?
    a. technical support
p.388 b. telecommuting
    c. mobile computing
    d. corporate computing

2. This category of remote LAN access addresses the need for field representatives to be able to access corporate information resources in order to offer superior customer service while working on the road.
    a. technical support
    b. telecommuting
p.388 c. mobile computing
    d. corporate computing

3. Which of the following remote LAN categories addresses the need to be able to dial-in to client systems with the ability to appear as a local workstation in order to diagnose and correct problems remotely?
p.389 a. technical support
    b. telecommuting
    c. mobile computing
    d. corporate computing

4. This form of remote client computing implies that the remote client PC should be able to operate as if it were locally attached to network resources.
    a. remote access
    b. remote control
    c. local control
p.391 d. remote node

5. Which of the following is a characteristic of remote node computing?
    a. redirector hardware/software is not required
    b. application processing is performed on the LAN-attached local PC
    c. it is the faster of the two remote computing methods
p.392 d. a full client NOS protocol stack is required on the remote client

6. Which of the following security related procedures for remote access computing would ensure that a remote user at an unauthorized site could not gain access to the LAN?
    a. password assignment and management
    b. intrusion responses
p.394 c. dial-back systems
    d. encryption

7. Which of the following security related procedures for remote access computing would ensure that an intercepted password would not be usable?
   a. password assignment and management
   b. intrusion responses
   c. dial-back systems
p.394 d. encryption

8. The token authentication scheme in which the server responds to the remote users PIN with a challenge number is called
   a. token ring
p.395 b. token response
   c. time synchronous
   d. random authentication

9. This alternative access for a remote PC user to gain access to the LAN comes with all necessary software pre-installed and therefore does not require additional remote control or remote node software.
p.397 a. LAN modem
   b. serial port of a LAN attached PC
   c. communications server
   d. access server

10. What is the most important advantage gained by using a communications server for remote access to/from a LAN?
    a. cost savings of a reduced number of modems
    b. cost savings of a reduced number of phone lines
p.398 c. control over the remote access to the LAN and its attached resources
    d. cost savings of a reduced number of software licenses

11. A key hardware component of a communications server is
    a. serial port
    b. CPU
    c. NIC
p.398 d. all of the above are key hardware components

12. This type of remote node server solution has a fully configured remote node server compatible with the existing network architecture and operating system.
    a. software-only solution
p.400 b. turnkey solution
    c. LAN modem
    d. dial-up server

186   Chapter 10

13. Which of the following is the industry standard software re-direction interrupt?
    a. Int2
    b. Int3
    c. Int5
p.403 d. Int14

14. This type of wireless transmission technology transmits at a particular frequency within the allowable range and adds at least ten bits to the data message in order to uniquely identify a particular transmission.
p.405 a. DSSS
    b. DSS
    c. FHSS
    d. ISS

15. This type of wireless transmission technology hops from one frequency to another throughout the allowable frequency range and tends to be less affected by interference.
    a. DSSS
    b. DSS
p.405 c. FHSS
    d. ISS

16. This IEEE standard has been proposed as the new wireless LAN standard.
    a. IEEE 802.1
p.406 b. IEEE 802.11
    c. IEEE 802.3
    d. IEEE 802.5

17. Which of the following wireless capabilities allows a user to transparently move between the transmission ranges of wireless LANs without interruption?
    a. CSMA/CD
    b. encryption
    c. roving
p.407 d. roaming

18. Which two pieces of software are needed by Mobile IP in order to support roaming?
p.407 a. mobile IP client and mobile IP home agent
    b. mobile IP client and mobile IP server
    c. mobile IP home agent and mobile IP server
    d. mobile IP server and mobile IP drivers

19. Which of the following statements is correct concerning remote control software?
    a. the guest is the remote PC and the host is the local server
    b. the guest is the local server and the host is the remote PC
p.408 c. the guest is the remote PC and the host is the local PC
    d. the guest is the local PC and the host is the remote PC

20. Windows NT RAS and NetWare Connect are examples of
    a. remote node server software
    b. software-only remote access solutions
p.411 c. a. and b. above
    d. none of the above

21. Remote node clients with the ability to link to servers running a variety of different NOSs are sometimes referred to as
    a. IP clients
    b. universal clients
    c. remote control clients
p.411 d. PPP clients

22. In producing mobile-aware applications, which of the following architectural components executes on the mobile client and acts as an interface between client applications requesting services and the wireless link over which the requests must be forwarded?
p.414 a. message manager
    b. message gateway
    c. agent event manager
    d. mobile middleware

23. In producing mobile-aware applications, which of the following architectural components acts as a holding station for messages to and from mobile clients which are temporarily unreachable?
    a. message manager
p.415 b. message gateway
    c. agent event manager
    d. mobile middleware

24. This emerging category of software seeks to offer maximum flexibility to mobile computing users while optimizing performance with the goal of offering transparency independent of client or server platform, applications and wireless services.
    a. mobile-aware applications
    b. mobile-aware operating systems
    c. mobile NIC drivers
p.415 d. mobile middleware

25. This remote access performance improvement technique allows only changes to screens, rather than entire screens, to be transmitted over the WAN link.
    a. network caching
    b. client caching
p.418 c. screen caching
    d. WAN caching

188   Chapter 10

26. This remote access performance improvement technique improves overall remote node performance up to five times by caching repetitive applications commands and systems calls.
p.418
a. network caching
b. client caching
c. screen caching
d. WAN caching

27. Which of the following is a type of wireless WAN technology?
a. frequency hop spread spectrum
b. direct sequence spread spectrum
p.418 c. cellular digital packet data
d. infrared transmission

28. This type of WAN service is typically used for transaction processing and database queries.
a. Circuit Switched Cellular
p.419 b. Cellular Digital Packet Data
c. Private Packet Radio
d. Personal Communications Services

29. This type of WAN service is typically used for large file transfers and faxes.
p.420 a. Circuit Switched Cellular
b. Cellular Digital Packet Data
c. Private Packet Radio
d. Personal Communications Services

30. This type of WAN service is typically used for short bursty messages and e-mail.
a. Circuit Switched Cellular
b. Cellular Digital Packet Data
p.420 c. Private Packet Radio
d. Personal Communications Services

31. A visionary concept of an evolving all-digital network architecture that could deliver a variety of telecommunications services transparently to users at any time regardless of their geographic location is
a. POTS
b. ISDN
c. POP
p.422 d. PCS

32. What would become the user's interface to PCS and the vast array of transparently available telecommunications services?
    a. API
p.424 b. PPN
    c. POP
    d. ISDN

33. Maximizing calls on minimum bandwidth, this type of access transmits digitized voice packets from numerous calls at different frequencies spread all over the entire allocated bandwidth spectrum by appending a code to each packet indicating which voice conversation it belongs to.
    a. TDMA
    b. FDMA
p.425 c. CDMA
    d. XDMA

34. Maximizing calls on minimum bandwidth, this type of access achieves more than one conversation per frequency by assigning timeslots to individual conversations.
p.424 a. TDMA
    b. FDMA
    c. CDMA
    d. XDMA

Fill-In the Blank Questions

1. The first step to designing a dial-in/dial-out capability for a local LAN, _____ determines what is to be accomplished in terms of LAN-based applications and use of other LAN-attached resources.

2. The term _____ is most often used to generally describe the process of linking remote PCs to local LANs without implying the particular functionality of that link.

3. As an alternative to having a dedicated PC at the corporate office for each remote user to dial into, remote users could attach to a dedicated multi-user server, known as a(n) _____ through one or more modems.

4. _____ modem capability is the ability of the communications software on the local clients to redirect all information for modems through the locally attached network interface card, across the local LAN, to the remote node server, and ultimately to an attached modem in a modem pool.

5. _____ is used as the MAC layer protocol for wireless LANs since collisions cannot be detected in wireless environments.

6. Operating systems which are able to easily adapt to different computing modes, such as stand-alone computing, remote access computing, and synchronization of files, with a variety of included supporting accessory programs and utilities, are referred to as _____ operating systems.

7. A specialized MIB called a(n) _____ MIB is required in order to store configuration and location information specific to remote users and can feed configuration and location information to enterprise network management systems via SNMP.

Answers

1. needs analysis p.390
2. remote access p.391
3. access server or communications server p.396
4. dial-out p.403
5. CSMA/CA p.413
6. mobile-aware p.413
7. mobile p.418

CASE STUDY AND ANSWERS

BIOTECH FIRM FINDS A WINNER IN WIRELESS

Activities

1. Top-down model:

Business	A biotech firm needed to provide its sales force with an automated system which would allow the salesperson to connect to the home office from places where phone jacks are out of reach.
	A messaging backbone with broad geographic coverage was needed by Univax Biologics.
	The system must be reliable and easy to use also.
Applications	The applications had to run on a laptop and provide file, print, fax and email services.
Data	Data consisted mostly of reports with email also being transferred between a server at the home office.
	Fax data was required.
Network	The network had to have no geographic boundaries.
	Security must be provided since data will be over wireless communication.
Technology	NEC Versa V laptops equipped with circuit-switched cellular wireless modems, Lotus cc:Mail Remote, Symantec Act for Windows and MobileWare client software were used for the client side.
	An NT 3.5 server with 48 MB of RAM and a 1GB hard drive running MobileWare, and NetWare 4.1 file, print and fax services with RSA Data Security encryption is the server configuration.
	The firm will be upgrading to Notes 4.0 in the future.
	The circuit-switched analog cellular modem provides a 9.6Kbps connection.

2. Unanswered questions:
   - Have the remote users notices any reliability or delay problems?
   - Will the remote systems accommodate any robust presentation packages or word processing software?
   - Will WWW access be available?
   - What are the client laptop hardware configurations?
   - Are there any protocol issues between NetWare 4.1 and NT 3.5 which must be dealt with?
   - What communication protocols were used?

Business
1. The primary business is selling a drug that helps prevent blood clotting in pregnant women.
2. The business has seen increased detail and frequency of reports sent from the field.
3. Wireless means that there is no delay in the home office receiving information or in providing information to its sales staff or customers.
4. Getting the information right away means someone at the home office can quickly fax over product information to a potential customer, forward an order to a distributor, respond to a customer's service issue or answer a query on how to use the product correctly.
5. Total cost was $58,000 or $2,900 per user.
6. Recurring monthly costs are about $70-$100 per user for wireless service.
7. Univax would like to bring outside distributors into the wireless electronics mail loop so they can be notified immediately of a new or changed order.
8. The design process included end users from the onset. Surveys were taken asking what the end users wanted to see in an ideal automation system.
9. Inclusion of the end user and training were the most important design decisions made. They provided buy-in and guaranteed a successful implementation.
10. A recent merger with another biotech firm has spread the aggregate user population across several cities in the U.S. and Canada. The users now put together more sophisticated messages with attachments requiring a more robust messaging/groupware system.

Application
1. The sales process was supported by the applications and network.
2. cc:Mail and MobileWare were chosen to support the business process.
3. MobileWare provides key services to ensure that applications run over the link reliably, efficiently and securely.
4. Modem connection applications were not necessary.
5. More robust applications such as Notes 4.0 are now being considered.

Data
1. RSA Data Security, Inc. encryption system is on the NT server.
2. Approximately 9.6Kbps of bandwidth is available.
3. Replication is important so that the user can work off-line without incurring connection charges.

Network
1. MobileWare software was used.
2. It provides broad geographic coverage, reliability and confirmation that messages were received, and it is easy to use by end users.
3. Broad geographic coverage was needed.
4. Sales personnel could contact the home office no matter where they were located.
5. Outside distributors may become users of the system so they can be notified immediately of a new or changed order.

Technology
1. NEC Versa V laptops equipped with circuit-switched cellular wireless modems, Lotus cc:Mail Remote, Symantec Act for Windows and MobileWare client software were used for the client side. An NT 3.5 server with 48 MB of RAM and a 1GB hard drive running MobileWare, and NetWare 4.1 file, print and fax services with RSA Data Security encryption is the server configuration. The firm will be upgrading to Notes 4.0 in the future. The circuit-switched analog cellular modem provides a 9.6Kbps connection. Communication protocols were not detailed in the article.

CHAPTER 11

Enterprise Networks & The Internet

ANSWERS TO CHAPTER REVIEW QUESTIONS

1. Figure 11-1 uses the top down model to summarize the factors influencing the required functionality of enterprise networks.

2. A business phenomenon known as the virtual corporation implies a business partnership among cooperating business entities which is electronically enabled via an enterprise network. In most cases, the virtual corporation implies that these business entities are sufficiently distant from one another that constant travel between locations in order to accomplish business objectives would not be possible. If the virtual corporation is considered a strategic business initiative, then the tactical fulfillment of that strategic objective is fulfilled via the establishment and support of virtual workgroups. By dynamically allocating people to projects based on expertise rather than location, the most qualified people can be more easily assigned to appropriate projects without concern for the expense and wasted productivity caused by extensive travel or frequent relocation. Although virtual workgroups members may be geographically dispersed, when they log in to corporate information resources, the enterprise network must treat them as if they are all connected to the same local LAN. Networks which can make geographically distributed users appear to be connected to the same local LAN are known as virtual LANs.

3. The term middleware is used to describe a wide variety of different types of software which enable transparent interoperability across enterprise networks. Architecturally, middleware fits between client/server applications and the enterprise network which delivers the messages linking those applications. Middleware's overall function is to provide whatever services are required to client/server applications in order to allow them to transparently interoperate across a variety of computing platforms and networks.

4. The key difference between a LAN switch which does not support virtual LANs and one that does is the treatment of broadcast and multicast messages. In a virtual LAN, broadcasts and multicasts are limited to the members of that virtual LAN only, rather than to all connected devices. This prevents propagation of data across the entire network and reduces network traffic. To simplify, virtual LANs are nothing more than logically defined broadcast/multicast groups within Layer 2 LAN switches since point-to-point traffic is handled by switched dedicated connections.

5. Rather than having to physically re-wire network connections for each change in workgroup configurations, a virtual LAN allows for flexible assignment of dedicated network resources to virtual workgroups by grouping users logically rather than according to physical network connections. While the original LAN switches delivered abundant bandwidth to locally attached workstations and segments, they lacked the ability to partition the switch into multiple segregated broadcast zones and to segment users into corresponding separate workgroups. Virtual LANs are software definable through configuration software contained within the LAN switch. The use of virtual LANs allows workgroup members to be assigned to more than one workgroup quickly and easily, if necessary. Subsequently, each virtual workgroup is assigned some portion of the LAN switch's backplane capacity. LAN switches which support virtual LANs use OSI layer 2 bridging functionality to logically segment the traffic within the switch into distinct virtual LANs.

6. A key limitation of virtual LANs is that when members of the same virtual LAN are physically connected to separate LAN switches, the virtual LAN configuration information must be shared between multiple LAN switches. Currently, no interoperability standards exist for transmitting or sharing virtual LAN information between layer 2 LAN switches. As a result, only proprietary switch-to-switch protocols between a single vendor's equipment is possible for multi-switch virtual LANs. Management and monitoring of virtual LANs is more difficult than traditional LANs due to the virtual LAN's dependence on LAN switches for physical connectivity. Because the switched LAN connections are established, used, and terminated in a matter of microseconds for most transmissions, it is difficult if not impossible to monitor these transmissions in real time by traditional means.

7. One solution to the management and monitoring dilemma is known as traffic duplication in which traffic between two switch ports is duplicated onto a third port to which traditional LAN analyzers can be attached. Standardization for interoperability will also help in a multi-LAN switch environment.

8. Transmission methods between Layer 2 switches differ between various switch vendors. In order to share virtual LAN information across Layer 2 switches, each must be able to talk to the other, necessitating standardization of switch to switch communication. IEEE 802.10 may be the necessary standard.

9. Originally conceived as a standard for secure data exchange on LANs which would allow workstations to set encryption and authentication settings, this standard is of interest to virtual LAN switch vendors because of the addition of a 32 bit header to existing MAC sub-layer frames. Instead of just holding security information, this additional 32 bit header could hold virtual LAN identifiers. In order to overcome the limitation on maximum data link layer frame length, IEEE 802.10 also includes specifications for segmentation and reassembly of any frames which should exceed maximum length due to the addition of the 32 bit header.

10. LAN switches are only able to offer the "forward-if-not-local" internetworking logic of bridges. In order to selectively transmit traffic between virtual LANs, routing functionality is required.

11. This routing functionality may be supplied by an external router or by specialized router software included in the LAN switch. LAN switches with built in routing capabilities are sometimes referred to as Layer 3 switches.

12. Layer 2 Virtual LANs are built using LAN switches which act as micro-segmenting bridges. A LAN switch which supports a layer 2 virtual LAN distinguishes only between the MAC addresses of connected workstations. No differentiation is possible based on layer 3, network layer, protocols. One or more workstations can be connected to each switch port. Layer 3 Virtual LANs are built using LAN switches which are able to process layer 3 network addresses. Such devices may be called routing switches. Since these devices are able to perform filtering based on network layer protocols and addresses, they are able to support multiple virtual LANs using different network layer protocols. Figure 11-5 details the functional differences between the two virtual LAN designs.

13. By creating a bandwidth hierarchy as part of a strategic network design, required bandwidth can be upgraded incrementally in a planned fashion rather than facing wholesale replacement of networking technology in reaction to a crisis of crippling network performance.

14. Distributed backbones were once the norm in which individual LAN segments are linked to a backbone LAN media via bridges and transceivers. These backbone networks often ran vertically between floors of a building while multiple, horizontal LAN segments were distributed throughout the building and attached to the backbone via bridges. Collapsed backbones, a more recent innovation, collapse the entire network backbone, which once spanned several floors of a building, into the backplane of a single internetworking device such as a router. The backplane of the router which is shared by numerous internetworking modules has enormous bandwidth capacity, usually in the gigabits per second range. Figure 11-7 contrasts distributed and collapsed backbone architectures for shared media internetworking.

15. One of the real benefits of ATM is its ability to switch LAN traffic without the need to make any hardware or software changes to LAN clients or servers. Another key benefit of ATM is its scalability both in terms of transmission speed and geographic scope of coverage. While ATM transmission speeds have been defined up to 2.4 Gbps (Gigabits per second) or more, its geographic scope of coverage spans from LAN based switches to wide area ATM network services offered by long distance carriers. The net effect of ATM's availability from the LAN to the WAN is that virtual LANs can be established over long distances using ATM switches as the virtual LAN bandwidth provider. In addition, ATM can transmit voice, video, data, and image simultaneously between network locations.

16. Through a process known as ATM LAN Emulation, virtual LANs are able to be constructed over an ATM switched network regardless of the geographic scope of that network. ATM LAN emulation is considered a bridging solution, like LAN switch-based virtual LANs, since traffic is switched based on MAC layer addresses. Unlike LAN switch-based virtual LANs, however, MAC layer addresses must be translated into, or resolved into, ATM addresses in a process known as ATM address resolution. In ATM LAN emulation, the ATM switching fabric adds an entire layer of its own addressing schemes which it uses to forward virtual LAN traffic to its proper destination. It is important to understand that ATM emulation, like other virtual LAN architectures built on layer 2 switching, is basically a bridged topology which suffers from the same limitations as other layer 2 switched networks:
    - Flat network topology
    - Broadcast storms (although limited to a particular virtual LAN)
    - No layer 3 filtering for security or segmentation

    On the other hand, because it does not discriminate between network layer (layer 3) protocols, ATM LAN emulation is able to support, or transport, multiple network layer protocols between virtual LANs. No hardware or software changes are required at workstations or servers.

17. The LEC (LAN Emulation Client) software which may be installed in a router with an ATM interface or some other type of ATM access device is also responsible for converting the LAN's data link layer protocols (Ethernet, Token Ring, FDDI) into fixed length ATM cells. Once the local LEC knows the ATM address of the remote LEC which is acting as an ATM proxy for the remote LAN destination, it sets up a switched virtual circuit, or switched network connection, to the remote LEC which subsequently delivers the information payload to the remote LAN workstation in a unicast (point-to-point) transmission. LAN Emulation Server (LES) software resides on a server or workstation which is directly attached to the ATM network and has a unique ATM address. The LES software performs three major tasks or services which can actually be accomplished by separate software programs executed on separate servers:

    LES Configuration Services are responsible for keeping track of the types of virtual LANs which are being supported over the ATM switching fabric and which LECs belong to which type of LAN. MAC addresses and corresponding ATM addresses of attached workstations are stored by the configuration server.

    LES Broadcast & Unknown Services (BUS) are responsible for handling requests for broadcasts and multicasts within the virtual LANs which exist across the ATM switching fabric.

    LES LAN Emulation Services receive address resolution protocol (ARP) requests from LECs seeking the ATM addresses of destination LAN workstations for which the MAC address is known.

18. MAC layer addresses must be translated into, or resolved into, ATM addresses in a process known as ATM address resolution.

19. LES Configuration Services are responsible for keeping track of the types of virtual LANs which are being supported over the ATM switching fabric and which LECs belong to which type of LAN. MAC addresses and corresponding ATM addresses of attached workstations are stored by the configuration server. LAN type (Ethernet, Token Ring, FDDI) is important to keep track of due to the variability of the maximum frame length accepted by workstations attached to each type of LAN.

20. LES Broadcast & Unknown Services (BUS) are responsible for handling requests for broadcasts and multicasts within the virtual LANs which exist across the ATM switching fabric. In addition, should a LEC not know the destination ATM address of a destination LAN workstation, it will forward that frame to the Broadcast & Unknown Server which will broadcast that frame throughout the virtual LAN on behalf of the LEC.

21. The goal of Classical IP over ATM is to allow IP networks, as well as all upper layer TCP/IP protocols, utilities, and APIs encapsulated by IP, to be delivered over an ATM network without requiring modification to the TCP/IP protocols. Using Classical IP over ATM, the ATM network is treated by IP like just another subnet or datalink protocol such as Ethernet or Token Ring. IP Routers see the entire ATM network as only a single hop, regardless of the actual size of the ATM network. IP subnets established over ATM networks using this protocol are known as Logical IP Subnets or LIS. A significant limitation of Classical IP over ATM is that it only works within a given subnet. As a result, in order to use IP addresses to properly route data between Classical IP subnets, an IP router must still be employed. Just as with ATM LAN emulation, Classical IP over ATM also requires address resolution. In this case a new protocol known as ATMARP (ATM Address Resolution Protocol) runs on a server in the logical IP subnet and provides address resolution between IP addresses and ATM addresses. ATM addresses may actually be the virtual circuit ID numbers of the virtual circuits or connections which are established between two ATM end-points on the ATM network. Understandably, Classical IP over ATM only supports IP as a network layer protocol over ATM networks. Other initiatives are underway to support multiple network layer protocols over ATM. The ATM Forum is currently working on MPOA (Multi Protocols Over ATM) which will not only support IP, IPX, Appletalk and other network protocols over ATM, but will also be able to route data directly between virtual LANs, thereby precluding the need for additional external routers. Routing implemented on switches using protocols such as MPOA is sometimes referred to as cut-through routing and uses ATM LAN Emulation as its Layer 2 switching specification. Like ATM LAN Emulation, MPOA operates transparently to end-devices and does not require any hardware or software changes to those end-devices or their applications. The IETF is currently working on RFC 1483, Multiprotocol Encapsulation over ATM Adaptation Layer 5. One of the significant contributions of this proposal is that it defines two different ways in which multiple network layer protocols can be transmitted simultaneously over an ATM network. The first method, LLC/SNAP Encapsulation, places indicators in the ATM data link layer frame to identify which network layer protocols are embedded within that data link layer frame. The second method, Virtual Channel-based Multiplexing, establishes a separate

virtual circuit, or connection, through the ATM network, for each network layer protocol transported from one workstation to another.

22. Routing implemented on switches using protocols such as MPOA is sometimes referred to as cut-through routing and uses ATM LAN Emulation as its Layer 2 switching specification.

23. IP switching technology distinguishes between the length of data streams and switches or routes accordingly on a case by case basis. In the case of long data streams associated with file transfers or voice or video transmissions, the IP switch sets up a virtual circuit through the ATM switching fabric and then forwards packets immediately via layer 2 switching to that virtual circuit. In the case or datagram-oriented, short messages, each message is forwarded through the layer 3 routing software located in the IP switch.

24. Protocols to distinguish between the types of transmissions and to decide whether to switch or route, are under development. IPsilon networks has proposed Flow Management Protocol (FMP) while Cisco Systems has proposed as alternative protocol known as tag switching.

25. A business might be interested in connecting to the Internet primarily for marketing rather than for sales purposes, since most people currently use the Internet for browsing rather than buying. Also, if existing or potential customers are Internet users, or enterprise partners such as key vendors or suppliers have and Internet presence, then a company should consider connecting to the Internet.

26. A bad reason to connect to the Internet would be if the business were expecting a lucrative untapped market for on-line electronic commerce and credit-card transactions.

27. Three major services include: the World Wide Web, Information Servers, and Global E-mail. The World Wide Web, which consists of servers offering graphical or multimedia presentations, is easy to access with a Web browser by both business employees and ordinary at-home users. Information Servers, which provide file transfer, remote login capabilities, and other information systems, are somewhat more difficult in that users must know the Internet address of the specific information server which they wish to access. The third service is Global E-mail, which offers a method for sending and receiving inter-company mail, and is generally easy to use, however proper security precautions must be taken.

28. The World Wide Web (WWW) is a collection of servers accessed via the Internet that offers graphical or multimedia (audio, video, image) presentations about a company's products, personnel, or services.

29. The information can be graphical and even multimedia, as well as interactive. In order to achieve this, Web browsers must be used and Web sites must be built by the company.

30. Information servers include: Telnet, a remote user login service of the TCP/IP protocol; FTP (File Transfer Protocol), which allows users to download, or transfer, information back to their client PCs; Gopher, which transparently searches multiple FTP sites for requested information and delivers that information to the Gopher client; WAIS (Wide Area Information Services, which offer multiple indexes to other Internet-attached WAIS servers; and UseNet, a type of newsgroup which shares text-based news items over the Internet.

31. Figure 11-10 contains a list of the benefits, advantages, and supporting trends of the Internet access business.

32. Figure 11-11 lists the disadvantages and obstacles to widespread use of the Internet by business.

33. IAP (Internet Access Providers) are primarily concerned with getting a subscriber company physically hooked up to the Internet. IPP (Internet Presence Providers) are primarily concerned with designing, developing, implementing, managing, and maintaining a subscriber company's presence on the Internet.

34. SLIP (Serial Line Internet Protocol) and the more recently released and more functional PPP (Point-to-Point Protocol) are used to support communication over serial or dial-up lines.

35. HTTP (HyperText Transport Protocol) is a specialized Web server protocol that supports multiple Web client requests for Web pages. HTML (HyperText Markup Language) is the programming language used to program text into Web pages.

36. Web browsers are a client-based category of software that are used to access not only Internet attached resources but also: local client-attached resources, local area network-attached resources, and enterprise or corporate network attached resources.

37. NetScape, MS Internet Explorer, and Mosaic are three popular Web browsers.

38. Figure 11-14 provides a good example of each term and how they interact together.

39. URLs (Uniform Resource Locators) allow location of indexed Web pages throughout the Internet as hot-clickable links from a given Web page. Hypertext refers to documents which have the ability to link to other documents.

40. An Internet gateway offers a LAN-attached link for client PCs to access a multitude of Internet-attached resources and is an access-oriented product. An Internet e-mail gateway provides translation between differing e-mail clients when e-mail is sent via the Internet, for instance, translating from Microsoft Mail to cc:Mail.

41. Figure 11-18 provides a list of advantages and disadvantages of an Internet gateway.

42. Both Figures 11-17 and 11-18 provide extensive information on the differences between accessing Internet services via an Internet gateway as opposed to Internet-enabled clients.

43. An Internet server offers Web services as well as Global E-mail, FTP/Telnet services, and UseNet NewsGroup services, while a Web server offers primarily Web services only.

44. CGI (Common Gateway Interface) is a standardized API which allows web applications to be written and potentially executed on multiple different Web servers.

45. A proxy server, which acts as a holding bin or repository for previously requested Web pages from distant Internet servers, can deliver the previously requested Web page quickly to the local client without the normal delay associated with downloading the Web page again in its entirety across the Internet, thus lightening the load on the network. The term proxy server is also used to describe an application layer gateway or firewall to protect corporate information resources from unauthorized access via the Internet.

TEST QUESTIONS

True/False Questions

1. Without the enterprise network, the virtual corporation would not exist. T/435

2. A business phenomenon known as the virtual workgroup implies a business partnership among cooperating business entities which is electronically enabled via an enterprise network. F/436

3. In a virtual LAN, broadcasts and multicasts are sent to all connected devices. F/438

4. Since standardized switch-to-switch protocols between different vendors' equipment exist, it is possible to build multi-switch virtual LANs. F/438

5. Layer 3 Virtual LANs are built using LAN switches which offer the "forward-if-not-local" internetworking logic of bridges. F/440

6. Layer 2 Virtual LANs are built using LAN switches which act as micro-segmenting bridges. T/441

7. One of the key benefits of ATM is its scalability both in terms of transmission speed and geographic scope of coverage. T/446

8. MPOA will support IP, IPX, Appletalk and other network protocols over ATM, as well as route data directly between virtual LANs, thereby precluding the need for additional external routers. T/449

9. The Internet is currently used very effectively as a sales tool by business. F/451

10. UseNet Servers share highly graphics-based information and news items over the Internet. F/453

11. Unfortunately, Global E-mail across the Internet is unable to handle inter-company e-mail needs. F/453

12. One of the major inducements for a business to establish an Internet gateway allowing access from all over the world is that the Internet is a highly secure network. F/453

13. EDI and EFT are technologies which preceded the existence of the world wide web. T/459

204   Chapter 11

14. A Web browser should offer transparency to users from concerns and compatibility issues such as geography, storage file format, hardware characteristics and operating system differences, and network or transport protocols. T/461

15. URLs are used within a given Web page to allow hypertext links to other related Web pages, documents, or services such as e-mail. T/461

16. The Internet's mail protocol is called HTTP. F/462

17. An IP address is a required component for Internet or Web server implementation. T/466

18. High speed RISC chips, such as the DEC Alpha, will be required for high performance Web servers. T/468

Multiple Choice Questions

1. Which of the following is **not** a challenge which must be addressed in order to effectively analyze, design, and implement enterprise networks?
    a. a lack of affordable wide area network bandwidth
 p.435 b. the single-vendor, multi-platform, single-protocol nodes typical of an enterprise network
    c. the quickly changing nature of the competitive business environment and downsizing
    d. quick, easy access to data regardless of physical location

2. In the top down model for enterprise networks, which of the following issues would have a business layer implication?
 p.436 a. extending the enterprise to include customers and vendors
    b. remote users require full access to corporate information resources
    c. remote users require data and files to be automatically synchronized each time they log in to corporate information resources
    d. distributed database replication imposes high bandwidth demands on the network

3. In the top down model for enterprise networks, which of the following issues would have an application layer implication?
    a. extending the enterprise to include customers and vendors
 p.436 b. remote users require full access to corporate information resources
    c. remote users require data and files to be automatically synchronized each time they log in to corporate information resources
    d. distributed database replication imposes high bandwidth demands on the network

4. In the top down model for enterprise networks, which of the following issues would have a data layer implication?
    a. extending the enterprise to include customers and vendors
    b. remote users require full access to corporate information resources
 p.436 c. remote users require data and files to be automatically synchronized each time they

log in to corporate information resources
d. distributed database replication imposes high bandwidth demands on the network

5. In the top down model for enterprise networks, which of the following issues would have a network layer implication?
   a. extending the enterprise to include customers and vendors
   b. remote users require full access to corporate information resources
   c. remote users require data and files to be automatically synchronized each time they log in to corporate information resources
p.436 d. distributed database replication imposes high bandwidth demands on the network

6. This phenomenon implies a business partnership among cooperating business entities and is known as the
   a. virtual workgroup
   b. virtual LAN
   c. virtual enterprise network
p.435 d. virtual corporation

7. Networks which can make geographically distributed users appear to be connected to the same local LAN are known as
   a. virtual workgroups
p.437 b. virtual LANs
   c. virtual enterprise networks
   d. virtual corporations

8. A virtual LAN is dependent on which of the following devices for its functionality?
   a. cabling
   b. shared-media hub
   c. NIC card
p.438 d. LAN switch

9. Virtual LANs are defined by which of the following?
p.438 a. configuration software contained within a LAN switch
   b. configuration software contained within a shared-media hub
   c. configuration software used to drive NIC cards
   d. configuration software used to control the wiring signals

10. This method used by switch vendors to share virtual LAN information uses virtual LAN tables which are broadcast periodically to all other switches.
    a. Frame tagging
p.440 b. Signaling message
    c. Time Division Multiplexing
    d. Frequency Division Multiplexing

206   Chapter 11

11. This method used by switch vendors to share virtual LAN information appends the virtual LAN number to the data link layer message which travels between LAN switches.
p.440
   a. Frame tagging
   b. Signaling message
   c. Time Division Multiplexing
   d. Frequency Division Multiplexing

12. This method used by switch vendors to share virtual LAN information assigns a specific portion of the bandwidth available on the LAN switches' backplanes for each virtual LAN's traffic.
   a. Frame tagging
   b. Signaling message
p.440 c. Time Division Multiplexing
   d. Frequency Division Multiplexing

13. Which of the following is a possible standard which could support virtual LANs because it allows for an addition of a 32 bit header to existing MAC sub-layer frames?
   a. IEEE 802.3
   b. IEEE 802.5
   c. IEEE 802.9
p.440 d. IEEE 802.10

14. Which of the following statements is correct concerning a Layer 2 Virtual LAN?
   a. It is more difficult to configure than a Layer 3 Virtual LAN.
p.443 b. It has no ability to differentiate between network layer protocols.
   c. It can do filtering at the network layer.
   d. It has the capability to route data.

15. This trend should allow virtual LANs to be more easily integrated into an enterprise network.
p.441 a. auto-configuring LAN switches
   b. non-auto-configuring LAN switches
   c. simple monitoring
   d. unsophisticated management tools

16. Condensing the entire network backbone, which once spanned several floors of a building, into the backplane of a single internetworking device such as a router is referred to as a
   a. distributed backbone
   b. distributed backplane
   c. compacted backbone
p.444 d. collapsed backbone

17. A fast switching technology whose benefit is its ability to switch LAN traffic without the need to make any hardware or software changes to LAN clients or servers.
    a. FDDI
p.446 b. ATM
    c. 100VGAnyLAN
    d. 100BaseT

18. Terminology used to describe the ability of network segments to offer required bandwidth as needed without having to re-write or modify the applications which will use those network segments, or to suddenly re-design the network.
    a. ATM
    b. Enterprise network
p.446 c. bandwidth hierarchy
    d. none of the above

19. Which of the following ATM LAN emulation architecture components/services appears to be an ATM end-station on behalf of the LAN clients it represents and is responsible for converting the LAN's data link layer protocols into fixed length ATM cells?
    a. LES Configuration Services
    b. LES Broadcast & Unknown Services
    c. LES LAN Emulation Services
p.447 d. LAN Emulation Client

20. Which of the following ATM LES software components is responsible for keeping track of the types of virtual LANs which are being supported over the ATM switching fabric and which LECs belong to which type of LAN?
p.447 a. LES Configuration Services
    b. LES Broadcast & Unknown Services
    c. LES LAN Emulation Services
    d. LAN Emulation Client

21. Which of the following ATM LES software components is responsible for handling requests for broadcasts and multicasts within the virtual LANs which exist across the ATM switching fabric?
    a. LES Configuration Services
p.447 b. LES Broadcast & Unknown Services
    c. LES LAN Emulation Services
    d. LAN Emulation Client

208 Chapter 11

22. Which of the following statements about ATM LAN emulation is correct?
    a. ATM LAN emulation discriminates between network layer protocols, supporting only one protocol at a time
p.449 b. ATM LAN emulation offers no routing capability
    c. ATM LAN emulation is built on Layer 3 switching
    d. ATM LAN emulation is unable to support, or transport, multiple network layer protocols between virtual LANs

23. Which of the following MPOA components which might be a kind of hybrid hub, switch, and router acts as an interface or gateway between LANs and the ATM network?
p.449 a. edge device
    b. route server
    c. ATM switch
    d. shared-media hub

24. Which of the following is a good reason for a company to start to think about developing a presence on the Internet?
    a. few of their customers use the Internet
    b. their enterprise partners do not use the Internet
p.452 c. existing or potential customers are Internet users
    d. the Internet provides a lucrative untapped market for on-line electronic commerce and credit-card transactions

25. Of the following, which is not a major category of Internet services?
    a. World Wide Web
p.452 b. BBS
    c. Information Servers
    d. Global E-mail

26. A client-based front-end software tool that allows access to WWW servers is know as a
    a. Web page
    b. Web crawler
    c. Web site
p.452 d. Web browser

27. A company would market itself or products on the WWW using which of the following?
    a. Web page
    b. Web crawler
p.452 c. Web site
    d. Web browser

28. Which of the following is used to access Internet-connected servers by allowing remote users to log into the server?
    a. FTP
p.453   b. Telnet
    c. Gopher
    d. WAIS

29. Which of the following allows users, through an anonymous user account, to download, or transfer, information back to their client PCs from and Internet-based server?
p.453   a. FTP
    b. Telnet
    c. Gopher
    d. WAIS

30. This type of information server is primarily used as a text-searching service.
    a. FTP
    b. Telnet
    c. Gopher
p.453   d. WAIS

31. Which of the following is an advantage or benefit of Internet access by business?
p.455   a. there are now improved browsers even novices can use, which are available for Internet access
    b. the information on the Internet is loosely organized
    c. the Internet will be fully maintained and funded by the government
    d. the Internet is unregulated

32. Which of the following is the most significant disadvantage or obstacle to widespread use of the Internet by business?
    a. browsers are not readily available for accessing the Web
p.456   b. the Internet is unregulated
    c. modem and ISDN technology do not offer enough bandwidth
    d. there are not enough local, regional, or national Internet access providers

33. If a company wanted a Web page on the WWW but did not want to invest in the required hardware and personnel to launch such a venture in-house, which of the following would the company likely contract?
p.456   a. IPP
    b. IAP
    c. local telephone company
    d. Internet Connectivity Provider

210   Chapter 11

34. Which of the following Web server connectivity alternatives is the least expensive?
    a. hiring a Web service provider
    b. in-house development and deployment
p.458 c. posting customer designed page on the access provider's server
    d. in-house development with leasing of line directly connected to Web

35. Specialized Web server software uses this protocol in order to handle the organization of servicing the multiple Web client requests for Web pages.
    a. HTMX
    b. HPPT
p.459 c. HTTP
    d. HTML

36. This is used to program text for Web pages.
    a. HTMX
    b. HPPT
    c. HTTP
p.459 d. HTML

37. This device acts as a translator, speaking a LAN-specific e-mail software protocol on one side and speaking the Internet's e-mail protocol on the other.
p.462 a. e-mail gateway
    b. SMTP
    c. Internet access provider
    d. Internet presence provider

38. What is a likely location for system bottlenecks due to the amount of processing involved with translating between mail protocols, especially at high traffic levels?
    a. Internet presence provider
p.463 b. e-mail gateway
    c. client front-end e-mail package
    d. LAN-attached client PC

39. Which of the following offers a LAN-attached link for client PCs to access a multitude of Internet-attached resources?
    a. Internet e-mail gateway
    b. client front-end browser
    c. client e-mail front-end
p.463 d. Internet gateway

40. Which of the following is an advantage of an Internet-enabled client?
    a. every client requires its own TCP/IP software
    b. it provides a single location of TCP/IP and client front-ends
p.465 c. it eliminates the Internet gateway as a potential bottleneck
    d. it doesn't require the use of local LAN transport protocols

41. An Internet transport protocol which supports communication over serial or dial-up lines is?
p.465
   a. SLIP
   b. TCP/IP
   c. IPX/SPX
   d. SLOP

42. The sole official authority in charge of issuing Internet IP addresses is
p.467
   a. InterNIC
   b. IAP
   c. IPP
   d. FCC

43. If a company wished to offer product information along with on-line technical support, which of the following would be required?
   a. Web server
p.467 b. Web server and gateway for file transfer and search engine software
   c. FTP server
   d. IAP

44. Which of the following would probably **not** provide an Internet (IP) address?
   a. Internet Presence Provider
   b. Internet Access Provider
p.472 c. Local Telecomm Provider
   d. none of the following would provide an IP address

Fill-In the Blank Questions

1. Using _____, people are dynamically allocated to projects based on expertise rather than location, ensuring that the most qualified people can be more easily assigned to appropriate projects without concern for the expense and wasted productivity caused by extensive travel or frequent relocation.

2. Layer 3 Virtual LANs are built around LAN switches, sometimes called _____ switches, since they are able to work with network layer protocols and addresses.

3. An alternative to adding routing capabilities to ATM switching fabrics _____ distinguishes between the length of data streams and switches or routes accordingly on a case by case basis.

4. The _____ is a collection of servers accessed via the Internet that offer graphical or multimedia presentations about a company's products, personnel, or services.

5. Although similar to the World Wide Web, _____ uses text-based information whereas the WWW's information is largely graphical.

6. A(n) _____ Provider is primarily concerned with getting a subscriber company physically hooked up to the Internet.

7. A(n) _____ Provider is primarily concerned with designing, developing, implementing, managing, and maintaining a subscriber company's presence on the Internet.

8. _____ is one of the three most popular Web browser front-end tools used.

9. A hot-clickable link to a Web page is known as a(n) _____.

10. The transport protocol used within the Internet that allows different types of computers and network access devices to exchange messages and deliver data and e-mail is known as _____.

11. A standardized API known as _____ allows web applications to be written and potentially executed on multiple different Web servers.

12. A _____ server acts as a holding bin or repository for previously requested Web pages from distant Internet servers.

13. Globally dispersed enterprises functioning as if all network-attached users are physically located in the same building would be known as a(n) _____.

Answers

1. virtual workgroups p.436
2. routing or multilayer p.441
3. IP switching p.450
4. World Wide Web (WWW) p.452
5. Gopher p.453
6. Internet Access p.455
7. Internet Presence p.456
8. Mosaic or NetScape or Internet Explorer p.457
9. URL (Uniform Resource Locator) p.461
10. TCP/IP p.465
11. Common Gateway Interface (CGI) p.468
12. Proxy p.468
13. Virtual corporation p.473

Chapter 11   213

CASE STUDY AND ANSWERS

LONG ROAD TO ONLINE COMMERCE

Activities
1. Top-down model:

Business	Burlington Coat Factory (BCF) wanted to create a Web site (virtual storefront) to compete against other businesses as well as draw customers into stores. A Web site would benefit stores that don't have enough space to carry certain items. Corporate re-engineering will be necessary to support Web commerce.
Applications	Web-conversion tools will be needed to set up and implement the Web site. In order to conduct Web commerce, security will need to be in place. Inventory applications will need to be developed. An order-fulfillment system will need to be developed. BCF's intranet must support groupware. Existing applications will need to be translated to a Web interface (browser).
Data	Data will need to be maintained dynamically in order to support Web commerce. Merchandise data, scanning of photos and other inventory data must be gathered in one place.
Network	The Web site must be available through standard Web browsers. Firewalls must be in place. Bandwidth requirements must allow for easy access from the Web. Both an internet and intranet must be supported.
Technology	BCF's external Web site was set up on a Sun Microsystems Inc. SPARCstation using NCSA Web-server software. TCP/IP and Internet E-mail are being used. Cisco Systems Inc. firewall router software is in place. BCF uses Novell Inc. Tuxedo transaction-processing software to log and update sales. An Oracle Corp. database is used for its online catalog of merchandise.

2. Unanswered questions:
   - What will the Return on Investment be?
   - How will the Web site measure the impact it is having on store sales?
   - How will the catalog merchandise be dynamically updated?
   - How will the system handle returns and credits?
   - What data analysis has been done to quantify types and amounts of data required to support the online catalog?
   - What security can be offered the customer when ordering online?
   - What network architecture is being used both for the LAN and WAN?
   - What training will be provided store and corporate personnel?
   - What are minimal client workstation configurations for both hardware and software?

Business
1. BCF is engaged in selling everything from coats to furniture through retail stores and now through an online Web site.
2. The company hoped to compete against companies like L.L. Bean Inc. and Spiegel Inc., draw customers into stores, and generate online sales with its electronic commerce application.
3. It hoped that online sales would increase in-store sales by encouraging customers to go to stores nearest them.
4. A warehouse and main distribution center support 250 stores nationwide.
5. It did not fulfill web-based online ordering because its operations rely largely on the warehouse and main distribution center which are not set up for ordering specific merchandise.
6. What to do when a store runs out of a item, how to ring up an online order shipped to a store nearest the customer, how to dynamically maintain the online catalog, and how to handle return sales, are a few of the sales policies which BCF will have to deal with in an electronic commerce mode.
7. A small group within the IS department is handling the effort with no new staff allocated.
8. A MIS Steering Committee, made up of top managers in the buying, distribution, and financial areas is responsible for overseeing the Web project.
9. BCF executives don't expect virtual shopping to replace the social interaction associated with in-store shopping. Primarily they expect the Web to promote the stores more aggressively by using the Web to advertise products and offer products at the push of a button.
10. That depends. Cost justification is not made clear in the article. Personnel support from the IS department is limited. This may not represent the ingredients for a successful implementation.

Application
1. The company was trying to deploy a web site on both its intranet and on the Internet.
2. Its own buyers must support this application.
3. Stocking, shipping, tracking merchandise along with returns appears to be the biggest application gap between the online ordering system and the current inventory and billing system.
4. Tuxedo is transaction-processing software which can be used to log and update sales and may be able to link the customer's electronic order on the Web to BCF's inventory and billing operations.

Data
1. The evolution of the BCF's Web site was to be an intranet server, but has moved to an online sales system which originally handled only corporate data and a store locator map, to an interactive catalog system.
2. The company will initially employ a toll-free number to handle all financial transactions; this is a method many businesses are using today for the delicate process of taking credit-card numbers. BCF eventually plans to deploy a financial-transaction model where credit-card data is handled directly by a bank, not by BCF.

Network
1. The original Web site used a Sun Microsystems Inc. SPARCstation running World Wide Web-server software from the NCSA.
2. The intranet Web site hosted a comprehensive corporate directory, store locator map, and a few IS reports.
3. BCF employed groupware such as Microsoft Excel.
4. It's intranet was not a dynamic system which the e-commerce web site will need to be.

Technology
1. Technological requirements include a move to making a Web browser its standard user interface and how to use the intranet for improving communication and training among 15,000 employees. Updating or making changes to its online catalog dynamically will be a requirement along with using a transaction processing system capable of handling it Web commerce inventory and billing operations.

CHAPTER 12

The Network Development Life Cycle

ANSWERS TO CHAPTER REVIEW QUESTIONS

1. The network development life cycle falls under the systems development life cycle in the network layer of the top-down model, while the systems development life cycle falls in the application layer of the top-down model. Figure 12-1 in the text illustrates this.

2. Ensure that network analysis and design is not performed in a vacuum. It is one step in an overall comprehensive information systems development cycle, commencing with business layer analysis and concluding with an analysis of the technology currently available to implement the system as designed. Following the top-down model in which requirements flow down and solutions flow up will also help.

3. By using analysis and design software to model their current network, companies are able to run optimization routines to reconfigure circuits and/or network hardware to deliver data more efficiently. Network optimization software can re-design networks which can save anywhere from thousands of dollars per month to millions of dollars per year depending on the size of the network. Some network design software can also verify carriers' billing and identify billing errors.

4. It can re-configure circuits and networking hardware yielding maximized performance, minimized price, or a combination of both.

5. Price, Performance

6. Yes, the cheapest solution is not always the most efficient and vice versa. There is a constant trade-off. Acceptable levels of performance and price are often business layer decisions determined by senior management.

7. CANE tools will use a standard known as CNIP or Common Network Information Platform which would allow any other CANE tool which could use the output to provide transparent integration with other CANE tools and would import the standardized, formatted data from CNIP.

8. Middleware and expert systems may enable vertical integration of CANE with I-CASE tools and business re-engineering software.

9. It is a good start for preparing an organized and comprehensive budget model to follow to prevent surprises! It identifies areas such as operational costs, future growth costs, training costs, etc. which are often overlooked in initial budgets.

10. Critical success factors are key behaviors or things to remember which can be of critical importance to the overall successful outcome of the network development life cycle. They are not associated with any particular step, but should be kept in mind throughout the process. Figure 12-5 in the text contains a list of 7 different critical success factors and explains each.

11. Process describes activities which should be taking place at any point during the development cycle, and the product is the outcome or deliverable from a particular stage of the overall cycle. A focus on product and process will facilitate the understanding of any systems development life cycle, not only the network development life cycle, and will also help keep the project on track.

12. Payload type analysis, transaction analysis, protocol stack analysis, time studies, mission-critical analysis, and traffic volume analysis.

13. All three fall under network analysis and design process and are the three major steps of the In-house network analysis and design phase. Circuit design is determined by results of the data traffic analysis. Network hardware is determined by results of circuit analysis and protocols.

14. The evaluation criteria should be set so that when the RFPs are answered by the vendors there will be a standard for comparison. The purpose of the Percent of Fit Goal is to set a minimum threshold of compliance for vendor proposals in order to warrant further consideration and invitations for demonstrations. It offers an element of objectivity to the proposal evaluation process.

15. The RFP assures that its priorities and unique business processes and requirements are fulfilled by the information system and network which is eventually installed. All vendor proposals are measured against the users' pre-defined requirements. The RFP assures that the delivered system, whether developed in-house or purchased from an outside vendor, will be flexible enough to change as business needs and requirements change.

16. Figure 12-10 in the text contains a Process-Product listing of the major components required for the RFP. Also, Figure 12-12 in the text contains a sample Table of Contents for and RFP.

17. Use the Percent of Fit Goal technique for evaluation. Establish evaluation criteria and assure buy-in from all effected parties.

18. Information about People:
    number of total employees
    number of employees performing each business function
    feeling about new system
    key political situations
    training
    Hardware-Software-Media
       current level of computerization
       current applications software
       current networking status
       local phone company
       availability of data services from local phone company
       software performance requirements
    Data
       number of customers
       number of inventory items
       number of open orders
       need for sharing data
       security needs
    Physical Plant
       condition of each remote site
       what additional physical systems will be needed

19. Buy-in at every stage by all affected parties must be stressed throughout the network analysis and design process in order to assure that everyone gets behind the new system and network and that everyone feels that they had an opportunity to make their thoughts known. The key element of system and network implementation is to assure that people-related needs such as management, support, and training have been thoroughly researched and appropriately addressed.

20. The cycle of monitoring, management, analysis, design, simulation and implementation is of an on-going nature.

21. CANE models current network configurations and can then run optimization routines to reconfigure circuits and/or network hardware to deliver data more efficiently. This is a continuing, cyclic process which must be used as the business needs continuously change.

22. The variance at different times or seasons may be quite great. The network must be designed to handle higher than normal demands during these peak seasonal times.

23. Outsourcing implies that vendors outside the company will be conducting the network analysis and design. This can be more objective and more thorough than in-house development. The outsourcing vendor may have more experience. On the other hand, the outsourcing vendor may not know the business needs well. The design must be built

around the business needs. Also, there might be a natural aversion to bringing in outside developers.

24. It is imperative to be aware of the corporate culture of an organization. The best planned network design may not be implemented if corporate politics are ignored. The network analyst must get the backing from the highest levels of management as well as ask the right questions at the right time to the right people.

25. Some corporations may be hierarchical, distributed, or open. Each of these corporate cultures will impact on the way the network analyst conducts business. There may need to be a requirement to be more formal and pass or not pass along certain information gained from interviews depending upon the corporate culture.

26. The approved results of one stage (buy-in) become the foundation or starting point for the next stage. If buy-in from all affected parties is assured at each stage, the presentation of the final proposal should be much smoother with a minimum of back-tracking or re-work required.

27. Use the Percent of Fit Goal to set a minimum threshold of compliance for vendor proposals in order to warrant further consideration and invitations for demonstrations. It offers an element of objectivity to the proposal evaluation process.

28. Before reaching any conclusions as to how various protocols are to be transported over the corporate network, those protocols must be accurately identified and documented. Once this is accomplished, the proper network device and its configuration can be determined. Also alternative circuit configurations can be designed.

29. Using the RFP assures that the network analyst has touched upon all the varied aspects of the potential design. Occasionally, problem definition reports or feasibility studies are presented to management for buy-in.

30. Baseline data is the current status of the system and network, from which to measure the eventual network impact. If the impact is not positive then the development was a failure! If you don't know where you started, how can you determine what you've accomplished?

31. By identifying the decision points and the exact information needed to make the correct business decisions, the network can be designed to provide the right information at the right time to the right decision maker. Too much information may cloud up the decision makers' ability to make the right decision.

32. The sole purpose of a network should be to solve business problems. If these are not articulated and understood, then the network designed will not answer or benefit the business, but will merely perpetuate current business problems.

33. The cost savings or revenue gained from the new network developed from the RFP can easily justify the work invested in the RFP. Also, in many cases, the RFP required a business process re-engineering project which may even streamline the business further.

34. Before taking time to prepare detailed proposals, many vendors appreciate knowing the implementation timetable of the proposed project. If the vendor already has projects underway or anticipated, they may lack sufficient manpower to meet the RFP's proposed implementation schedule.

35. The information gathered will help determine the unique data and processing requirements for those locations. This will assure the proposals address all situations, not just the overall business problem. This information will also be used later on in the detailed budget generation.

36. Does the vendor have significant experience in developing and implementing systems of a similar nature to the one described in the RFP? Does the vendor have a sufficiently large organization to support the smooth and successful implementation of such a system? Is the vendor financially solvent so as not to be likely to declare bankruptcy in the middle of the project implementation?

37. At vendor demonstrations, it is important for the users, rather than the vendors, to be in charge. Ask to see each and every feature stated in the RFP demonstrated.

38. The difficulties can be assessed by performing data traffic analysis, circuit analysis and configuration alternatives, and network hardware analysis and configuration alternatives to see that voice, data and video are not the same when it comes to networking. See Chapters 4 and 8 for more specifics.

39. ATM, mentioned in Chapter 8, _may_ possess the ability to simultaneously transport data and voice over both LANs and WANs.

40. By compiling the results of the Data Traffic Analysis Report and the Circuit Configuration Diagram in an I-P-O Diagram, the required processing ability of the sought-after device can be documented. Figure 12-18 in the text illustrates this.

41. Operational costs and anticipated growth should not be overlooked. By including these costs in the budget, the network analyst may prevent surprises, such as required or anticipated facilities upgrades and any legitimate need which was identified in the location-by-location survey.

42. The designers of the network simulation software have had to make some fairly radical changes in the ease of use as well as the sophistication of the software. An example of this increased sophistication is the ability to model particular make, model and manufacturer's network devices.

43. It is the result when the network implications of the deployment of new network-intensive applications are known before the actual release of the software. Thus, although current technology may not possess the capability, the business information system of the future may interface to the strategic business planning system in order to meet the strategic business objectives without disrupting current networks.

44. Return on Investment (ROI) is perhaps the most traditional approach to measuring cost/benefit and is well suited to incremental upgrades of existing systems. However, for entirely new or innovative projects, although costs may be accurately projected, projected benefits are more intangible and are far more difficult to quantify in real terms. Total Cost of Ownership (TCO) is another popular measure for objectively comparing the relative costs of alternative approaches or potential technology strategies. However, there are no universally accepted methods for calculating TCO and, as a result, the factor has become widely used as a marketing tool by vendors trying to convince corporations to migrate to a particular technology platform. Furthermore, TCO ignores the benefit side of the equation. Consequently, Total Benefit of Ownership (TBO) tries to quantify the usability and associated benefits of technological options. TBO attempts to quantify productivity increases as well as cost reduction. However, in order to properly quantify increased productivity, one must first measure current levels of productivity by developing evaluation criteria so that baseline data can be gathered.

TEST QUESTIONS

True/False Questions

1. A focus on the process allows one to focus on a milestone indicating completion of one stage of the development cycle and a readiness to proceed with subsequent stages. F/483

2. Although considered a cycle, the network development life cycle usually starts at the management phase when a network is designed from scratch. F/484

3. The cycle of monitoring, management, analysis, design, simulation, and implementation of the network development life cycle is an on-going process. T/484

4. A good network analysis and design methodology treats both in-house personnel as well as outside consultants as potential service providers by clearly documenting requirements in a formalized RFP and expecting compliance with those requirements. T/486

5. If communication from all affected parties is assured at each stage, the presentation of the final proposal should be much smoother with a minimum of back-tracking or rework required. T/487

6. If management's initial charge is, "Look into this problem and get back to me," then a feasibility study with management buy-in and approval before further study is clearly appropriate. T/491

7. The importance of the strategic system performance evaluation criteria lies in their ability to measure the extent to which proposed information systems designs deliver on strategic business goals. T/493

8. One advantage of being an in-house systems development group is that they do not have to submit a proposal in compliance with the requirements outlined in the RFP because they probably helped develop the RFP. F/502

9. Seasonality of transaction volume counts how often and at what time of day, week, or month a given transaction or process is normally executed. F/506

10. Total Cost of Ownership (TCO) tries to quantify the usability and associated benefits of technological options. F/513

224 Chapter 12

Multiple Choice Questions

1. With regard to the top-down model, the Network Development Life Cycle fits in which layer?
   a. business
   b. application

   p.482 c. network
   d. data

2. Which key component of the systems development effort describes activities that should be taking place at any point during the development cycle?

   p.483 a. process
   b. product
   c. place
   d. parameters

3. Which key component of the systems development effort is the outcome or deliverable from a particular stage of the overall cycle?
   a. process

   p.483 b. product
   c. place
   d. parameters

4. One milestone from the technology layer of the Information Systems Development Process could be a
   a. database design

   p.483 b. detailed network diagram
   c. network requirements document
   d. strategic business plan

5. A milestone of the business layer of the Information Systems Development Process could be a
   a. database design
   b. detailed network diagram
   c. network requirements document

   p.483 d. strategic business plan

6. Key behaviors or things to remember which can be of an overriding importance to the overall successful outcome of the network development life cycle are called
   a. requests for proposals
   b. political factors

   p.486 c. critical success factors
   d. none of the above

7. Awareness of the corporate culture can have a large impact on a project's success and is known as
   a. buy-in
   b. process/product awareness
p.486 c. political awareness
   d. communication

8. As each stage is concluded, agreement as to conclusions from all affected customer groups is of critical importance, and is known as
p.487 a. buy-in
   b. process/product awareness
   c. political awareness
   d. communication

9. When conducting a problem definition brainstorming session, the consultant should start with which of the following items articulated by senior management?
   a. network design charts
p.489 b. strategic business goals
   c. database design
   d. application software selection

10. The current status of the system and network, from which to measure the network is called
   a. application software
   b. database objects
   c. strategic information
p.490 d. baseline data

11. The product of the analysis phase of the network analysis and design methodology, in addition to the strategic information system design itself, is the
   a. perceived problem
   b. buy-in of management
p.492 c. evaluation criteria by which the proposed new system will be judged
   d. baseline data

12. Which of the following might be considered examples of a corporation's strategic business goals?
   a. enable improved inventory control
   b. enable shorter shelf re-stocking cycles
   c. allow for more efficient use of labor
p.493 d. all of the above

226   Chapter 12

13. As users from different functional areas get together and brainstorm problems that seemed deeply imbedded in current systems and solve them as new or modified business actions or steps, this is referred to as

p.494
- a. business process reengineering
- b. reverse engineering
- c. business functional criteria
- d. decision points

14. Which of the following provides the information that is required for the decision-maker to make an informed decision?
- a. opportunity points
- b. evaluation criteria

p.495
- c. decision points
- d. none of the above

15. One of the key areas in which user group members can contribute is in the identification of _____, which can be enabled by the strategic information system design, and can lead to improved corporate performance.

p.495
- a. opportunity points
- b. evaluation criteria
- c. decision points
- d. none of the above

16. This assures that the delivered system, whether developed in-house or purchased from an outside vendor, will be flexible enough to change as business needs and requirements change.
- a. feasibility study
- b. decision point
- c. buy-in

p.497
- d. RFP

17. In an RFP, this information is supplied to the vendors to show that some modules of the overall strategic information systems design are more critical than others.
- a. company profile
- b. overall system characteristics

p.500
- c. project phase prioritization
- d. proposed project schedule summary

18. This is an important inclusion in the RFP because if the vendor already has projects underway or anticipated, they may lack a sufficient labor force to meet this RFP's proposed implementation schedule.
- a. company profile
- b. overall system characteristics
- c. project phase prioritization

p.500
- d. proposed project schedule summary

19. Background information from potential vendors may be requested in the RFP because
p.502
   a. we might want to see if the vendor has enough experience
   b. we will need to know if their bid is within our price range
   c. we may want to hire their personnel
   d. none of the above

20. Which of the following offers an element of objectivity to the proposal evaluation process?
p.502
   a. percent of fit goal
   b. critical success factors
   c. references
   d. vendor experience

21. Examining all aspects and characteristics of the data that will be passed between corporate locations over the proposed network is known as
   a. circuit analysis and configuration alternatives
   b. network hardware analysis and configuration alternatives
   c. protocol stack analysis
p.504 d. data traffic analysis

22. Once the nature of the data is thoroughly understood, which of the following explores the possibilities for delivering that data in a reliable and effective manner?
p.504
   a. circuit analysis and configuration alternatives
   b. network hardware analysis and configuration alternatives
   c. protocol stack analysis
   d. data traffic analysis

23. Finally, which of the following explores the possible data communications hardware devices that may be required to tie the various circuit configurations together into a reliable, manageable network?
   a. circuit analysis and configuration alternatives
p.504 b. network hardware analysis and configuration alternatives
   c. protocol stack analysis
   d. data traffic analysis

24. Which data traffic analysis type combines all types of transactions with the results of the time study and produces a time-sensitive traffic quantity/amount requirements profile?
   a. payload type analysis
   b. transaction analysis
   c. protocol stack analysis
p.505 d. traffic volume analysis

228   Chapter 12

25. If certain mission-critical transactions cannot tolerate an occasional faulty data circuit, then what must be designed into the initial network design configuration?
    a. multiple protocol stacks
    b. encryption methods
p.506 c. redundant links
    d. none of the above

26. There are several performance evaluation criterion for network configurations, such as
    a. how fast the vendor can implement the design
p.508 b. whether sufficient redundancy implemented to support mission critical applications
    c. whether the network is capable of interoperating with a Wide Area Network
    d. should a network consultant be hired

27. By compiling the results of the data traffic analysis report and the circuit configuration diagram on this diagram, the required processing ability of the sought-after device can be documented.
    a. H-S-M
    b. OSI
    c. ISDN
p.508 d. I-P-O

28. Which of the following is a product of the implementation phase when wrapping up the network analysis and design methodology?
    a. prepare a detailed, comprehensive budget
    b. final buy-in by all affected parties
p.510 c. detailed list of tasks and responsible parties with due dates
    d. comprehensive systems and networking budget model

29. Networking and systems budgets typically focus only on which costs of the new system?
p.512 a. acquisition costs
    b. operations costs
    c. incremental change/anticipated growth costs
    d. none of the above

30 The most important element of any systems or networking implementation is
    a. networking hardware
    b. networking software
p.514 c. people
    d. training

31. Which type of software is used to automate the entire network development life cycle process?
    a. CASE
p.514 b. CANE
    c. SANE
    d. INSANE

32. Performance engineering software tools model the overall network performance using a series of mathematical formulae and are also known as
    a. maintenance software
    b. CASE software
p.517 c. simulation software
    d. none of the above

33. With regard to proactive LAN management software, which are desired limits of certain performance characteristics which are set by the user?
p.519 a. thresholds
    b. baseline performance statistics
    c. what-if network analysis statistics
    d. object oriented network objects

34. To aid in network management, some management systems can record normal performance characteristics over an extended period of time, which are known as
    a. thresholds
p.519 b. baseline performance statistics
    c. what-if network analysis statistics
    d. object oriented network objects

35. A common network information platform (CNIP) used by vendors of computer-assisted network engineering software merely to pass the output from their particular software product to a neutral data platform enables
    a. CASE tools
    b. vertical integration
p.519 c. horizontal integration
    d. baseline performance statistics

36. Which of the following is perhaps the most traditional approach to measuring cost/benefit and is well suited to incremental upgrades of existing systems?
    a. TBO
p.513 b. ROI
    c. TCO
    d. IPO

230   Chapter 12

37. Which of the following is a popular measure for objectively comparing the relative costs of alternative approaches or potential technology strategies?
   a. TBO
   b. ROI
p.513 c. TCO
   d. IPO

Fill-In the Blank Questions

1. Two key components to any systems development effort are the process and the _____ of each stage of that development life cycle.

2. The network analysis and design methodology is consistent with previous information systems development models in that business, application, and data requirements definition are prerequisites to _____ design activities.

3. One of the first things an outside consultant, sometimes called a(n) _____, should do when conducting an investigation into a problem is to identify all parties potentially affected by the perceived problem.

4. The problem definition and its associated recommendations for further study are sometimes referred to as a(n) _____.

5. By organizing the strategic information system design information into an understandable format and by adding detailed information concerning performance evaluation criteria for the data and network layers, a document known as (an) _____ is produced.

6. The _____ sets a minimum threshold of compliance for vendor proposals in order to warrant further consideration and invitations for demonstrations.

7. Following all of the vendor demonstrations comes time for the _____ decision.

8. _____ allows information systems and networking administrators to hire outside contractors to operate and maintain corporate information systems and networks.

9. In a comprehensive networking and systems budget, the _____ include estimated monthly costs for leased line or dial-up line usage as well as the estimated cost for the additional electricity required to run the new equipment.

10. _____ are a popular way to safely roll out new systems or networks by bringing only one part of the business or a single store on-line before implementing the new network throughout the business.

Answers

1. product p.483
2. network p.486
3. facilitator p.489
4. feasibility study p.491
5. RFP or Request For Proposal p.497
6. percent of fit goal p.502
7. make-or-buy p.503
8. Outsourcing p.503
9. operations costs p.512
10. Pilot tests p.513

232   Chapter 12

CASE STUDY AND ANSWERS

LONG ROAD TO ONLINE COMMERCE

Activities
1. Top-down model:

Business	Large projects have large budgets, multiple teams, often span the globe, and include several vendors. Network administrators are often trained on technical issues, but need training in order to manage high-stakes projects. IS specialty shops must now become business departments. Only two-thirds of applications development projects actually were completed with only 16 percent finished on time and budget. Project management statements should spell out the business case, list the people involved, and identify the people with the most influence over the project.
Applications	IS can no longer be stuck in the maintenance mode as they tended to legacy applications. Project management software should be used.
Data	n/a
Network	Many network administrators can manage a large WAN, but do not have the proper skills to run a business project from a business vice technical design standpoint.
Technology	Use of automated tools such as Microsoft Project and Workbench will help the manager keep control over large projects. Use of groupware can enhance the success of a project and keep it on time and budget.

2. Unanswered questions:
   More specific technological components need to be identified.
   What authority does a network administrator have in order to manage a large multi-faceted business project?
   How does a distributed client/server architecture affect the management of a large project?
   How does one develop a plan for how much time a large project should take?
   What are the components of a prototype system?

Business
1. They must juggle hefty budgets and allocate resources. Their work is often not seen by the user making it difficult for upper management to understand. Their projects often span the globe with team members on several continents. They must also work with several vendors.
2. Due to downsizing, many network managers have been pressed, untrained, into service as project managers.
3. Order enough pizzas for the team, and it'll come up with something.
4. You must get the work done through others, and must usher in all of a project's elements on time. Key would be developing a vision, defining a mission statement and following a process.
5. Training from and certification by the Project Management Institute is available.
6. The key to a solid mission is creating a sense of urgency. Team synergy is important, but you need a strong leader to keep the team moving.

Application
1. One-third of projects were canceled. Of those that saw completion, a scant 16 percent finished on time and on budget. The cost of corporate bungling is estimated to be $81 billion for canceled projects for 1995.

Data
1. n/a

Network
1. Network development projects tend to not be as sexy or flashy. They also span the globe with members on several continents and include several vendors, making it difficult to manage and coordinate a project.

Technology
1. Microsoft Project and Workbench can be used to manage a project. Lotus Notes 4.0 can facilitate communication among project teams.
2. Common sense is the best criterion for choosing project-management aids. Find a methodology that fits the situation.

CHAPTER 13

Network Security

ANSWERS TO CHAPTER REVIEW QUESTIONS

1. As interest and activity concerning the Internet has mushroomed, and as telecommuters and remote users are increasingly in need of access to corporate data, network security has become a dominant topic in data communications.

2. As illustrated in Figure 13-1, the SPDLC is aptly depicted as a cycle since evaluation processes validate the effectiveness of original analysis stages. Feedback from evaluation stages cause renewed analysis with possible ripple effects of changes in architecture or implemented technology. The feedback provided by such a cycle is ongoing, but will only work with proper training and commitment from the people responsible for the various processes depicted in the SPDLC.

3. In order to begin to define security requirements and the potential solutions to those requirements, a network analyst can create a matrix grid mapping all potential user groups against all potential corporate information resources. The security requirements assessment grid is meant to provide only an example of potential user groups and information resource categories. The grid should be modified to provide an accurate reflection of each different corporate security environment. Furthermore, the grid should be used as a dynamic strategic planning tool. It should be reviewed on a periodic basis and should be modified to reflect changes in either user groups or information resources. Only through on-going auditing, monitoring, evaluation, and analysis, can a security requirements assessment plan remain accurate and reflective of a changing corporate network environment.

4. Security measures that are too stringent can be just as damaging to user productivity as can a total lack of enforced security measures. The optimal balance point that is sought is the proper amount of implemented security process and technology that will adequately protect corporate information resources while optimizing user productivity.

5. Throughout the initial stages of these security policy development efforts, it is essential to remember the Critical Success Factors of the network development life cycle described in Chapter 12. Before proceeding blindly with a security policy development project, it is important to properly define the scope or limitations of the project. Figure 13-13 summarizes some of the critical success factors for network security policy implementation.

6. One way to organize an approach to security policy and architecture development is to use a model or framework such as ISO 7498/2 , the OSI Security Architecture. This framework maps fourteen different security services to specific layers of the OSI 7 Layer Reference Model. The OSI Model Security Architecture can be used as an open framework in which to categorize security technology and protocols, just as the OSI 7 Layer Model can be used to categorize internetworking technology and protocols. Although more specific and varying slightly in terminology from the five fundamental values listed in Figure 13-5, the OSI Security Architecture is consistent with and includes all of these fundamental values. As illustrated in Figure 13-6, the ISO 7498-2 Security Architecture could be used as a grid or checklist to assess whether or not the listed security service has been provided for each associated OSI Model layer protocols and by what technologies each service is to be provided. Not all services will necessarily be provided to all suggested layers in all corporate settings. This does not diminish the value of the OSI Security Architecture as a planning framework however.

7. Assets are corporate property of some value that require varying degrees of protection. In the case of network security, assets most often include corporate data and the network hardware, software, and media used to transport and store that data. Threats are processes or people that pose a potential danger to identified assets. A given asset can be potentially threatened by numerous threats. Threats can be intentional or unintentional, natural or man-made. Network related threats include hackers, line outages, fires, floods, power failures, equipment failures, dishonest employees, or incompetent employees. Vulnerabilities are the manner or path by which threats are able to attack assets. Vulnerabilities can be thought of as weak links in the overall security architecture and should be identified for every potential threat/asset combination. Vulnerabilities that have been identified can be blocked. Once vulnerabilities have been identified, a network analyst should proceed in developing defenses to these vulnerabilities. Which vulnerabilities should be dealt with first? How can a network analyst determine an objective means to prioritize vulnerabilities? By considering the risk, or probability of a particular threat successfully attacking a particular asset in a given amount of time via a particular vulnerability, network analysts are able to quantify the relative importance of threats and vulnerabilities. A word of caution however, risk analysis is a specialized field of study, and quantification of risks should not be viewed as an exact science. In identifying the proper prioritization of threats and vulnerabilities to be dealt with, network analysts should combine subjective instincts and judgment with objective risk analysis data. Once the order in which threats and vulnerabilities will be attacked has been determined, protective measures are designed and taken that effectively block the vulnerability in order to prevent threats from attacking assets. Among the major categories of potential protective measures are: virus protection, firewalls, authentication, and encryption.

8. Recalling that multiple vulnerabilities (paths) may exist between a given asset and a given threat, it should be obvious that multiple protective measures may need to be established between given threat/asset combinations.

9. Refer to figures 13-9, 13-10, and 13-12 for the roles of executives, management and users in the successful development and implementation of security policy.

10. Auditing as it relates to network security policy may be either automated or manual. Manual audits can be done by either internal or external personnel. Manual audits serve to verify the effectiveness of policy development and implementation, especially the extent to which people understand and effectively execute their assigned processes in the overall corporate security policy. Manual audits are also referred to as policy audits or off-line audits. Automated audits, otherwise known as event detection or real-time audits depend on software that is able to assess the weaknesses of your network security and security standards. Most audit software depends on capturing large amounts of event data and then filtering that data for exceptional or unusual events.

11. Most audit software depends on capturing large amounts of event data and then filtering that data for exceptional or unusual events. Captured events can be telephone calls, login attempts, network server directory access attempts, access to Internet news groups or web sites, or remote access attempts via dial-up lines. In order to generate meaningful exception reports, audit software allows users to create filters that will allow only those events deemed exceptional by the users to appear on reports. Intrusion detection systems test the perimeter of the enterprise network through dial modems, remote access servers, web servers, or internet access. In addition to merely detecting intrusions, such as unsuccessful login attempts over a pre-set limit, some tools are also able to provide automated responses to these intrusion attempts. Also, some of the more sophisticated intrusion detection systems are dynamic or self-learning and are able to become better at detecting intrusions or to adjust exception parameters as they gain experience in a given enterprise network environment.

12. Rather than passively gathering network statistics like auditing tools, security probes actively test various aspects of enterprise network security and report results and suggest improvements.

13. The term computer virus is generally used to describe any computer program or group of programs that gains access to a computer system or network with the potential to disrupt the normal activity of that system or network.

14. Viruses that are triggered by the passing of a certain date or time are referred to as time bombs while viruses that require a certain event to transpire are known as logic bombs.

15. When the actual virus is hidden inside an otherwise benign program and delivered to the target system or network to be infected it is known as a trojan horse.

16. Polymorphic viruses change their appearance each time an infected program is run in order to avoid detection.

17. Although specific to web technology and Java embedded programs, hostile applets could still be considered viruses. Attack applets are intent on serious security breaches, while malicious applets tend to be annoying rather than destructive. Hostile applets are unknowingly downloaded while web surfing.

18. As collaborative applications such as groupware have become more commonplace in corporations, a new method of virus infection and virus re-infection has emerged. Since groupware messages and data are stored in a shared database, and since documents can be distributed throughout the network for document conferencing or workflow automation, the virus is spread throughout the network. Moreover, since groupware servers usually replicate their databases in order to assure that all servers on the network are providing consistent information, the virus will continue to spread. Even if the virus is eliminated from the originating server, responses from still-infected replicated servers will re-infect the original server as the infection/re-infection cycle continues.

19. Virus scanning is the primary method for successful detection and removal. However, virus scanning software most often works off a library of known viruses, or more specifically the unique digital signatures of these viruses, while new viruses are appearing at the rate of nearly 200 per month. Because of this, it is important to buy virus scanning software whose vendor supplies updates of virus signatures at least once per month. In an effort to be more proactive than reactive, emulation technology attempts to detect as yet unknown viruses by running programs with a software emulation program known as a virtual PC. In so doing, the executing program can be examined in a safe environment for any unusual behavior or other tell-tale symptoms of resident viruses. The advantage of such programs is that they identify potentially unknown viruses based on their behavior rather than by relying on identifiable signatures of known viruses. Because of their ability to monitor behavior of programs, this category of anti-virus technology is also sometimes known as activity monitors. Such programs are also capable of trapping encrypted or polymorphic viruses that are capable of constantly changing their identities or signatures. In addition, some of these programs are self-learning, thereby increasing their knowledge of virus-like activity with experience.

20. The shortcoming of CRC and hashing checkers as anti-virus technology is that they are only able to detect viruses after infection, which may already be too late.

21. In order to prevent unauthorized access from the Internet into a company's confidential data, specialized software known as a firewall is often deployed. Firewall software usually runs on a dedicated server which is connected to, but outside of the corporate network.

22. A filter is a program which examines the source address and destination address of every incoming packet to the firewall server. Network access devices known as routers are also capable of filtering data packets. Filter tables are lists of addresses whose data packets and embedded messages are either allowed or prohibited from proceeding through the firewall server and into the corporate network. A filtering program which only examines

source and destination addresses and determines access based on the entries in a filter table is known as a port level filter or network level filter or packet filter. Application level filters, otherwise known as assured pipelines, application gateways, or proxies go beyond port level filters in their attempts to prevent unauthorized access to corporate data. While port level filters determine the legitimacy of the party asking for information, application level filters assure the validity of what they are asking for. Application level filters examine the entire request for data rather than just the source and destination addresses. Secure files can be marked as such and application level filters will not allow those files to be transferred, even to users authorized by port level filters.

23. Proxies are capable of approving or denying connections based on directionality. Users may be allowed to upload files but not download. Proxies introduce increased latency as compared to port level filtering.

24. An architectural variation of an application gateway that offers increased security is known as a dual-homed gateway. In this scenario, the application gateway is physically connected to the private secure network and the packet filtering router is connected to the nonsecure network or the Internet. Between the application gateway and the packet filter router is an area known as the screened subnet. Also attached to this screened subnet are information servers, WWW servers, or other servers that the company may wish to make available to outside users. However, all outside traffic still goes through the application gateway first, and then to the information servers. TCP/IP forwarding is disabled, and access to the private network is only available through one of the installed proxies. Remote logins are only allowed to the gateway host. Also refer to Figure 13-18.

25. An alternative to the dual-homed gateway that seeks to relieve all the reliance on the application gateway for all communication, both inbound and outbound, is known as a trusted gateway or trusted application gateway. In a trusted gateway, certain applications are identified as trusted and are able to bypass the application gateway entirely and are able to establish connections directly rather than be executed by proxy. In this way, outside users can access information servers and WWW servers without tying up the proxy applications on the application gateway. Again, refer to Figure 13-18.

26. Refer to Figure 13-18 for a clear and graphical differentiation between a trusted gateway and a dual homed gateway.

27. Internal firewalls include filters that work on the datalink, network, and application layers to examine communications that occur only on a corporation's internal network, inside the reach of traditional firewalls. Internal firewalls also act as access control mechanisms, denying access to any application for which a user does not have specific access approval. The fact that an estimated 60% of security attacks occur inside the firewall is the primary motivation for internal firewalls.

28. Authentication assures that users attempting to gain access to networks are really whom they claim to be.

29. Challenge-response token authentication involves the following steps:
    1. The user enters an assigned user ID and password at the client workstation.
    2. The token authentication server software returns a numeric string known as a challenge.
    3. The challenge number and a Personal ID Number are entered on the hand held Smart Card.
    4. The Smart Card displays a response number on the LCD screen.
    5. This response number is entered on the client workstation and transmitted back to the token authentication server.
    6. The token authentication server validates the response against the expected response from this particular user and this particular Smart Card. If the two match, the user is deemed authentic and the login session is enabled.

    Time synchronous token authentication uses slightly more sophisticated technology in order to simplify the challenge-response procedure somewhat. The result is that in time synchronous token authentication, there is no server to client challenge step.
    1. Every 60 seconds, the time synchronous Smart Card and the server-based software generate a new access code.
    2. The user enters their UserID, a Personal ID Number, and the access code currently displayed on the Smart Card.
    3. The server receives the access code and authenticates the user by comparing the received access code to the expected access code unique to that Smart Card that was generated at the server in time synchronous fashion.

    Figure 13-21 differentiates between challenge-response token authentication and time synchronous token authentication.

30. Biometric authentication can authenticate users based on fingerprints, palm prints, retinal patterns, voice recognition or other physical characteristics.

31. Perhaps the most well known combination authentication/authorization software is Kerberos, developed originally at Massachusetts Institute of Technology and marketed commercially by a variety of firms. The Kerberos architecture is illustrated in Figure 13-22. As illustrated in Figure 13-22, a Kerberos architecture consists of three key components: Kerberos client software, Kerberos authentication server software, and Kerberos application server software

32. Kerberos enforces authentication and authorization through the use of a ticket-based system. An encrypted ticket is issued for each server to client session and is valid only for a pre-set amount of time. The ticket is only valid for connections between a designated client and server, thus precluding users from accessing servers or applications for which they are not properly authorized.

33. With private key encryption the decrypting device must use the same algorithm or method to decode or decrypt the data as the encrypting device used to encrypt the data. For this reason private key encryption is sometimes also known as symmetric encryption.

The encryption key customizes the commonly known algorithm to prevent anyone without this private key from possibly decrypting the document. This private key must be known by the both the sending and receiving encryption devices and allows so many unique combinations (nearly 2 to the 64th power), that unauthorized decryption is nearly impossible. The safe and reliable distribution of these private keys among numerous encryption devices can be difficult. If this private key is somehow intercepted, the integrity of the encryption system is compromised. In Public Key Encryption, the sending encryption device encrypts a document using the intended recipient's public key and the originating party's private key. This public key is readily available in a public directory or is sent by the intended recipient to the message sender. However, in order to decrypt the document, the receiving encryption/decryption device must be programmed with their own private key and the sending party's public key. In this method, the need for transmission of private keys between sending and receiving parties is eliminated. As an added security measure, Digital Signature Encryption provides an electronic means of guaranteeing authenticity of the sending party and assurance that encrypted documents have not been altered during transmission. Figure 13-23 illustrates the differences between private key encryption, public key encryption, and digital signature encryption, while Figure 13-24 summarizes some key facts about currently popular encryption standards.

34. Public key dissemination must be managed in such a way that users can be assured that public keys received are actually the public keys of the companies or organizations that they are alleged to be. This added level of assurance is provided by public key certificates. X.509 is an international standard for public key certificates. Third party key certification services, or certificate authorities (CA), issue the public keys along with a certificate assuring the authenticity of the key. Such certification authorities issue public keys of other organizations, along with certificates of authenticity, assured by their own digital signature. VeriSign is one example of a trusted third party issuer of X.509 public-key certificates. The U.S. Postal Service has also announced plans to begin issuing public key certificates.

35. Authentication products must be integrated with existing information systems and applications development efforts. APIs (Application program interfaces) are the means by which authentication products are able to integrate with client/server applications. Beyond APIs are application development environments or software development kits that combine an application development language with the supported APIs. APIs or application development environments must be compatible with the programming language in which applications are to be developed. The alternative would be that security software would have to be "hard-coded" into applications.

36. Remote Authentication Dial-In User Service (RADIUS) is supported by a wide variety of remote access technology and offers the potential to enable centralized management of remote access users and technology. The RADIUS architecture is illustrated in Figure 13-25. RADIUS allows network managers to centrally manager remote access users, access methods, and logon restrictions. It allows centralized auditing capabilities such as

keeping track of volume of traffic sent and amount of time on-line. RADIUS also enforces remote access limitations such as server access restrictions or on-line time limitations. For authentication, it supports Password Authentication Protocol (PAP), Challenge Handshake Authentication Protocol (CHAP), and SecurID token authentication.

37. Secure HTTP is a secure version of HTTP which requires both client and server S-HTTP versions to be installed for secure end-to-end encrypted transmission. S-HTTP, based on public key encryption, is described as providing security at the document or application level since it works with the actual HTTP applications to secure documents and messages. S-HTTP uses Digital Signature Encryption to assure that the document possesses both authenticity and message integrity. SSL is described as wrapping an encrypted envelope around HTTP transmissions. Whereas S-HTTP can only be used to encrypt Web documents, SSL can be wrapped around other Internet service transmissions such as FTP, telnet, and Gopher as well as HTTP. SSL is a connection level encryption method providing security to the network link itself. SSL Version 3 (SSL3) added support for more key exchange and encryption algorithms as well as separate keys for authentication and encryption. SSL and S-HTTP are not competing or conflicting standards although they are sometimes viewed that way. In an analogy to a postal service scenario, SSL provides the locked postal delivery vehicle while S-HTTP provides the sealed, tamper-evident envelope which allows only the intended recipient to view the confidential document contained within.

38. Password Authentication Protocol is the simpler of the two authentication protocols designed for dial-in communication. PAP repeatedly sends the user ID and password to the authenticating system in clear text pairs until it is either acknowledged or the connection is dropped. There is no encryption performed with PAP. Challenge Handshake Authentication Protocol provides a more secure means for establishing dial-in communication. It uses a three-way challenge that includes the user ID, password and also a key that encrypts the ID and password. The process of sending the pair to the authentication system is the same as with PAP, but the encryption reduces the chance that someone will be able to pick-up the ID and password and use it to access a system.

39. An Internet E-Mail specific encryption standard which also uses digital signature encryption to guarantee the authenticity, security, and message integrity of received e-mail is known as PGP which stands for Pretty Good Privacy. PGP overcomes inherent security loopholes with public/private key security schemes by implementing a Web of Trust in which e-mail users electronically sign each other's public keys to create an interconnected group of public key users. Digital signature encryption is provided using a combination of RSA and MD5 (Message Direct Version 5) encryption techniques. Combined documents and digital signatures are then encrypted using **IDEA** (International Data Encryption Algorithm) which makes use of one-time 128-bit keys known as session keys. PGP/MIME overcomes PGP's inability to encrypt multimedia (MIME) objects.

40. Secure Electronic Transactions (SET) are a series of standards to assure the confidentiality of electronic commerce transactions. These standards are being largely promoted by credit card giants VISA and MasterCard. SET standards are specifically aimed at bank-card transactions over the Internet.

41. In order to provide virtual private networking capabilities using the Internet as an enterprise network backbone, specialized tunneling protocols needed to be developed that could establish private, secure channels between connected systems. One shortcoming of the proposed specification is that it does not deal with security issues such as encryption and authentication.

42. IPsec is a protocol that ensures encrypted communications across the Internet via virtual private networks through the use of manual key exchange. IPsec supports only IP based communications. IPsec is a standard that, in theory at least, should enable interoperability between firewalls supporting the protocol. Although firewalls of the same brand seem to interoperate sufficiently via IPsec, that does not seem to be the case between different brands of firewall technology.

43. Transport Mode ESP is used to encrypt the data carried by the IP packet. The contents of the data field of an IP (network layer) packet are the upper layer or transport layer protocols TCP (connection-oriented) or UDP (connectionless). These transport layer envelopes encapsulate upper layer data. Tunnel Mode ESP encrypts the entire IP packet including its own header. This mode is effective at countering network analyzers or sniffers from capturing IP address information. Tunnel mode is most often used in a network topology that includes a firewall that separates a protected network from an external non-secure network.

44. In order to maintain proper security over a widely distributed enterprise network, it is essential to be able to conduct certain security related processes from a single, centralized, security management location. Among these processes or functions are the following:
Single Point of Registration (SPR) allows a network security manager to enter a new user (or delete a terminated user) from a single centralized location and assign all associated rights, privileges, and access control to enterprise resources from this single point rather than having to enter this new user's information on multiple resources distributed throughout the enterprise.
Single Sign-On (SSO) also sometimes known as Secure Single Sign-On (SSSO) allows the user to login to the enterprise network and to be authenticated from their client PC location. It is not necessary for the user to remember a variety of different userids and passwords to the numerous different enterprise servers from which they may request services. Since this is the single entry point onto the enterprise network for this user, auditing software can be used to keep non-repudiatable records of all activities and transactions. Any of the variety of authentication technologies discussed earlier can be used in support of single sign-on.

Single Access Control View allows the user's access from their client workstation to only display those resources that the user actually has access to. Any differences between server platforms should be shielded from the user. The user should not need to memorize different commands or control interfaces for the variety of enterprise servers that a user may need to access.

45. The primary focus of the Orange Book is on providing confidential protection of sensitive information based on six fundamental requirements: Security Policy, Marking, Identification, Accountability, Assurance, and Continuous Protection. It is broken into two primary parts; the first is illustrated in Figure 13-28. It specifies the criteria that must be met in order to achieve a specific rating. The criteria are defined in hierarchical fashion, with four different ratings possible. The 'A' rating is the most secure possible and the 'D' rating corresponds to the least secure rating possible. Specifically, C2 rating defines protection as controlled access, encapsulating resources and providing login and explicit autiding.

46. The Clipper Chip initiative proposed that every phone and data communications device in the United States would be equipped with a Clipper Chip to support encryption. The part of the proposal that had businesses and individuals concerned was that the government would hold a spare set of keys that could decrypt any message encrypted by a Clipper Chip device.

47. A key recovery mechanism will offer a back door into encrypted data for the government. Key recovery schemes basically assure that a spare set of encryption keys are always available. With key recovery, the actual information used to reconstruct a key travels with the message header. However, someone with the key decryption codes (the spare set of keys) must combine the decryption codes with the key information in the message header in order to decrypt the message.

48. The big question with key recovery seems to be, "Who will hold the keys?" Key Escrow agencies, otherwise known as Trusted Third Parties, are the most commonly proposed solution.

49. If key recovery were to be extended to a domestic basis, the implications could be phenomenal. Everyone who uses the Internet for communication would need a key and a key escrow agent. This could mean tens of millions of keys unless some type of key sharing was initiated.

TEST QUESTIONS

True/False Questions

1. Enterprise network security goals must be set by network managers. F/529

2. To help the network analyst define security requirements and potential solutions the security requirements assessment grid should be used. T/530

3. Network vulnerabilities are processes or people that pose a potential danger to identified assets. F/536

4. Policy audits depend on software that is able to assess the weaknesses of your network security and security standards. F/543

5. Viruses that are triggered by the passing of a certain date or time are referred to as time bombs while viruses that require a certain event to transpire are known as logic bombs. T/545

6. The most common physical transport mechanism of the spread of viruses is the diskette. T/545

7. The overall purpose of authorization is to assure that users attempting to gain access to networks are really whom they claim to be. F/555

8. Encryption involves the changing of data into an indecipherable form prior to transmission. T/560

9. CHAP provides a secure means for establishing dial-in communication by using a three-way challenge that includes the user ID, password and also a key that encrypts the ID and password. T/566

10. C-2 certification and C-2 compliance are one and the same. F/572

Multiple Choice Questions

1. Assuring that implemented policy and technology are meeting initial goals would fall under which of the following Security Policy Development Life Cycle processes?
    a. Identification of business related security issues
    b. Architecture and process design
p.531   c. Audit impact of security technology and processes
    d. Evaluate effectiveness of current architecture and processes

2. This fundamental value of network security policy development assures that even authorized users are only allowed access to those information and network resources that they are supposed to access.
   a. Authorization
   b. Privacy
   c. Data integrity
p.534 d. Access control

3. This fundamental value of network security policy development assures that data is genuine and cannot be changed without proper controls.
   a. Authorization
   b. Privacy
p.534 c. Data integrity
   d. Access control

4. Which of the following terms is used to define corporate property of some value that require varying degrees of protection?
p.536 a. assets
   b. threats
   c. vulnerabilities
   d. risks

5. Which of the following terms is used to define the manner or path by which threats are able to attack assets?
p.536 a. vulnerabilities
   b. risks
   c. protective measures
   d. certification programs

6. Which of the following protective measures would be used against a trojan horse attack?
   a. passwords
   b. service filtering
p.538 c. firewalls
   d. authentication

7. This area for development of acceptable use policies deals with access of offices, computer rooms and visitor policies.
   a. remote access policy
p.540 b. physical access policy
   c. software license policy
   d. password protection and management policy

8. An auditing technique which depends on software that is able to assess the weaknesses of your network security and security standards is known as a(n)
   a. manual audit
   b. policy audit
   c. off-line audit
p.543 d. real-time audit

9. SATAN, which actively tests various aspects of enterprise network security and reports results is a type of
   a. virus protection
p.543 b. security probe
   c. firewall
   d. gateway

10. Virus protection must include which of the following in order to be effective?
    a. policy
    b. people
    c. technology
p.544 d. all of the above must be included

11. This term is used to define any computer program or group of programs that gain access to a computer system or network with the potential to disrupt the normal activity of that system or network.
p.544 a. virus
    b. proxy
    c. security probe
    d. gateway

12. A virus which requires a certain event to transpire is called a
    a. trojan horse
    b. time bomb
p.545 c. logic bomb
    d. polymorphic virus

13. A virus which hides inside an otherwise benign program and is delivered to the target system or network is called a
p.545 a. trojan horse
    b. time bomb
    c. logic bomb
    d. polymorphic virus

248   Chapter 13

14. This type of virus can change its appearance each time an infected program is run in order to avoid detection.
    a. trojan horse
    b. time bomb
    c. logic bomb
p.546 d. polymorphic virus

15. Which of the following is the primary method for successful virus detection and removal?
    a. firewalls
    b. packet filtering
p.548 c. virus scanning
    d. password protection

16. If the point of attack for a virus is the client PC, which of the following protective measures would be most effective?
p.549 a. strict diskette scanning policy with auto-scan at system start-up
    b. firewalls
    c. strict policy with respect to linking to the corporate network after linking to other sites
    d. rigorous backup in case of major outbreak

17. If the point of attack for a virus is through remote access users, which of the following protective measures would be most effective?
    a. strict diskette scanning policy with auto-scan at system start-up
    b. firewalls
p.549 c. strict policy with respect to linking to the corporate network after linking to other sites
    d. rigorous backup in case of major outbreak

18. If the point of attack for a virus is the server, which of the following protective measures would be most effective?
    a. strict diskette scanning policy with auto-scan at system start-up
    b. firewalls
    c. strict policy with respect to linking to the corporate network after linking to other sites
p.549 d. rigorous backup in case of major outbreak

19. This type of filter examines the entire request for data rather than just the source and destination addresses.
    a. port level filter
    b. network level filter
p.550 c. application level filter
    d. packet filter

20. This type of gateway is physically connected to the private secure network and the packet filtering router is connected to the nonsecure network or the Internet.
    a. packet filter firewall gateway
    b. trusted gateway
    c. application gateway
p.551 d. dual-homed gateway

21. This type of gateway seeks to relieve all the reliance on the application gateway for all communication, both inbound and outbound.
    a. packet filter firewall gateway
p.551 b. trusted gateway
    c. internal firewall gateway
    d. dual-homed gateway

22. Which of the following firewall functional characteristics deals with how the firewall will react when illegal access has been detected?
    a. proxy isolation
    b. attach protection
p.554 c. violation notification
    d. system monitoring

23. Which of the following authentication processes uses a one-time-use session password but eliminates the server to client challenge step?
p.556 a. time synchronous token authentication
    b. biometric authentication
    c. challenge response token authentication
    d. challenge asynchronous token authentication

24. Which of the following authentication processes is based on fingerprints, palm prints, retinal patterns, voice recognition or other physical characteristics?
    a. time synchronous token authentication
p.557 b. biometric authentication
    c. challenge response token authentication
    d. challenge asynchronous token authentication

25. The condition when a biometric authentication device's comparison algorithm is set too sensitively which results in valid users being denied access is known as
    a. false accepts
    b. false readings
    c. exceptions
p.558 d. false rejects

26. If the biometric device comparison algorithm is not set sensitively enough these will occur when impostors are allowed access because the comparison was not detailed enough.

p.558
a. false accepts
b. false readings
c. exceptions
d. false rejects

27. Which of the following terms is used to assure that properly authenticated users only access the network resources for which they are properly authorized?
a. authentication
b. login authentication

p.558 c. authorization
d. encryption

28. Kerberos enforces authentication and authorization by issuing one of these for each server to client session, and is valid only for a pre-set amount of time.
a. realm
b. token
c. brokered authorization

p.559 d. ticket

29. In this method of encryption, the need for transmission of private keys between sending and receiving parties is eliminated.
a. private key encryption

p.561 b. public key encryption
c. digital signature encryption
d. symmetric encryption

30. This type of encryption provides an electronic means of guaranteeing authenticity of the sending party and assurance that encrypted documents have not been altered during transmission.
a. private key encryption
b. public key encryption

p.561 c. digital signature encryption
d. symmetric encryption

31. Authentication products can be integrated with existing information systems and applications development efforts through the use of

p.563
a. APIs
b. public key certificates
c. certificate authorities
d. digital IDs

32. With regard to remote access security which of the following is **not** one of the three tiers used in the RADIUS architecture?
    a. remote access devices
    b. enterprise databases
    c. RADIUS authentication server
p.565 d. X.509 public key certificate authorities

33. This standard for encrypting traffic on the WWW is based on public key encryption and is described as providing security at the document or application level since it works with the actual HTTP applications to secure documents and messages.
p.565 a. S-HTTP
    b. SSL
    c. PAP
    d. CHAP

34. In the analogy to a postal service scenario, this standard for encrypting traffic on the WWW provides the locked postal delivery vehicle.
    a. S-HTTP
p.566 b. SSL
    c. PAP
    d. CHAP

35. This standard for encrypting traffic on the WWW is described as wrapping an encrypted envelope around HTTP transmissions.
    a. S-HTTP
p.565 b. SSL
    c. PAP
    d. CHAP

36. Which of the following authentication protocols repeatedly sends the user ID and password to the authenticating system in clear text pairs until it is either achkowledged or the connection is dropped?
    a. S-HTTP
    b. SSL
p.566 c. PAP
    d. CHAP

37. Which of the following authentication protocols uses a three-way challenge that includes the user ID, password and also a key that encrypts the ID and password?
    a. S-HTTP
    b. SSL
    c. PAP
p.566 d. CHAP

38. This encryption technique is targeted primarily toward on-line commerce and financial transactions.
    a. SSL
p.566 b. PCT
    c. PGP
    d. PEM

39. Which of the following is an Internet e-mail specific encryption standard which also uses digital signature encryption to guarantee the authenticity, security and message integrity of received e-mail?
    a. SSL
    b. PAP
p.566 c. PGP
    d. PEM

40. This virtual private network tunneling protocol ensures encrypted communications across the Internet via virtual private networks through the use of manual key exchange and supports only IP-based communications.
    a. PPTP
    b. PPP
p.568 c. IPsec
    d. IPTP

41. Which of the following processes used to maintain security over a widely distributed enterprise network allows the user to login to the enterprise network and to be authenticated from their client PC location?
    a. Single Point of Registration
p.569 b. Single Sign-On
    c. Single Access Control View
    d. C-2 Certification

42. Which of the following standards making organizations is the U.S. representative to the ISO?
    a. NIST
    b. NSA
p.570 c. ANSI
    d. OSI

43. The Orange Book certification class which provides controlled access using encapsulated resources, login and explicit auditing.
    a. D
    b. A1
    c. B3
p.572 d. C2

44. This encryption technology concept would allow a back door into encrypted data for the government by allowing the government to hold a spare set of keys that could decrypt any message encrypted by this technology.
    a. key recovery mechanism
p.573 b. Clipper Chip initiative
    c. key escrow agencies
    d. none of the above

Fill-In the Blank Questions

1. _____ is the probability of a particular threat successfully attacking a particular asset in a given amount of time via a particular vulnerability.

2. Policy audits, also called _____ audits, serve to verify the effectiveness of policy development and implementation, especially the extent to which people understand and effectively execute their assigned processes in the overall corporate security policy.

3. Rather than passively gathering network statistics like auditing tools, _____ actively test various aspects of enterprise network security and report results and suggest improvements.

4. In order to prevent unauthorized access from the Internet into a company's confidential data, specialized software known as a(n) _____ is often deployed.

5. A _____ is a program which examines the source address and destination address of every incoming packet to the firewall server.

6. _____ authentication technology provides one-time-use session passwords that are authenticated by associated server software.

7. Changed, unmeaningful encrypted data is known as _____.

8. The Internet security standard, promoted by credit card giants VISA and MasterCard, aimed at bank-card transactions is known as _____.

9. _____ Mode ESP encrypts the entire IP packet including its own header.

10. A vendor can claim C2 _____ even if they have not gone through the entire C2 security certification process with their product.

Answers

1. risk p.536
2. manual p.542
3. security probes p.543
4. firewall p.548
5. filter p.550
6. Token p.555
7. ciphertext p.560
8. SET or Secure Electronic Transactions p.567
9. Tunnel p.569
10. compliance p.572

CASE STUDY AND ANSWERS

TACKLING INTERNET SECURITY

Activities

1. Top-down model:

Business	Adequate security must be provided in order to move a business to the Internet using TCP/IP.
	A piecemeal approach to information security cannot provide adequate security for business
Applications	Security must be transparent.
	Security is complicated when no integration of products is possible.
	Security standards must be set up for applications to interoperate properly.
	Configuration and testing of security software is difficult.
Data	Data needs to be encrypted without impacting severely on performance.
	Different types of data require different security.
Network	Security should be transparently built into the network
	Security must be an end-to-end process whenever a connection is made.
	Network standards must include security such as IPsec for point-to-point encryption between firewalls.
Technology	Some specialized hardware may be needed in order to deliver true security.
	Firewalls must be integrated with other technologies such as encryption and digital certificates.
	Security should be integrated with LAN equipment.

2. Unanswered questions:

   How much does security cost the business?
   When will integrated, standardized security products be available?
   How will security be built in to hardware, and what cost will this have in terms of performance and dollars?
   How will firewalls be integrated with other technologies such as encryption and digital certificates?

Business
1. Security products lag behind other Internet products in terms of interoperability and integration with network software and hardware and are difficult to test and configure as well as a proliferation of firewalls without the development of other aspects of security management all contribute to the problem.
2. A piecemeal approach to information security along with a lack of standards are sources to the problem.
3. Integrating firewalls, encryption, and authentication, and developing standards will help solve the security problems.
4. The long term trend will be to integrate firewall technology into the network hardware and software.
5. Standards should help in the integration and interoperability of network products as well as configuration, to provide transparent security to the business.

Application
1. Security products lag behind other Internet products in terms of interoperability and integration with network software and hardware.
2. Refer to figures 13-19, 13-20, and 13-24 in the text.

Data
1. Firewalls do not integrate with digital certificates and data encryption technologies and need to become standardized in network applications.
2. Standardization of security protocols should help.

Network
1. Firewalls, digital certificates, and data encryption technologies must become better integrated.
2. IPsec is a protocol that ensures encrypted communications across the Internet via virtual private networks through the use of manual key exchange.
3. ISAKMP (Internet Security Association Key Management Protocol) is a standard which defines a security architecture for managing the cryptographic keys necessary for electronic commerce and virtual private networks.

Technology
1. Firewalls are not standardized nor are they integrated with network hardware and software. They require configuration and testing and if not properly configured, they will not work properly.
2. Standardization seems to be the best solution along with building in security into the network hardware and software.

CHAPTER 14

Network Management

ANSWERS TO CHAPTER REVIEW QUESTIONS

1. Network managers must simultaneously deploy new services, control costs, provide competitive advantage and provide guaranteed quality of service in an increasingly complicated, multi-vendor, multi-platform, multi-protocol environment. The response to these pressures is to combine the processes embedded in the top down model and the network development life cycle. The top down model forces the network manager to constantly evaluate business objectives, the nature of the applications that will meet those business objectives, the nature of the data that will support those applications, the functional requirements of the network that will deliver that data, and finally, the configuration of the technology that will provide the required network functionality. The network development life cycle forces the network manager to engage in an on-going process of network monitoring, planning, analysis, design, modeling, and implementation based on network performance. Figure 14-1 helps to explain further cost containment.

2. Outsourcing some network management duties can be cheaper especially if in-house talent is unavailable, however one must clearly identify the processes to be outsourced, establish communication and evaluation mechanisms along with penalties or bonuses based on performance.

3. Systems Administration focuses on the management of client and server computers and the operating systems and network operating systems that allow the client and server computers to communicate.
Enterprise Network Management focuses on the hardware, software, media, and network services required to seamlessly link and effectively manage distributed client and server computers across an enterprise.

4. Refer to figure 14-4 which lists and explains the five OSI categories of network management.

5. Figure 14-5 clearly describes the components which make up a consolidated service desk. A consolidated service desk has an approach which offers a number of benefits over previous network management technologies:
    - As a single point of contact for all network and application problem resolution, appropriate personnel processes can be matched with associated network management technologies. This match of standardized processes with technology yields more predictable service levels and accountability. CSD software should include features

to support problem escalation, trouble ticketing and tracking and productivity management reporting. Users should be able to easily check on the status of the resolution of reported problems.
- The consolidation of all problem data at a single location allows correlations between problem reports to be made, thereby enabling a more proactive rather than reactive management style. Incorporated remote control software will allow CSD personnel to take over end-user computers and fix problems remotely in a swift manner.
- Resolutions to known user inquiries can be incorporated into intelligent help desk support systems in order to expedite problem resolution and make the most effective use of support personnel. On-line knowledge-bases allow users to solve their own problems in many cases.
- The consolidated services desk can also handle other processes not directly related to problem resolution such as inventory and asset tracking, asset optimization through the use of such technology as license metering software, and can also coordinate hardware and/or software upgrades. Software upgrades could be centrally handled by electronic software distribution technology. The management of these systems changes is referred to as change management.
- Network security policies, procedures, and technology can also be consolidated at the CSD.
- Eliminates or reduces "console clutter" in which every monitored system has its own console. In large multinational corporations, this can lead to well over 100 consoles. Recalling, that all of these consoles must be monitored by people, console consolidation can obviously lead to cost containment.

6. Important advantages of server management software are shown in figure 14-6. Some server management software runs on the managed servers and can have an impact on performance. Some also require a dedicated management workstation. The software can be complicated to install, configure and control.

7. Because the consolidated service desk is held accountable for its level of service to end-users, it is essential that help desk management technology be able to gather the statistics necessary to measure the impact of the consolidated service desk. Since a significant amount of the interaction with a consolidated service is via the phone, it is important for help desk management software to be able to interact with call center management technology.

8. The heart of any help desk management software package is the knowledge base, that contains not just the resolutions or answers to problems, but the logic structure or decision tree that takes a given problem and leads the help desk staff person through a series of questions to the appropriate solution. The portion of the software that sifts through the knowledge base to the proper answer is sometimes referred to as the search engine. Both components are necessary to provide effective help desk services.

9. Policy-based management tools in their simplest form are able to automate certain tasks by using job scheduling utilities to schedule background and after hours jobs. Another key point about these tools is that they are able to administer multiple different types of client platforms such as DOS, Windows 3.X, Windows 95, Windows NT, OS/2, HP-UX, AIX, SunOS, Solaris, to name but a few. More advanced tools not only automate administrative tasks, but also provide an interface for managing the corporate desktop configuration policies themselves. Administrators are able to set policies for an entire global enterprise, for specified domains or for individual workstations.

10. Desktop management is primarily concerned with the configuration and support of desktop workstations. The overall desktop management architecture is known as the DMI or Desktop Management Interface and is illustrated in Figure 14-9.

11. Desktop management software is primarily concerned with the configuration and support of desktop workstations while enterprise network management software is concerned with the entire enterprise including the network devices, communications lines, and the servers. DMI-compliant desktop management systems store performance and configuration statistics in a (Management Information Format), and enterprise management systems employ a MIB. Desktop management technology offerings from different vendors are best characterized as suites of associated desktop management applications. Current offerings differ in the variety of management modules include within a given suite as well as the extent of integration between suite modules.

12. A lack of effective application management tools and underlying application management protocols that can expose an application's dependencies and measure numerous aspects of performance, and a lack of standards of what application performance information should be gathered and how that information should be reported are limitations faced by distributed application management.. A standard API called application response measurement (ARM) and an IETF proposed standard for web-based enterprise management help to overcome the limitations.

13. Agents from the numerous individual networking devices forward network management information to Enterprise Network Management Systems which compile and report network operation statistics to the end user, most often in some type of graphical format. Enterprise Network Management Systems are really management application programs running on a management server. An alternative to the centralized enterprise management console approach known as the distributed device manager (DDM) has begun to emerge. DDM takes more of an end-to-end full network view of the enterprise network as opposed to the centralized enterprise management console architecture that takes more of an individual device or element focus.

14. As originally conceived, the enterprise management console would collect the performance data from all of the devices, or elements, comprising an enterprise network in a single, centralized location. However, as networks grew in both complexity and size,

and the numbers of devices to be managed exploded, the amount of management traffic flowing over the enterprise network has begun to reach unacceptable levels.

15. The network management information gathered must be stored in some type of database with an index and standardized field definitions so that network management workstations can easily access this data. A MIB, or Management Information Base as these databases are known, can differ in the fields defined for different vendor's networking devices. These fields within the MIBs are known as objects. One fairly standard MIB is known as the RMON MIB, which stands for Remote Network Monitoring MIB. Finally, a protocol is required to encapsulate the management data for delivery by network and transport layer protocols. Partly due to the dominance of TCP/IP as the internetworking protocol of choice, SNMP (Simple Network Management Protocol) is the defacto standard for delivering enterprise management data.

16. Distributed network probes gather information from a variety of network devices manufactured by multiple vendors and relay that information to numerous distributed device manager consoles. Probes are strategically placed throughout the enterprise network, especially at junctions of LAN and WAN segments in order to isolate the source of network traffic problems. Management traffic is minimized and remains localized rather than monopolizing enterprise network bandwidth supplying the centralized enterprise management console. Agents and RMON probes run on various networking devices and forward their network management information to a centralized Enterprise Network Management system.

17. A proposed protocol currently under development by the DMTF (Desktop Management Task Force) that would support HMMS is known as CIM or Common Information Model. CIM would permit management data gathered from a variety of enterprise and desktop voice and data technology to all be transported, processed, displayed, and stored by a single CIM-compliant web browser. Management data to be used by CIM would be stored in MOF (Modified Object Format) as opposed to DMI's MIF format or SNMP's MIB format. Figure 14-15 illustrates the interaction of the various types of management data.

18. Another possible standard for distributed application management is a proposed IETF standard known as web-based enterprise management (WBEM) that integrates SNMP, HTTP, and DMI (desktop management interface) into an application management architecture that can use common web browser software as its user interface. The WBEM logical architecture is illustrated in Figure 14-14. The overall intention of the architecture is that the network manager could manage any networked device or application from any location on the network, via any HMMP (Hypermedia Management Protocol)-compliant browser. Existing network and desktop management protocols such as SNMP and DMI may either interoperate or be replaced by HMMP. Management data from a variety of software agents would be incorporated into the web based enterprise management architecture via the HMMS (Hypermedia Management Schema). All web-based management information is stored and retrieved by the request broker known as HMOM

(Hypermedia Object Manager). The WBEM architecture is only a logical design at this point and implemented products and protocols are yet to become reality.

19. The original SNMP protocol required internetworking device specific agents to be polled for SNMP encapsulated management data. Alarm conditions or exceptions to pre-set thresholds could not be directly reported on an as-needed basis from the agents to the enterprise network management software. The lack of ability of agents to initiate communications with Enterprise Network Management Systems causes constant polling of agents to transpire. As a result of the constant polling, considerable network bandwidth is consumed. Also, the original SNMP protocol did not provide for any means of manager to manager communication. As a result, only one enterprise network manager could be installed on a given network forcing all internetworked devices to report directly to the single enterprise network manager. Hierarchical arrangements in which regional managers are able to filter raw management data and pass only exceptional information to enterprise managers is not possible with the original SNMP.Another major shortcoming of the original SNMP is that it was limited to using TCP/IP as its transport protocol. It was therefore unusable on NetWare (IPX/SPX), Macintosh (Appletalk) or other networks. Finally, SNMP does not offer any security features which would authenticate valid polling managers or encrypt traffic between agents and managers. Through a new SNMP2 procedure known as Bulk Retrieval Mechanism, managers can retrieve several pieces of network information at a time from a given agent. This precludes the need for a constant request and reply mechanism for each and every piece of network management information desired. Agents have also been given increased intelligence which enables them to send error or exception conditions to managers when requests for information cannot be met. SNMP2 allows the establishment of multiple manager entities within a single network. As a result, large networks that were managed by a single manager under SNMP can now be managed by multiple managers in a hierarchical arrangement in SNMP2. Overall network traffic is reduced as network management information is confined to the management domains of the individual network segment managers. SNMP2 works transparently with Appletalk, IPX, and OSI transport protocols. Increased security in SNMP2 allows not just monitoring and management of remote network devices, but actual remote of those devices as well. Furthermore, SNMP2 or a variation of SNMP known as Secure SNMP, will allow users to access carriers' network management information and incorporate it into the wide area component of an enterprise network management system. Perhaps the most significant SNMP2 development in terms of implication for distributed client-server management is the ability to deploy multiple agents per device. Also,, rather than having merely distributed enterprise network management, the entire distributed information system could be managed, with each major element of the client-server architecture managed by its own management infrastructure.

20. Some people feel that features of SNMP2, especially the security aspects, are too difficult to implement and use while others blame the delay on concerns over marketing position and competitive advantage from technology vendors.

21. While the original RMON MIB only required compatible technology to be able to collect and analyze statistics on the physical and data link layers, RMON2 requires collection and analysis of network layer protocols as well. In addition, RMON2 requires compatible technology to be able to identify from which applications a given packet was generated.

22. Point products also known as element managers - are specifically written to address a particular systems administration or network management issue. The advantage of point products is that they are narrow in scope, provide the sought after solution, and are usually relatively easy to install and understand. The disadvantage to point solutions is that they do not necessarily integrate with other systems administration and network management tools. Any necessary correlation between point products must be done by network management personnel. Frameworks - offer an overall systems administration or network management platform with integration between modules and a shared database into which all alerts, messages, alarms, and warnings can be stored and correlated. Perhaps more importantly, most frameworks also offer open APIs or an entire application development environment so that third-party application developers can create additional systems administration or network management modules that will be able to plug-in to the existing framework and share management information with other modules. The advantage of a well-integrated framework is that it can offer the network administrator a single, correlated view of all systems and network resources. The disadvantage of frameworks is the development or integration of modules within the framework can be difficult and time consuming. In addition, not all management modules may be compatible with a given framework. Integrated Suites - could perhaps be looked upon as a subset of frameworks. The difference between integrated suites and frameworks is that integrated suites are filled with their own network management and systems administration applications rather than offering the user an open framework into which to place a variety of chosen applications. The advantage of integrated suites is that the applications are more tightly integrated and linked by a set of common services which tend to offer the user a more consolidated view of network resources. The disadvantage of integrated suites is that they do not offer the open pick-and-choose architecture of the framework.

23. Figure 14-20 provides a list of the most important functional characteristics of enterprise network management systems.

24. Figure 14-21 lists the important functional characteristics of network analyzers.

25. Layer 1 testers are more commonly known as cable scanners or cable testers, while devices that test layers 2 through 7 are often called protocol analyzers.

26. Network baselining tools are able to track network performance over extended periods of time and report on anomalies or deviations from the accumulated baseline data.

27. All simulation systems share a similar trait in that the overall network performance which they are able to model is a result of the net effect of a series of mathematical formulae. The value of a simulation system is in its ability to predict the performance of various networking scenarios otherwise known as what-if analysis. Simulation software uses the current network configuration as a starting point and applies what-if scenarios. The benefits of a good network simulation package include:
    - Ability to spot network bottlenecks such as overworked servers, network failures, or disk capacity problems
    - Ability to test new applications and network configurations before actual deployment. New applications may run well in a controlled test environment, but may perform quite differently on the shared enterprise network
    - Ability to re-create circumstances in order to reproduce intermittent or occasional network problems.

    Ability to replicate traffic volume as well as traffic transaction type and protocol mix.

28. Any simulation needs traffic statistics in order to run. How these traffic statistics may be entered can make a major difference in the ease of use of the simulation system. Possibilities include: Manual Entry by users of Traffic Data collected elsewhere, Traffic Data entered "live" through a direct interface to a protocol analyzer, a Traffic Generator which generates simulated traffic according to the user's parameters, or auto discovery from SNMP and RMON data generated by enterprise network management systems.

29. Some of the value that network auditing tools can provide is in such areas as consolidated services desks, inventory management, network management, and security. What network auditing tools all seem to have in common is the ability to provide records of which network files have been accessed by which users.

30. Network auditing tools can provide help in such areas as consolidated services desks, inventory management, network management, and security. Other capabilities include: Keep time logs of file accesses, Determine which users are deleting files that just seem to disappear, Audits when users copy files to diskettes, Ability to audit which software programs (authorized and unauthorized) are installed and/or running on any computer, Ability to audit only specified files and/or specified users, Ability to integrate with security, systems management, or help desk products, Report output format, text-based, graphical, Able to export to spreadsheet, word processing or database products, Ability to track and report on configuration changes, and Ability to track logins and logouts.

TEST QUESTIONS

True/False Questions

1. The network development life cycle forces the network manager to engage in an on-going process of network monitoring, planning, analysis, design, modeling, and implementation based on network performance. T/581

2. Enterprise network management focuses on the management of client and server computers and the operating systems and network operating systems that allow the client and server computers to communicate. F/584

3. Ultimately, in order to be especially useful in meeting overall goals of systems reliability and end-user satisfaction, server management software must provide server capacity planning capabilities by monitoring server performance trends and making recommendations for server component upgrades in a proactive manner. T/588

4. Desktop management is primarily concerned with the configuration and support of servers linked through the network using enterprise network management tools. F/595

5. LAN management tools tend to be more focused on problem identification than enterprise-wide consolidated service desk software with characteristics such as problem diagnosis or problem avoidance. T/599

6. The original SNMP protocol, through the use of agents, provided for the means of manager to manager communication. F/604

7. The most significant SNMP2 development in terms of implication for distributed client/server management is the ability to deploy multiple agents per device. T/605

8. One of the difficulties recently overcome by most enterprise network management systems was a lack of interoperability between different enterprise network management systems and third party network management systems. F/610

9. The major cause of the lack of interoperability between a given enterprise network management system and the variety of third party network management systems is the lack of common APIs between them. T/611

10. LAN and WAN network analyzers are able to capture network traffic in real time without interrupting normal network transmission. T/611

266   Chapter 14

Multiple Choice Questions

1. Which of the following is a key component to successful outsourcing?
    a. identifying processes which can be most appropriately outsourced
    b. managing outsourced processes by establishing communication and evaluation mechanisms
    c. choosing the right outsourcing provider for the right job
p.583   d. all of the above are key components

2. This component of network management focuses on the hardware, software, media, and network services required to seamlessly link and effectively manage distributed client and server computers across an entire company or corporation.
    a. systems administration
    b. network administration
p.584   c. enterprise network management
    d. systems management

3. Under which OSI category of network management would the monitoring of the network or system state fall?
    a. accounting management
    b. performance management
    c. configuration management
p.586   d. fault management

4. Under which OSI category of network management would compiling an accurate description of all network components fall?
    a. accounting management
    b. performance management
p.586   c. configuration management
    d. fault management

5. Under which OSI category of network management would determination of quality of service parameters fall?
    a. accounting management
p.586   b. performance management
    c. configuration management
    d. fault management

6. Which of the following is **not** a benefit of a consolidated service desk approach to end-user and infrastructure support?
    a. a single point of contact for all network and application problem resolution
    b. consolidation of all problem data at a single location
    c. reduces "console clutter"
p.587   d. handles only processes directly related to problem resolution

7. This component of the help desk management software package contains answers to problems and the decision tree that takes a given problem and leads the help desk person through a series of questions to the appropriate solution.
   a. search engine
p.591 b. knowledge base
   c. IVRU
   d. third party help desk telephone number

8. Using this type of software in an enterprise precludes users from having to remember multiple passwords.
   a. policy-based management tool
   b. management interface API
p.593 c. single sign-on
   d. agent

9. This component of the Desktop Management Interface Architecture is the DMI application which resides on each desktop device to be managed.
   a. Component Interface API
   b. Management Interface API
   c. Desktop Interface API
p.595 d. DMI Services Layer

10. This component of the Desktop Management Interface Architecture is designed to interface to the desktop system management program which will consolidate the information from this client with all other desktop components.
    a. Component Interface API
p.596 b. Management Interface API
    c. Desktop Interface API
    d. DMI Services Layer

11. This component of the Desktop Management Interface Architecture is designed to interface to the individual application programs or desktop components which are to be managed and monitored on the local client.
p.596 a. Component Interface API
    b. Management Interface API
    c. Desktop Interface API
    d. DMI Services Layer

12. Which functional characteristic of a desktop management system is responsible for supporting the setting of threshold limits for CPU activity, remaining disk space, etc.?
    a. network monitoring
p.597 b. server monitoring
    c. license metering
    d. network operating system compatibility

268   Chapter 14

13. Which functional characteristic of a desktop management system is responsible for watching and reporting upon data link layer traffic?
p.597 a. network monitoring
       b. server monitoring
       c. alarms
       d. network operating system compatibility

14. Which functional characteristic of a desktop management system is responsible for notifying the manager of changes to files, configuration changes, or violations of pre-set thresholds?
       a. network monitoring
       b. server monitoring
p.598 c. alarms
       d. network operating system compatibility

15. This enterprise network management component is software which runs on networking devices such as servers, bridges, and routers to monitor and report the status of those devices.
       a. MIB
p.601 b. agent
       c. RMON MIB
       d. object

16. The enterprise network management system stores information from network devices in a database called a(n)
       a. RMON
       b. object
       c. agent
p.601 d. MIB

17. The de facto protocol for delivering enterprise network management data to the enterprise network management system is
       a. SMTP
       b. STP
p.602 c. SNMP
       d. SNP

18. These are relied on by the DDM architecture to gather information from a variety of network devices manufactured by multiple vendors and relay that information to numerous distributed device manager consoles.
p.602 a. distributed network probes
       b. agents
       c. MIBs
       d. RMON objects

19. This proposed protocol may finally achieve transparency of enterprise management technology.
   a. SNMP
   b. DMI
   c. HMMP
p.603 d. CIM

20. Which of the following was the reason for SNMP consuming a considerable amount of network bandwidth?
   a. SNMP was limited to using TCP/IP as its transport protocol
p.604 b. SNMP required device specific agents to be polled for encapsulated management data
   c. SNMP did not offer security features
   d. SNMP was limited to using IPX/SPX as its transport protocol

21. Which of the following SNMP problems was corrected through a new SNMP2 procedure known as Bulk Retrieval Mechanism?
p.605 a. alarm conditions not directly (as they occur) reported to the enterprise management system
   b. no manager-to-manager communication
   c. unusable with IPX/SPX
   d. no security features for authenticating valid polling managers

22. RMON2 compatible agent software which resides within internetworking devices and reports performance statistics to enterprise network management systems is referred to as a(n)
   a. SNMP probe
   b. Database MIB
   c. Application MIB
p.606 d. RMON probe

23. This Application MIB group of variables would store background information concerning applications such as application name, manufacturer, version, release, installation date and license number.
p.607 a. Definition variables
   b. State variables
   c. Relationship variables
   d. SNMP variables

24. This Application MIB group of variables would report on the current status of a given application.
   a. Definition variables
p.607 b. State variables
   c. Relationship variables
   d. SNMP variables

270 Chapter 14

25. This Application MIB group of variables would define all other network attached resources on which a given distributed application depends.
   a. Definition variables
   b. State variables
p.607 c. Relationship variables
   d. SNMP variables

26. Which of the following network management technology architectures is used to address a particular systems administration or network management issue?
   a. frameworks
   b. integrated suites
p.608 c. point products
   d. none of the above

27. Which of the following network management technology architectures offers open APIs so that third-party modules will be able to be plugged-in to it?
p.609 a. frameworks
   b. integrated suites
   c. point products
   d. none of the above

28. Which of the following network management technology architectures offers tightly coupled applications linked by set of common services, however the services are not linked by open APIs?
   a. frameworks
p.609 b. integrated suites
   c. point products
   d. none of the above

29. Which of the following is **not** typically a functionality found in a cable scanner?
   a. pinpoints locations of cable breaks
   b. check for attenuation
p.613 c. display actual text being transmitted across the medium
   d. determine if NeXT exists

30. Which of the following is used to track network performance over extended periods of time and report on anomalies or deviations from the accumulated baseline data?
   a. network modeling tools
p.615 b. network baselining tools
   c. network simulation tools
   d. network auditing tools

31. Which of the following is used to provide records of which network files have been accessed by which users?
    a. network modeling tools
    b. network baselining tools
    c. network simulation tools
p.616 d. network auditing tools

Fill-In the Blank Questions

1. Guarantees of proper execution and delivery of end-user applications are sometimes quantified in terms of _____ guarantees.

2. The selective hiring of outside contractors to perform specific network management duties is known as _____.

3. The overall integration of computer-based software and telephony equipment is known as _____.

4. _____ is the name used to define the overall desktop management architecture proposed by the DTMF.

5. Embedded performance metrics are sometimes referred to as _____.

6. A(n) _____ is a piece of software that collects performance statistics and properly formats them for transmission to the application management console or any SNMP-based administrative program.

7. An alternative to the centralized enterprise management console approach, _____ takes more of an end-to-end full network view of the enterprise network as opposed to the centralized enterprise management console architecture that takes more of an individual device or element focus.

8. Through a new SNMP2 procedure known as _____, managers can retrieve several pieces of network information at a time from a given agent.

9. _____ serve as repositories for enterprise network performance information to be displayed in meaningful format by enterprise network management systems.

10. _____ are network analyzers which operate primarily at layer 1 of the OSI model only.

Chapter 14

Answers

1. QOS or Quality of Service p.581
2. outsourcing p.583
3. CTI or Computer Telephony Integration p.591
4. DMI or Desktop Management Interface p.595
5. instrumentation p.600
6. agent p.600
7. DDM or Distributed Device Manager p.602
8. Bulk Retrieval Mechanism p.605
9. MIBs or Management Information Bases p.605
10. Cable scanners p.613

CASE STUDY AND ANSWERS

TACKLING INTERNET SECURITY

Activities

1. Top-down model:

Business	Pepsi's restaurant chains needed to have their management systems integrated with Pepsi's main management structure to provide the divisions with centralized-management design to ensure no changes to the network can be made that would affect other divisions.
	Pepsi believes bringing in management responsibility for the chains will save on resources by sharing equipment and expertise.
	They want to try to standardize hardware, software and procedures as much as possible.
Applications	Pepsi had developed it own management systems.
	The company will spread the information among three data centers to place less of a burden on the database in Somers and provide remote administrators with the management information they need.
Data	Remote data will be used as well as centralized data, but will be distributed.
	They don't want a database to become too large because it won't be fast enough when querying information.
Network	LAN, WAN, and remote services will be required.
	Events/alarms must be kept to a minimum so as not to use up expensive wide area bandwidth.
	Currently all events and traps are sent to the same location, however this will be changed so that the events and traps are spread across three data centers.
	Improved performance when accessing information is needed.
	Proactive network management is a goal.

274   Chapter 14

Technology   Currently there are 24,000 nodes which will increased to 30,000 when the restaurant divisions are added to the management information system.
Pepsi is upgrading to and HP Tornado management platform, HP OpenView 4.1.
Over 1,000 events are received each day from 172 sites and it's help desk in Winston-Salem receives notification of events from another 135 offices.
Seagate Technology Inc.'s NerveCenter is used to filter repeat alarms.
Other management tools used include Optivity, CiscoWorks, Network Helth Trakker, and Action Request System.
The database is on an HP G70 server and an HP K220 and HP D350 will be added at two other sites.
Cisco router, DSU/CSU connections, and WAN links from 56Kbps to 1.544 Mbps have been set up.

2. Unanswered questions:
What is the budget or cost analysis for this project?
What operating systems will be used for both the clients and the new servers?
What is the hardware/software configuration needed for the average client?
How will the data at the three sites be backed up?
How will fault tolerance be provided throughout the system?
How will proactive network management be achieved (details)?

Business
1. Pepsi is a major player in the soft drink area, with several large restaurant chains.
2. Pepsi wants to network its restaurant chains with the corporation's main management system.
3. Pepsi's main management structure would provide the divisions with a centralized management design to ensure not changes to the network can be made that would affect other divisions.
4. They have pre-planned implementation of standards and procedures to ensure a smooth implementation.

Application
1. Currently HP OpenView 3.31 is used with a planned upgrade to 4.1 which will allow a distributed implementation.
2. Somers manages 172 sites across the country.
3. Winston-Salem manages 135 sites.
4. Once the net has been expanded, three central data sites responsible for 30,000 nodes and 360 remote sites will be managed.
5. The management data will be shared across three data centers located in Somers, Dallas, and Winston-Salem.

Data
1. HP OpenView 4.1 will let the company divide network information among the data centers.
2. The network management system can be used in a centralized manner or decentralized, and is distributed as described in the article.
3. 1,000 alarms are received per day.
4. The alarms are filtered by NerveCenter from Seagate Technology Inc.
5. Filtering removes repeat alarms and reduces the amount of bandwidth used as well as reducing the number of problems the network managers need to view.
6. The database currently resides in Somers.
7. The data will be distributed to three sites.

Network
1. The network objective was to allow for proactive rather than reactive network management.
2. 30,000 nodes are on Pepsi's network after the expansion.
3. Currently, the management team is responsible for the WAN links, routers, and computers that hold the management software.
4. The management team may become responsible for the servers (500-600 file servers).
5. 30,000 nodes could have an adverse impact on network bandwidth because of the amount of management information taking up too much bandwidth, not leaving enough for data.
6. The polling can be minimized by using HP OpenView 4.1's distributed approach, resulting in a reduction of bandwidth use by two-thirds.

Technology
1. HP OpenView with NerveCenter to determine alarms and repeats, Optivity works with Bay Networks' hardware, CiscoWorks is used with Cisco routers, Network Health Trakker and Action Request System are used to automatically generate trouble tickets.

COMMENTS FOR SELECTED FIGURES

CHAPTER 1 - COMMENTS FOR SELECTED FIGURES

Figure
   #

1-1 Data Communications is a complex topic consisting of many interacting components as illustrated. Each of these components can have an interaction with another. For instance, you might add on sub-components for CARRIERS, in the areas of CABLE (on-demand) and FILM INDUSTRY. Then explain how these interact with the TECHNOLOGY/RESEARCH component which is trying to provide cable video on demand. Under MERGERS/ACQUISITIONS, refer to recent articles in such journals as *NETWORK WORLD* to review recent actions such as the McCaw/AT&T merger.

1-7 Recently the name for CCITT has changed to ITU (International Telecommunications Union) and plays an important part in standards making since products and services are increasingly more global in nature requiring connectivity and interoperability internationally.

1-9 This figure provides a business perspective for the interacting components of Figure 1-1. Remember Goldman's Law 4: If the network doesn't make good business sense, it probably makes no sense. Thus, interaction between components from a supply and demand perspective can help the data communications professional plan for the future.

1-10 *This is the most important figure in the text*! This model is extremely valuable since the data communications is such a rapidly changing field. Using this model, business demands are passed down the with solutions passed back up. Objectives of each layer are met by the solution of the layer underneath. Physical network design is part of the technology layer, while logical network design is a function of the network layer and above. This top-down approach will be used throughout the book especially if you use the case studies.

1-11 To help the student work with the top-down model, this Figure provides details of what happens in each of the layers. Many new students think that a course in data communications and networking consists only of discussing the technology layer. This, of course, is the easy part. Goldman's Law 4 requires that a top-down approach be followed, or more than likely, the networking project will not succeed.

1-12 After you've defined the terms interface, protocol, and compatibility, use this figure to show an example of each. If possible, bring in some of the hardware used as physical interfaces such as serial and parallel cables.

1-13 <u>One of the most important Figures in the book</u>. The OSI reference model provides the framework or an architecture in which standards can be developed, compared, and understood. It allows data communications technology developers as well as standards developers to talk about the interconnection of two networks or computers in common terms without dealing in proprietary vendor jargon. Each layer is independent from the other. For instance, layer 1 media can vary independently from layer 2 protocol. Remember, it is a framework (workbench) not a protocol. It is empty and only defines the 7 layers you can then define protocols for. We can use it to compare systems which may need to communicate to each other.

1-16 Understanding and communicating technical information is just a part of the job for a data communications professional. Technical "weenies" abound, however professionals are able to understand the business needs of a company by using their interpersonal skills, and then provide answers to these needs through their understanding of data communications technology.

CHAPTER 2 - COMMENTS FOR SELECTED FIGURES

Figure #

2-1 This figure represents a roadmap for the entire chapter. It could be used as a good outline or even as a study guide.

2-6 Serial is often either a 25 or 9 pin male/RS-232 connection while parallel is 25 DB female. Parallel cables are also often called Centronics. Serial speed is approximately 19.2Kbps while parallel is approximately 100Kbps. Distance limitation is usually 50ft. for serial and high speed parallel is around 16ft.

2-8 Use this figure along with the descriptions of the most commonly used RS-232 signals in figure 2-9 and have students explain the use of each of the commonly used pins/lines of the connection. Which signals are not supported on the DB-9?

2-13　Explain the difference between discrete/digital and wavelike/analog waves. Also explain that in the I-P-O model, the processing details need not be known as long as they produce the output needed. For instance, there are many modems which can change analog to digital and vice versa.

2-19　This figure, while first appearing somewhat busy, provides the graphical information to explain the difference between baud rate and transmission rate (bps), as well as the relationship between the physical representation of a wave and its graphical representation as a constellation point.

2-21　With asynchronous transmission it is important to note the use of start/stop bits and that we are not constantly in time, so we must resync transmission for each character. With synchronous transmission we are always in time (done with a clock) and we do not need to constantly resync the devices. Because of this, efficiency for synchronous transmission is much higher as shown in the figure.

2-22　Explain the importance of full-duplex over half-duplex and the speed of transmission gain. Even more important is that you must know what the modem at the other end of the line is transmitting at: full or half-duplex. Full-duplex transmission is only possible on a two wire circuit with echo cancellation.

CHAPTER 3 - COMMENTS FOR SELECTED FIGURES

Figure
#

3-1　This is an excellent example of how to apply the top-down model to a business situation. Stress that you always begin with the business layer and its requirements which will be passed down to the other layers which in turn will pass up solutions. In this case the business layer requirements are : faster, more efficient, more reliable, and more service.

3-3　This figure provides a list of technical innovations used to support ever faster mode transmission rates. Go over each innovation with the students. Also, ask the students to research more current technological innovations they may find in current PC magazines.

3-9　Parity is calculated both horizontally and vertically. Change a single bit as if a character had taken a hit to show how parity is checked to catch the error. Change 2 bits in a single character to show how it will not be caught by simple one-directional parity checking, but will be caught by longitudinal redundancy checking.

3-10   Which of the trends listed appear to be favored currently by vendors? Which ones are being tested/used in your geographic locations? Have you students call cellular, phone, and cable companies to see what technologies they are preparing to use.

3-15   It is important to point out that asking the right question is more important than knowing only some of the technology issues. As an example, let's say that you wanted to be able to access the files on your PC at work from your computer at home. Run through the Question and Implication/Options to find which ones actually apply. Ask how this could then translate into a business decision.

3-16   An excellent summary of the file transfer protocols. Have your students do a comparative study of communications software specifically to identify which packages support which protocols, their price and other functionalities, putting the information together in a technology analysis grid format.

3-17   The Technology Analysis Grid will be used throughout the text. Functionality (going across) refers to the WHAT from the Network Layer. Communications software refers to the HOW TO from the Technology Layer. Cross-referencing these can lead to the proper decisions for acquisition of the right communications software to meet business needs.

CHAPTER 4 - COMMENTS FOR SELECTED FIGURES

Figure
  #

4-3 & 4-4   These Figures represent the different methods used to digitize voice signals. PCM and ADPCM are the most popular voice digitization techniques.

4-9   Call your local PBX vendors and get comparative pricing for the different features listed in this Figure. What features does your institution and its PBX have?

4-12   What are the people issues behind each of these services or devices? For instance, what are some of the frustrations associated with and automated attendant? Has anyone ever interacted with a voice processor? Did they encounter any problems?

4-13   CTI is becoming very popular with today's businesses. Have your students do a Web search of CTI to find the latest applications being used. You might also conduct your own Web search of CTI implementations and present an actual case study showing the business value CTI can bring to a company.

4-20   Use the figure to ask your students to identify the strengths and weaknesses of IP-based voice transmission. Pay particular attention to business requirements and technology bottlenecks.

4-25   Have your students find the costs involved with the two pictures in this figure. Remind them that they must have compatible equipment at both ends. List the costs in a side-by-side comparison chart. Remember that ISDN requires a special ISDN line. Is ISDN available in your area? Is it available through to the destination? Are their intermediate costs for ISDN delivery across different LATAs? What are the modem costs for both technologies? What is the business need for either technology?

CHAPTER 5 - COMMENTS FOR SELECTED FIGURES

Figure
  #

5-3   Business needs are the overriding factor when considering a LAN solution. If the LAN solution doesn't make business sense, then it makes no sense at all. Add that in today's competitive business atmosphere, doing more with fewer people and providing your people with more and better information should be one of the business needs that a LAN may be able to meet.

5-4   This figure again represents one of the most important concepts in the entire book. The OSI model is often used as a means by which to organize comparative information regarding alternative network architectures. Use this figure to explain each of the layers functionalities. Protocols can be introduced using this model. Especially important is to explain that each layer of the OSI model relies on lower layers to perform more elementary functions and to offer transparency to the intricacies of those functions. In particular, note the first four layers deal with establishing and assuring reliability. The physical and Data Link layers deal with point-to-point, while the Network and Transport layers accomplish similar functions for end-to-end network connections.

5-5   Encapsulation and de-encapsulation of data for each layer can be visually understood using this figure.

5-6   Token Passing access methodology is easily understood by using this figure. Perhaps you can have four different students represent stations A, B, C, and D, and let them explain what they are doing by passing around a sheet of paper which represents a free token. Try having one of the students (station B) send a message. Ask them what has to happen before they can send it and after they are done. Another interesting exercise is to have station A send the message but drop out of the ring before the message returns. You can then explain the function of the active monitor (assuming station A wasn't the active monitor) to show how a data token is kept from going around the ring forever.

5-8   A good figure for explaining the difference between the older Ethernet II frame type and the newer IEEE 802.3 with IEEE 802.2 LLC data unit standard now used.

5-14 One of FDDI's most important features is its reliability. This figure can be used to demonstrate how dual counter-rotating rings provide reliability in the event of a break. The need for the dual rings to be counter rotating should be especially evident.

5-19 This figure can be used to explain several concepts about 100VG-AnyLAN: network architecture, demand priority access, round robin polling scheme, and priority delivery.

5-21 This figure provides a simple way to explain the bandwidth usage of the 16.144 Mbps Iso-Ethernet network. Use it to also explain the three different service modes as well as its compatibility with ISDN.

CHAPTER 6 - COMMENTS FOR SELECTED FIGURES

Figure
#

6-1   A good figure to begin the discussion of LAN hardware. It puts it all in one place. Use this figure and bring in a computer to point out and possibly pass around the different components mentioned.

6-3   An excellent example to help students understand why switches are able to improve the overall throughput of a LAN. For instance, in the same amount of time, the shared media hub might be able to pass 10Mbps while the switched media hub is passing 30Mbps.

6-6   This figure demonstrates the different data transfer methods of today's computer systems. It is important to note that to use bus mastering DMA the NIC and expansion bus must be bus master-enabled. Keep in mind that bus mastered NICs may be more expensive than non-bus mastered. Refer to Black Box, Glasgal, and 3Com catalogs for the most current information and throughput rates. Perhaps have the students do this creating a technology analysis grid similar to the one presented in figure 8-4.

6-10 If possible, work through the steps on an actual computer demonstrating how a monolithic driver is used and then how an NDIS driver is configured.

6-12 A good figure to base a discussion of the differences between stand-alone, stackable, and enterprise hubs. Require your students to use the Internet and explore Web sites which might have information about each type of hub. Ask them to bring that information to class. If possible, have them print out or make overheads of the devices they find on the Web.

6-16 Probably the most rapidly expanding area of LAN hardware is the LAN switch. Pick four or five different switches from catalogs like Glasgal, Black Box and 3Com, and have your students use this figure to make a comparison of the features. Give them a scenario they could then use to decide which of the switches would be the right business choice to employ for the given situation.

6-19 Use this figure to discuss the different UTP specifications. Bring samples of each category of wiring to class and show the students the differences, such as twisting, bending and compare UTP to STP and fiber if you can acquire any.

CHAPTER 7 - COMMENTS FOR SELECTED FIGURES

Figure
   #

7-1   A good figure to begin the discussion of software used on a local area network. If you have a LAN available to you, ask the students to fill in specific vendor/products for each of the boxes listed on the LAN software architecture diagram.

7-3   To start the discussion of LAN operating systems, use this figure to explain the difference between the functionalities offered by a peer-to-peer and client/server system. Find examples of each from PC magazines to compare features and prices.

7-4 Use this figure to explain the business reasons why new service requirements are emerging for network operating systems. Explain the importance of each item under the emerging requirements columns. For instance, "all network objects defined in single location and shared by all applications" has become important as companies become more dispersed and distributed, especially from a management point of view.

7-10 Provides an excellent graphical description of the difference between real-mode and API/VxD drivers. Note especially the difference between shared and individual addressing sub-systems. Ask the students which type (shared or individual) is supported by Windows 3.1, Windows '95 and Windows NT.

7-12 An excellent figure for pulling many of the concepts described in the chapter together. Note the OSI model layers are listed. Use this to reinforce the reasons the OSI model is used by network analysts, so that they may discuss different network operating system solutions.

7-13 A good summary of client network operating system features. This figure can be used to see if the student really understands the various concepts presented. Formulate scenarios in which one of the client network operating systems would be a better choice than the others, and then ask the students why. For instance, you need access to files stored on a Windows NT server, but your client workstations are very limited in memory capacity (4MB RAM).

7-16 This figure is useful in demonstrating the differences between server and client network operating systems. Ask the students to give you an example of each block in the client and server diagrams.

7-17 This figure shows how Unix, combined with TCP/IP, and NFS can be thought of as a full network operating system capable of working with clients and servers. Note the two upper layers of the client side. If possible, demonstrate a database or spreadsheet front-end tool and X-Windows.

7-18 Use this figure to demonstrate Unix's two chief positive attributes of portability and modularity. Explain the importance of the kernel being written in C and interfacing with the hardware through device drivers rather than directly. Ask the student to find out why different versions of Unix and different shells have been developed, and how they fit into the architectural diagram in this figure.

7-19 Go over this diagram and discuss what a root, absolute path, relative path, and link are. Then, ask the students to draw a similar diagram in which a subdirectory called "courses" has several other subdirectories for some of the classes at your college. Under each of the course subdirectories, have files for course instructor, students, etc. Also, in one of the subdirectories ask the students to provide a link between two course instructors.

7-25 As remote access becomes more popular, Windows NT's ability to support users remotely through RAS is something to discuss in class. Perhaps you can demonstrate a dial-up session and explain how all the OSI layers and steps are needed to remotely access a local area network. What special security issues does remote access introduce?

7-27 The Windows NT Security model is important to its recent certification as C-2 compliant by the government. Ask your students to find out what C-2 compliance means, and how Windows NT conforms to it. The requirements for a C-2 secure system are found in the U.S. National Security Agency's National Computer Security Center (NCSC) in the publication Trusted Computer System Evaluation Criteria, also known as the "Orange Book." Have your students access the World Wide Web at Novell, Microsoft and the government for more information! What is the difference between the Red book and the Orange book? Stress the difference between C-2 compliance and C-2 certification.

CHAPTER 8 - COMMENTS FOR SELECTED FIGURES

Figure
#

8-2 The arrow joining the two trucks can be considered the actual Wide Area Network "cloud". We don't always know or care how the packets got from one user to the destination user between the trucks so we often represent this as a cloud. Note also that items are placed in packages (packets) and then grouped together for transport (multiplexing).

8-3 With FDM, notice that a portion of the total bandwidth is available 100 percent of the time to a connected terminal. Frequencies are high and low and generally mux 2 channels over a 2 wire system.

8-4 With TDM the mux slices time and gives equal time to each attached device. It waits whether or not the terminal puts anything into the mux. You must have the same type of mux at the other end to separate the composite message frame. You can use a modem with a TDM. Also see Newton's Telecom Dictionary for an excellent description of TDM.

8-5 Sometimes called stat muxes, they dynamically allocate time slices to devices which are more active, paying more attention to terminals that need it, eliminating idle time on the link from devices which do not have any data to send. STDMs also have buffers for holding data.

286 Comments for Selected Figures

8-8 This Figure summarizes the two primary switching techniques used to deliver messages from here to there. Use this figure to review the differences between each. In particular, note the PAD which formats data and adds a destination address in the packet header.

8-10 One of the main points to emphasize is the overhead of each. With connectionless PSNs error detection is done by the end devices only, while connection-oriented PSNs need more overhead for call set-up and teardown and error detection which is provided by the network. That is why connection-oriented is considered reliable with point to point error detection and correction.

8-12 A good summary of Narrowband ISDN architectural information. ISDN is digital and the D channel allows for control information such as caller ID. The level of service can be adjustable.

8-29 This Figure can help to identify BECN and FECN as well as noting that the payload is a variable length. This will be important to note when Frame Relay is contrasted to ATM.

8-33 Note that ATM is fixed length. This allows ATM switches to control more through hardware rather than software, which increases the speed as compared to Frame Relay. The payload (information packet) is 48 octets because the U.S. is heavily ethernet and wanted 64 bytes, while the French wanted 32 bytes mainly due to their commitment to ISDN. Since they couldn't agree 48 became the payload size.

CHAPTER 9 - COMMENTS FOR SELECTED FIGURES

Figure
   #

9-1 This figure presents an excellent overview of the internetworking possibilities today's network manager faces. Have your students look through trade magazines, such as LAN Times, and find case studies with configurations close to those presented by this figure. Then ask them why one solution was picked over other possible solutions.

9-4 Key to understanding how routing works, this figure can be used with some sample packets/frames in order to demonstrate how the router works in an internetworked environment.

9-5 It is important that students understand at what level of a protocol stack each type of internetworking device operates. This figure presents a generic overview of the OSI layer at which each internetworking device will process packets of information. Since the data link layer deals with only point-to-point addressing, that explains why bridges fit at this layer. Note that as you move up the OSI layers, the internetworking devices become more complicated, but they can only process at the layer they are on or below. Have your students prepare a technology analysis grid listing functions of internetworking down the side and the internetworking devices across the top. They should refer to the book, WWW and vendor catalogs to fill in the grid.

9-9 Have your students provide actual products for each category of bridge. Possibly, provide several scenarios, asking the students to decide which type of bridge technology would be appropriate as well as providing actual vendor product information supporting their decision.

9-14 This figure supports a growing trend in today's internetworking solutions: "Switch when you can, route when you must", and "Switch for bandwidth; route for filtering and internetwork segmentation." Possibly combine this figure with the case study at the end of this chapter to support or critique the solution used in the case study.

9-21 Understanding that LAN-to-LAN and LAN-to-mainframe internetworking are two very different prospects, use this figure to present the parallel networks model which many businesses and universities still must support today. Ask the students what the disadvantages of such a network are and use your discussion as an introduction to the four SNA/LAN integration solutions presented next in the chapter text.

CHAPTER 10 - COMMENTS FOR SELECTED FIGURES

Figure
#

10-2 This figure provides a basic understanding of the differences between remote node and remote control. Students must understand the difference in order to continue the chapter's discussion on both topics. Perhaps demonstrating software such as PCAnywhere or Carbon Copy would help cement down the differences between remote node and remote control. Use the points made in figure 10-1 to explain this figure.

10-3   Another important issue for students to understand is the difference in underlying protocols when using remote control and remote node links. Point out that remote control uses proprietary protocols between guest and host remote control software, while remote node uses redirector software.

10-5   Ask students to research each of these physical topologies in terms of cost, technical expertise required, advantages and disadvantages. Have the students bring specific advertisements to class for each alternative. Good places to find such information are PC Magazine, Byte and the Web.

10-10 Often described as a solution looking for a problem, wireless technologies are becoming more popular. Using this figure, ask your students to make a list of problems or scenarios which each of these could solve. Make sure that they pay particular attention to the throughput and distance columns as well as addressing security and cost.

10-16 Have your students prepare a case study in which they find an article on the use, in a company, of one of the wireless WAN services listed above this figure. Ask them to answer the questions in this top-down model based on the information in the article. If they can't find the information for a question in the article, what other questions must they ask in order to find the information if they were able to talk to the author?

10-17 A good figure comparing the various wireless WAN services discussed in the chapter. Assign your students to find a recent article or two on each of these services highlighting the advantage(s) and disadvantag(s) of using the particular service.

10-20 Explain the broader issues of PCS. It's not just a cordless phone. Distance, multi-vendor services, billing, etc. are all issues which need to be dealt with before PCS can become a reality along with standards and frequency allotment.

10-21 Bandwidth is an important issue in PCS. Each of these multiple access methods offers a way around limited bandwidth.

CHAPTER 11 - COMMENTS FOR SELECTED FIGURES

Figure
#

11-1   A good figure to start your discussion of enterprise networks. Use this figure to expand earlier chapters' top down models in order to see the business needs and required functionality of enterprise networks. Perhaps you can assign one of the readings at the end of the chapter and use this figure as a basis for discussion of the article.

11-3   Using the figure you can illustrate the differences between LAN switches and Virtual LANs. Ask the students how a shared-media hub is managed. Then ask them to look at the figure and explain how a switch is managed, especially in a virtual LAN configuration. This will accent one of the current disadvantages in today's VLANs.

11-6   Ask your students to use this figure to help analyze your network, or some other company's network, to see what the enterprise network bandwidth hierarchy should be and what it actually is. Ask them to explain why the current environment is set up the way it is and what a structured bandwidth hierarchy design would be for a strategic network plan.

11-8   ATM LAN Emulation (LANE) is described in this figure. Use the Jeffries article in DATA COMMUNICATIONS, September 21, 1994, to help you further explain the various components of the ATM LAN Emulation architecture shown in this figure. Ask the students to form groups and do research into LANE and present their findings to the class.

11-10 Prepare an imaginary business scenario for a small, medium, and large business that currently does not use the Internet. Be specific in the type of business. Then have the students list reasons why each of the businesses should or should not become involved with using the Internet. Be sure to include scenarios that are not just selling a product, but might also be providing a service, such as a travel agency.

11-12 Use this figure to discuss the major differences between an Internet Presence Provider, Internet Access Provider, especially as it applies to home use as opposed to a business LAN situation. Explain the advantages and disadvantages each provides. Also, assign students to research which of the providers are locally available.

11-20 This figure is a good way to analyze a company's needs for Internet access. Find a case study from a magazine, and ask the students to apply the information found in each layer of this top-down model. They must pay particular attention to ensuring that the technology layer meets the needs ultimately passed down from the business layer.

11-21 As you work your way down through each function, ask the students to explain what each means. You may be able to find a Web ad or commercial ad in a magazine or local paper that describes a provider's services. Use it, along with this figure, to decide what type of Internet provider the business is.

CHAPTER 12 - COMMENTS FOR SELECTED FIGURES

Figure
  #

12-1 This is where the Network Development Life Cycle (NDLC) fits into the big picture. The network analyst working on NDLC must have a good working knowledge of the other layers. How could the analyst gain the knowledge?

12-2 The Product or Milestone column represents the deliverables from the particular layer. Remember, always start at the business layer and work down passing requirements to lower layers, which in turn pass solutions up to the level above.

12-3 During the Analysis phase the business objectives must be determined. This is an information gathering phase. The Design phase is the physical layout of the network developed during the Analysis phase. Simulation uses software to represent the network, looking for possible problem areas and bottlenecks. It tests the design to see if it will actually work. Prototyping allows for testing, in an "off-line" manner. Implementation is the actual placement of the network into production. Monitoring will help to ensure that analysis and design specifics have been met and passes information to the management phase. This phase is not really the end, but rather the input to starting the cycle all over again.

12-4 Notice the overlap of the top-down layers. The application and data layers can be thought of as strategic level issues so that we can do the network and technology design. The network layer is the logical design, while the technology layer is the physical design.

12-5 Why are these issues important? Ask the students for examples where not addressing one or several of these success factors had jeopardized a project. There are more questions which can be asked here, such as where does the real power lay in a company? Is the company hierarchical or decentralized/open door in label and reality?

12-7 Development of a feasibility study relies on a thorough definition of the problem. This Figure can help in gathering the information needed to develop the feasibility study. The use of the process/product model should be stressed.

12-10 To prepare the request for proposal these eight issues can help the network analyst do a thorough job. Are there others you or your students might suggest?

12-12 Although not exhaustive, this sample table of contents highlights the major issues which must be contained in an RFP. Briefly describe what is meant by each in more detail.

12-15 Least expensive is not always best. This sample vendor information request form can help the analyst and management make sound decisions which are often not looked at by companies. Discuss the reason for each of these with your students.

12-17 Conduct a data traffic analysis on a location by location or node by node basis to be thorough. Payload type analysis is determining what type of payload, voice, video, data, image, or fax will be placed on the network. Traffic Volume Analysis = Payload + Transactions + Time. Protocol stack analysis looks at the OSI seven layer model and the interfacing which must occur resulting in the determination of what data communications hardware will be used.

12-18 People know what they want (Output - is a potential WAN service) and analysis can determine what we already have and will have by way of input. Hence, Processing is what it will take to get from the input to the output desired.

12-19 This is a summary of the key points of wrapping up the Network Analysis and Design Methodology. Briefly discuss each point and its importance.

CHAPTER 13 - COMMENTS FOR SELECTED FIGURES

Figure
  #

13-2   Use this figure to break the class into six different groups. Assign each group to one of the processes of the Security Policy Development Life Cycle. Have the group then research their assigned process and apply it to a real life business. Perhaps you can use your school's Information Systems Department. When completed, each group can then give an overview of what they found, both in terms of strengths and weaknesses for each process.

13-7   Ask your students to provide other examples of actual assets, threats, vulnerabilities, risks, and protective measures as they might apply to grades, product information, or credit cards.

13-11 Use this figure to explain each of the potential areas for development of acceptable use policies. Research your school's policy for each area and discuss any strengths or weaknesses noted by students.

13-17 Using this figure to help develop functionalities needed by anti-virus software, ask your students to prepare a technology analysis grid comparing the functionalities of today's most popular anti-virus software.

13-23 When describing Private Key, Public Key and Digital Signature Encryption, use this figure to show strengths and weaknesses of each. Have your students pick one of the three encryption methods, explore it on the Web and write a report to be briefly discussed in class and then turned in.

13-28 Although this figure simplifies the security certifications, it is actually much more detailed. An excellent article on C2 certification and what it means can be found in Network Computing, December 01, 1996, titled "C2 Security: Does It Matter?" Also, at the Web site - http://netware.novell.com/discover/compete/casecuri.htm, a good discussion can be found explaining the differences between Novell's Red Book C2 certification and Microsoft's Orange Book C2 certification. Thus, not only is there a difference between certification and compliance, but also between types of certification.

CHAPTER 14 - COMMENTS FOR SELECTED FIGURES

Figure
 #

14-1   Have your students work individually or in teams. Using this figure, assign them to prepare an actual cost containment analysis of a real network. It can be a business or possibly your schools network. Task them to provide specific detailed information for each of the five cost containment issues.

14-4   As in figure 14-1 above, have your students design a questionnaire they could use to ask network managers how they provide network management in the five OSI categories listed. Then have the students conduct interviews of network managers and report on their findings in class.

14-12 Use this figure to define each of the elements in the enterprise network management architecture. If possible, arrange for a guest lecturer who actually is responsible for managing a network to give a demonstration or provide overheads of how their system uses agents, SNMP, and MIBs to help provide the information needed to effective manage their network using a network management software package.

14-16 Although somewhat complicated, this figure contains the major components that make up the overall enterprise network management architecture and protocols as well as the move to SNMP2 manager-to-manager communication. Ask your students what the significance of manager-to-manager communications is.

14-21 Explain the difference between a cable scanner and protocol analyzer using this figure. Additional information may be found in catalogs by Black Box and Glasgal. Assign your students to use the Web to find information about different cable scanners and what the vendor says about the layer 1 capabilities. Do the same for protocol analyzers from various vendors. Possibly have them present their investigation in the form of a technology analysis grid, with functionality on the vertical axis and the particular product on the horizontal axis. Why is there such a broad range of pricing for products with similar names?